When Ziggy Played Guitar

David Bowie and Four Minutes that Shook the World

DYLAN JONES

WINDMILL BOOKS

1 3 5 7 9 10 8 6 4 2

Windmill Books
20 Vauxhall Bridge Road
London SW1V 2SA

Windmill Books is part of the Penguin Random House group of companies
whose addresses can be found at global.penguinrandomhouse.com.

Copyright © Dylan Jones 2012, 2016, 2018

Dylan Jones has asserted his right to be identified as the author of this Work in
accordance with the Copyright, Designs and Patents Act 1988.

Extract on pp. 178–80 from *To Major Tom: The Bowie Letters* © Dave Thompson

First published by Preface Publishing in 2012
First published in paperback by Windmill Books in 2018

www.penguin.co.uk

A CIP catalogue record for this book is available from the British Library.

ISBN 9781786090638

Typeset in 11/16 pt Minion by Jouve (UK), Milton Keynes
Printed and bound in Great Britain by Clays Ltd, Elcograf S.p.A.
Designed by David Eldridge

FOR DAVID BOWIE AND ROBIN DERRICK

CONTENTS

DAVID BOWIE
8 JANUARY 1947 – 10 JANUARY 2016

For myself and members of my generation, the Bowie generation, his death is more momentous than John Lennon's. Of course it would be invidious to compare the two, but it is still difficult even now for me to grasp just how much he meant to me. I was a teenager in the Seventies, and was one of the many people who saw his performance of 'Starman' on *Top Of The Pops* in the summer of 1972 (I had just turned twelve), one of the many millions whose lives were altered at such an impressionable age.

For my generation, it is almost impossible to overemphasise just how important David Bowie was to us, not just in terms of music and fashion, but also in terms of how we carried – and continue to carry – ourselves in the world. I remember exactly where I was when I heard about John Lennon's death, but Bowie's passing will stay with me in a different, more permanent way. I knew Bowie a little, and unlike many famous people who can have a little of the sheen rubbed off of them when you meet them, Bowie became even more intriguing when I did. Bowie was even more fascinating in person, because his curiosity, his obsession for 'the new' appeared to be innate. He was as important to the Seventies as the Beatles were to the Sixties, and yet his reach and his influence continue today in a way that we have yet to quantify, try as we might.

'I Think I Saw You In An Ice-Cream Parlour, Drinking Milk Shakes Cold And Long'

WHEN ZIGGY STARDUST CAME TO CALL, 1972

Many of those who saw David Bowie perform 'Starman' on the BBC in the summer of 1972 have never forgotten it, and it sits there, on a tatty old loop in our memory bank, reminding us that we were once both very young.

'In memory everything seems to happen to music'
Tennessee Williams, *The Glass Menagerie*

IT WAS A GOLDEN, ephemeral moment, and after that moment, on Thursday 6 July 1972, music would never really be the same again. This was the evening – a completely unexpected evening, at that; there was nothing inevitable about it – when David Bowie appeared on BBC One's *Top Of The Pops*, playing 'Starman', the first single from *The Rise And*

Fall Of Ziggy Stardust And The Spiders From Mars, and going some way to shaping a nation's youth in the process. Recorded the day before at BBC TV Centre in London's White City, it was broadcast as live, causing havoc in millions of sitting rooms all over Britain, changing the life of the performer as much as the lives of those watching him. The single had been released almost two months previously, but after this performance it would shoot up the charts as though propelled by stardust and Bowie himself.

This particular performance is one remembered by hundreds of thousands of my generation, an event that helped lure them into adolescence, the day that made many of us go out and get our hair cut, or dyed orange, or both – the day that helped kick-start punk, that would make many of us start peering over the horizon into our own futures, a pop-shock moment as important as watching Elvis Presley on *The Dorsey Brothers Stage Show,* or the Beatles on *The Ed Sullivan Show.* Or, later, as important as staring aghast at the Sex Pistols, acting like gibbons and swearing like parrots, on Thames TV's *Today,* presented by the hapless Bill Grundy. In the same way that people can remember exactly where they were when they first heard Bob Dylan, Leonard Cohen, Pink Floyd, Donna Summer, the Clash, or the Stone Roses, so they can recall when they first heard David Bowie. And for many of us it was 6 July 1972.

When he appeared on *Top Of The Pops* that night he would help nudge a culture of adoration that would be incubated in housing estates, garden suburbs, and bedsits all over the country. In short, Ziggy Stardust caused a tectonic shift in pop culture, providing, in the words of *Rolling Stone*, 'a model of courage to millions who had never been embraced by a popular culture before. He helped set others free in unexpected ways, even if he couldn't do the same for himself.'

In 1972, the world was a place that was best seen through a television, then at the very height of its power, and the only way that most of us could vicariously experience a world on the other side. For me, and for the many other innocents who saw Bowie perform that night, the world we were shown was transgressive: sexual androgyny, impious glam rock, the edge of all we knew. It was thrilling, slightly dangerous, transformative. For me, and for those like me, it felt that the future had finally arrived. It may have been dystopian (which at the time was rather confusing in itself), it may have been slightly confusing, and have come in the form of a flame-haired, sapling-thin scarecrow from Bromley, but when you're a callow twelve-year-old you take your cultural salvation in any shape it comes. And at 7.25 that evening, it came in the shape of twenty-five-year-old David Robert Jones. Thirty-five minutes later, life was rather different; a screen door had been opened, one through which many of us ran as fast as our skinny little legs would carry us.

Britain at the time still felt like it was immersed in the Fifties, a long slow black and white film that wasn't quite finished. London in particular was full of post-war prefabs and pre-war sensibilities, a grey city apparently even in springtime. Not that 1972 was uneventful. This was the year of *The Godfather*, the year of Frederick Forsyth's *Day Of The Jackal*, the year of *M*A*S*H*, the year Stan Smith beat Ilie Nastase in the Wimbledon Men's Singles Final, the year Carole King cleaned up at the Grammy Awards (taking Record, Album, and Song of the Year), the year five White House operatives were arrested for breaking into the offices of the Democratic National Committee, and the year the Black September group hijacked a Lufthansa Boeing 707 over Turkey, demanding the release of three comrades still held for the massacre of Israeli athletes during the Munich Olympic Games a few months earlier. As a snapshot of global attrition in the Seventies, July 1972 was as good as any: India's Indira Gandhi and Pakistan's Zulfikar Ali Bhutto nervously signed an agreement to peacefully negotiate future disputes; North and South Korea negotiated a futile agreement to discuss reunification; and the much anticipated chess match between the Soviet Union's Boris Spassky and the US champion Bobby Fischer finally began in Reykjavik, nine days after the official start date. No decade was better at binary conflict, and any subversive cultural behaviour seemed to happen in spite of it, rather than – as had happened in the Sixties – because of it. The space race provided the greatest conflict of all, a metaphor for the global struggle of the free world's way of life against whatever it was that was happening behind the Iron Curtain. When Neil Armstrong and Buzz Aldrin bobbed along the lunar surface at one-sixth normal gravity on 20 July 1969, the race was won, which back on Earth only made the cold war worse.

American television history was made on Saturday 19 February, when, towards the end of an episode of the most popular show of the time, *All In The Family* (which had been loosely based on Johnny Speight's hugely successful UK series *Till Death Us Do Part*), Sammy Davis Jr planted a kiss on the right cheek of Archie Bunker, the show's extraordinarily bigoted lead character, played by Carroll O'Connor. This split second made headlines all over the country, and instantly became the stuff of television legend. The script demanded that Davis joke that he had a clause in his contract requiring him to kiss white celebrities and, as he did so, Bunker was sent reeling.

It was a busy year in music. On 17 January, Highway 51 South in Memphis, Tennessee, was renamed 'Elvis Presley Boulevard'. Three days later, a year before it was actually released, Pink Floyd attempted the first performance of *The Dark Side Of The Moon* at The Dome in Brighton, only to fall foul of technical difficulties, forcing the band to abandon it and play it in its entirety the following night. That same night, Keith Richards jumped on stage to jam with Chuck Berry at the Hollywood Palladium, but his idol ordered him off for playing too loud. Berry later claimed that he didn't recognise Keith, and would not have thrown him off the stage had he known. On 9 February, Paul McCartney's new group Wings made their live debut at the University of Nottingham; it was McCartney's first public concert since the Beatles' performance in San Francisco's Candlestick Park in August 1966. Ten days later he would cause a furore when Wings' debut single, 'Give Ireland Back To The Irish', was banned by the BBC. On 31 March, the official Beatles fan club closed down. This was also the year in which the term 'Krautrock' was used for the first time, by Ian Mac-Donald in his piece 'Germany Calling' in the *New Musical Express*. On 2 May, Stone the Crows guitarist Les Harvey was electrocuted on stage during a show in Swansea by touching a poorly connected microphone, and died in hospital a few hours later. Led Zeppelin's untitled fourth studio album, the 'Runes' LP, which was released on 8 November 1971, was already on its way to becoming the best-selling album of 1972, as well as the fourth best-selling album of all time.

The previous six months had been tumultuous in other ways: George Harrison had organised the first all-star charity concert in the form of The Concert For Bangladesh, at Madison Square Garden, and starring Bob Dylan, Ravi Shankar, Leon Russell, Ringo Starr, and Eric Clapton; the second Glastonbury festival had taken place (the first to be held over the Summer Solstice), featuring Traffic, Fairport Convention, Hawkwind, and a relatively subdued David Bowie; and the Doors' Jim Morrison had been found dead in a bathtub in Paris at the age of twenty-seven.

Black Power had yet to fracture, and, inspired by the civil rights movement and the increasing number of Vietnam protests, black activism was on the rise. In musical terms, Eugene McDaniels (once called 'the black Bob Dylan' by industry legend Jerry Wexler) was one of the lower profile exponents of the movement, and while he would go on to write Roberta Flack's massive 1974 hit 'Feel Like Making Love', his 1971 album *Headless Heroes Of The Apocalypse* would become renowned less for its songs (which would have to wait twenty years to be appreciated, and sampled, by the likes of A Tribe Called Quest and the Beastie Boys), and rather more for its political influence. Atlantic Records were forced to stop promoting the album when 39th US Vice President Spiro Agnew contacted them, protesting about the album and demanding to know why they had released such a disturbing and seditious record.

Thirties decadence was given a Hollywood sheen in the shape of *Cabaret*, Bob Fosse's somewhat extraordinary evocation of Berlin during the Weimar Republic in 1931 under the cloud of the National Socialist Party. The film made stars – rock stars – out of Liza Minnelli and Joel Grey, both of whom were so well groomed, spangly, and libidinous, they made Mick Jagger, Lou Reed, and Iggy Pop look like mime artists in rep.

Elsewhere, *The French Connection* won Best Picture at the Academy Awards, Gloria Steinem launched *Ms.* Magazine, and *Apollo 17*, the last manned moon landing to date, returned to Earth with 250 pounds of lunar samples. Time Inc. transmitted HBO for the first time, the first pay cable network, Pulsar produced the first digital watch, Atari introduced the arcade version of Pong, the first video game, Idi

Amin expelled 50,000 Asians from Uganda, Bangladesh gained independence from Pakistan, and John Lennon began his long battle to stay in the US when his immigration visa expired. In Laguna Niguel, in California, a group of seven men from Ohio broke into a branch of the United California Bank and looted the safe deposit boxes, making off with thirty million dollars, at the time an unprecedented amount. They were eventually apprehended by the FBI.

And Clint Eastwood became the biggest box office star in the world.

In Britain – where the likes of Clint Eastwood, Robert Redford, and Burt Reynolds represented a world that could only be imagined – there were two debilitating miners' strikes, the sort of industrial action that would eventually go some way to defining the decade. The first strike began on 9 January and soon involved a quarter of a million miners, systematically mobilising themselves and using flying pickets to successfully disrupt coal supply. Eventually Ted Heath was forced to declare a state of emergency, resulting in power cuts and the infamous three-day week. During 1972 alone, over twenty-three million working days were lost due to industrial action by civil servants, firemen, building workers, railwaymen, and ambulance drivers. We all ate by candlelight, listening to our battery-powered transistor radios. Heath's government was unable to successfully deal with the increasing militancy of the unions, and the impasse made industrial relations the worst they'd been since 1926.

Sectarian violence was escalating in Northern Ireland,

reaching a sickening crescendo when, on 30 January, thirteen unarmed demonstrators were shot dead in Londonderry by members of the Parachute Regiment. Bloody Sunday helped feed anti-British sentiment (the *Guardian* called it 'Britain's My Lai'), a colonial battle of wills that would keep percolating throughout the rest of the decade and beyond.

The picket line was not producing great art – unless you counted 'Part Of The Union' by the Strawbs, and few did – and any musical zeitgeist wasn't the result of, or a response to, the agitprop of the time. Rather it was born in a vacuum. There was little appetite for the aftershocks of the Sixties among a new generation who were already taking the counter-cultural victories of the previous decade for granted. Squint, and we could have been back in the Fifties, where orthodoxies had yet to be challenged, and where consumerism was king. 'The A-bomb's apocalyptic revelation precipitated a new kind of global consciousness and a new kind of psychology,' wrote Jon Savage in *Teenage: The Creation Of Youth 1875–1945*. 'Faced with the prospect of instant vaporisation, many began to focus totally on the present, if not the instant. The new psychology – soon to be culturally interpreted as existentialism – privileged living in the moment and was materially oriented.' Faction fighting was everywhere, as there was also a war of attrition developing between the cultural radicals of the Sixties and the flag-wavers of the traditional left, a split between idealism on the one hand, and the pragmatic matter of household economics on the other.

Closer to home, Paul McCartney had just released his

second solo album, much to the ire of the critics (his 'Irish' single still being some months away). *Ram* was a collection of half-baked whimsical sketches that appeared to pay no mind to his legacy. He even had the audacity to credit his wife Linda on some of the songs. 'Obviously I was used to having a collaborator and I felt the pinch after John,' said McCartney in his defence. 'I was used to writing solo stuff too, of course, but some of them I'd get a bit stuck on – like I would with John – and Linda would change some of the words, alter a little piece here and there, write a line or two, give me ideas. It was just me and her in the studio most of the time, there together all day.' He was attacked as much as Lennon had been for daring to involve his wife in his creative output, the world not being ready for a former Beatle singing about domesticity and sheep.

This is the world that Ziggy Stardust landed in, beamed down to a sullen, punitive, disgruntled grey country that hadn't been Great for some time, a country full of sullen, disgruntled people who by rights shouldn't have taken too kindly to a pop singer dressed up as a gay alien in a quilted jumpsuit. But take to him is exactly what they did.

'No one has seen anything like this before,' Bowie boasted, just a few weeks after the release of *Ziggy Stardust*. 'That's what's missing in pop music right now, entertainment. There's not much outrageousness left.'

Bowie's performance on *Top Of The Pops* was a very personal rite of passage, one seen by millions and shared by hundreds of thousands of people – a moment in the culture that would go on to define its time. It had an effect on a generation that would grow up to define their own music in their own times – the Clash, the Sex Pistols, Boy George, Duran Duran, U2: all were influenced by watching David Bowie and the Spiders From Mars that night, shocked out of their teenage stupor, and giddy with a sense of relief that none of them really understood. Suddenly, we all had a shared mythology, one we could call our very own. As for Bowie himself, 1972 was the year in which he started to straddle his constituencies, appealing to both the long in tooth and the short of trouser, to the pubescent consumers of seven-inch singles and the greatcoat-wearing longhairs who carried their albums under their arms like the next generation would one day carry man bags.

Bowie not only had scale, he had depth. Ziggy Stardust introduced an era of fashion, theatricality, sex, and intelligence to pop, themes and attitudes that are still copied today. Not only did Bowie's success with Ziggy properly launch the Seventies, but he inadvertently set in motion a generational shift that would see an extraordinary commodification of pop culture, one that accelerated like greased lightning throughout the Eighties, helping create a hydra-headed consumer lifestyle in the process. Bowie's Ziggy Stardust years – with the glamour shock and three-minute blitzkrieg pop – are some of the most enduring in British youth culture, emerging during a time of excessive musical indulgence, sartorial apathy, and increasing American cultural imperialism, while predating punk rock by a good four years.

Blade Runner. Grace Jones. *The Face. i-D.* Madonna. Lady Gaga. None would have happened without Bowie. If postmodern style was a gestural symphony of absurdity and retro-futurism, then this was Bowie incarnate – the ultimate hyper-real star. And if your idea of postmodernism was simply 'Anything goes', then this could hold true, too. (Without Bowie, there would have *been* no Eighties: 'The Americans are very confused by the sex of the new British bands,' spluttered an editorial in the *Daily Mirror* in 1983. 'First they thought Boy George was Girl George and that Yazoo's Alf was really an Alfred. Now they are convinced that Eurythmics' lovely Annie Lennox is actually a he.') Before 7.25 p.m. on 6 July 1972, the world looked relatively straightforward. At 8 p.m., after *Top Of The Pops* had finished, we all wanted to be rock stars. And, ridiculously, some of us thought we deserved to be rock stars, too.

We didn't know it at the time, but this was a moment that would almost immediately be enshrined in adolescent folklore, a moment that just popped out of the box, like a free plastic toy. There was no nobrow in 1972, and the chasms between the familiar categories of high and low culture were not bursting with content; instead of carefully drawn lines in the sand there were deep, brick-lined trenches, huge empty cavities guarded by armed blue-stockings wielding fountain pens and frosty looks.

On 6 July, all that went.

Ziggy Stardust was the first real postmodern pop star, a bisexual beat messiah, a flame-haired yob in lip gloss and mascara, silver jumpsuit and platform boots – a strange hybrid of androgynous spaceman, rent-boy Elvis, and rock 'n' roll glitter queen. Bowie was a combination of thin-lipped calculation and burning vocation, to borrow a phrase from James Wolcott, like Bob Dylan after he had outgrown his Woody Guthrie breeches and began playing his personas like a cardsharp. He could commune with the past, present, and future, and do it differently each time.

'I TOOK THE IDEA OF FABRICATION AND HOW IT HAD SNOWBALLED IN POPULAR CULTURE,' SAID BOWIE. 'REALISM AND HONESTY HAD BECOME BORING TO MANY JADED PEOPLE BY THE EARLY SEVENTIES . . . IT WAS A WAY OF CREATING MYSELF.'

'There's not much outrageousness left any more, apart from me and Marc Bolan,' said Bowie in January that year. 'The Beatles were outrageous at one time, and so was Mick Jagger, but you can't remain at the top for five years and still be outrageous . . . you become accepted and the impact has gone.'

It was Bowie's time, and the silver saxophones weren't about to refuse him. Ziggy's ambidextrous android was the forerunner of punk's glam savages and the first pop star with genuine built-in obsolescence. He was a star in quotation marks, crossing barriers of gender and genre in an attempt to capture the signs of the times.

'I took the idea of fabrication and how it had snowballed in popular culture,' said Bowie in 1990. 'Realism and honesty had become boring to many jaded people by the early Seventies. I think the band only half understood what I meant, but I thought it would be such great fun to fabricate something so totally unearthly and unreal and have it living as an icon. So the story of Ziggy came out of that thinking. A lot of it came out of my own problems. It was a way of creating myself.'

Bowie had an innate ability to plunder – some would say it was a defining characteristic – and with his latest creation (he'd been at it for years, not that any of us knew) all that work, all that digging, had paid off. Ziggy Stardust was the jigsaw man, created out of bits of this, and pieces of that. And then dressed up in some fancy satin and tat. Bowie didn't care if he came across as phony, and was even boastful about creating the first fabricated pop star. 'I wasn't at all surprised Ziggy Stardust made my career,' he said. 'I packaged a totally credible plastic rock star – much better than any sort of Monkees fabrication. My plastic rocker was much more plastic than anybody's.' Flippancy was all the rage: 'I'm an instant star,' he said with a smile, 'Just add water and stir.' There was a 2-D quality about Ziggy that Bowie was extremely proud of, maybe because he figured he couldn't compete in any other way. This was one of the reasons we all liked him so much – we liked the artificiality of it all. To those a tad older, to the folkies and beardies for whom insurrection was a lifestyle choice as much as a by-product of the age, Bowie was confrontational. He was an affront to the virtuoso industry, to the Deadheads, and to those for whom the Sixties were an end, rather than any kind of beginning.

Some artists are diminished by the fuss surrounding their work; others, like Bowie, are energised by it. He certainly was at the time. And after his performance on *Top Of The Pops*, he was a star.

What was it that Brian Eno once said? 'Some people say Bowie is all surface style and second-hand ideas, but that sounds like a definition of pop to me.'

Great pop *Ziggy Stardust* most certainly is, music that not only defined an era, but jump-started a generation, music made by pop's most enduring alter-ego, one we continue to embrace; Ziggy still graces magazine covers, still gets played on the radio, still initiates feisty conversation. When Marcel Duchamp said that art is created partly by its maker, partly by its audience, he was unwittingly anticipating the whole Ziggy hysteria. Ziggy Stardust is undoubtedly Bowie's greatest creation, but the durability of his legacy, and the almost impertinent way in which he dropped into our lives that night begs one very important question: Does David Bowie own Ziggy Stardust's death mask, or do we?

ONE

'Didn't Know What Time It Was, The Lights Were Low'

LONDON, DEAL, THE MOON, 1968–1972

'Space Oddity' accompanied the saturated television coverage of the Apollo 11 moon landing, turning its writer into a one-hit wonder in the process. Back here on Earth, life was slow, often tense, and monochrome.

'The future cannot be predicted, but futures can be invented'
Dennis Gabor, creator of the hologram

LONDON IN 1972 looked not so different from how it looked in 1952, even to eyes that hadn't seen it first hand. The city was anthracite, smoke-grey, the belching chimneys and London fog lending a gauze to everything from Tower Bridge to Earls Court. I don't remember anyone ever having a suntan, even if they'd just been abroad (not that I really knew people who went abroad, to be honest, not unless they were posted there, and even then they never returned with a tan), and most of the time it was like living in black and white. It was as though the Sixties had never happened, as if the decade of colour, social upheaval, psychedelic drugs, and free love had actually only been a film, a film that was no longer showing. Not at any cinema that I knew of, anyway, and certainly not where I lived. I have vivid memories of wandering around London with my father in the early part of the decade, and all the memories are grey. I distinctly recall going to a Lyons Corner House near the Strand, and even that memory – the bustle, the excitement, the almost exotic nature of the food – now seems as though it was filmed completely in black and white, by a second unit BBC film crew, for broadcast on an early evening local news programme. Even the West End I remember as pallid, wet, and pretty much without sensation.

In the early Seventies, a lot of London was still covered in weed-filled bombsites, and if you travelled across the city you would see Edwardian pubs sitting proudly in the middle of acres of wasteland, or Victorian tenements forlornly lining holes in the ground the size of football pitches, or maybe they were guarding them. Elegant stucco rubbed up against towering new office blocks which bordered huge swathes of urban scrubland. In central London, Westminster Council and the GLC were starting large slum clearance and re-habilitation schemes – glacially, you felt, as while the landscape filled with armies of cranes, few of them appeared to be making much difference to the mess around them.

Even the advertisements in the *Radio Times* hinted at a different age, when aspirations were far more tempered than they would soon become: Nescafé instant coffee, gas fridges, electric fridges, smokers' toothpowder, Pyrex jars, Army Junior Leaders, National Savings Certificates, the NatWest Bank, a Lucky Strike mint competition ('Win two Hillman Avengers and a Mediterranean holiday courtesy of Lunn Poly!'), Sanatogen multivitamins, the Vauxhall Victor Transcontinental, the Provincial Building Society, Halfords, hearing aids, the Leeds Permanent Building Society, savings bonds, and furniture stretch covers. Just about the only ad that hinted at a world beyond the square walls of the room containing your television was one for Schweppes dry ginger ale.

London in the early Seventies was like the Bakerloo Line – all brown and Bakelite and dark even when lit. Decimalisation, which was meant to hint at the white heat of modernisation, had only encouraged us to think that we were all slightly worse off than we'd been before it was introduced the previous year. A gallon of petrol was 35p, a pint of beer 13p – figures that were still new to people. A pensioner interviewed on the BBC News couldn't understand 'why they didn't wait for us old people to die out' before changing the currency.

It wouldn't be enough to say that every day in London in the early Seventies was like Sunday; specifically they were like any Sunday in November between the hours of four and five o'clock in the afternoon. It was almost as if the country had been brushed with a charcoal wash. On our small black and white televisions, in our over-inked black and white newspapers, in magazines that only sparingly used colour, the world was held at a safe monochromatic distance. As the writer Chris Bohn pointed out in the *New Musical Express*, when looking back at 1972, 'Psychedelic colour had fast faded into uniform blue denim and fledgling heavy metal; love and peace had come to stand for passiveness and eventual apathy; the spirit of '68 was doused once it was channeled into the conventional left.'

Perhaps my memories have been tainted by the fact that the only photographs I have of the period are black and white. I'm not sure why, as nearly all of our family photographs from 1965 onwards are in colour, but the pictures I have from 1970 to 1972 are all monochromatic.

Prime Minister Edward Heath's 1972 budget (delivered on Tuesday 21 March) was a critical moment in his government, as he tried to reflate the economy to reverse the rise in unemployment figures (which passed one million in January that year), making the generation who had been told by Harold Macmillan fifteen years earlier that they'd never had it so good, feel as though they'd never had it so bad. Even the new slavishly aped the old: in 1972 the two best-selling cars in the country were both made by Ford – the Cortina and the Escort, both ugly versions of old American cars.

Yet if you put your ear to the ground, or had your finger on the pulse, you might be able to tell that change was afoot. 'What makes 1972 special goes beyond folk memories of a glorious summer lived out to the sound of a then-hip Rod Stewart singing "You Wear It Well",' wrote David Lister in the *Independent* not so long ago. 'What makes that year special is that it marked a borderline between the Sixties – the years of affluence, experiment, sex and drugs, and hippie, idealistic, and, yes, flaky politics – and the real Seventies, the years of inflation, unemployment, changing attitudes to gender and sexuality, radicalisation, and the first mentions of words that were much later to become commonplace: terrorism and terror.'

I didn't know *anything* was afoot.

At the time of the 6 July broadcast I was living eighty miles from London, in Deal, sitting uncomfortably between Sandwich and Dover on the south coast. Kent was meant to be the garden of England; in my mind it was more like the scullery. Deal had a pier, although to me it looked too much like an unfinished underpass, the sort you might find in the Elephant and Castle, only pointed instead at the dishwater sea. Deal didn't even have a proper beach, as it had shingle instead. The local ice cream

AT THE TIME OF THE 6 JULY BROADCAST I WAS LIVING EIGHTY MILES FROM LONDON, IN DEAL, SITTING UNCOMFORTABLY BETWEEN SANDWICH AND DOVER ON THE SOUTH COAST. ALL YOU COULD SMELL WAS BRINE, WAFTING ACROSS TOWN LIKE CHEAP COLOGNE.

won lots of awards, although for some reason it was granulated; here, even the sand was in the wrong place. Deal had its fair share of seagulls, obviously, sad weather-beaten birds that always gave me the impression they'd be much happier living in Brighton. We all did. I'm fairly sure both my parents felt that the place was beneath them, although to be fair, I never knew a time when this wasn't the case.

All you could smell was brine, wafting across the town like cheap cologne.

There was the Deal Beach Parlour, the Rock Shop, some small amusement arcades (how arcane that expression sounds now), a few teashops and a parish hall, an angling association and plenty of stray dogs. There were the caravan parks that looked identical to the parks the caravans were bought from (why did their owners bother attaching them to their cars and moving them?). When Caesar first came to Britain, he landed at Walmer, which sits directly next to Deal on the coast, and frankly it's a wonder he ever came back. By the eighteenth century the town had become a notorious haunt of smugglers and thieves, and you can still find local magazines publishing two-hundred-year-old gazette pieces trumpeting the fact: 'There are said to be in the town of Deal not less than two hundred young men and sea-faring people, who are known to have no visible way of getting a living, but by the infamous trade of smuggling . . . This smuggling has converted those employed in it, first from honest industrious fishermen, to lazy, drunken and profligate smugglers.'

In 1972 there may have been fat red-cheeked men in the fish and chip shops, but outside in the rain there were leaden seas and washed-out skies. Turn around and walk into the streets, and mostly what you'd find was Anaglypta and pebble dash.

We lived in Middle Deal, in the centre of town, not far from the industrial estate, and just a spit from the local pub, the Bowling Green Tavern (once known as the Gun Inn). Ours was a narrow house, just one bedroom wide – long and thin like an upturned bungalow. My bedroom was full of nylon and vinyl. Pale blue nylon sheets, dark blue nylon pyjamas, and a box of seven-inch singles. There was myself, twelve, brother Daniel, five, and my forty-something parents, Audrey and Michael. And my mother's mother, Ada. My father only visited at weekends, as he was away working, in London, in High Wycombe, in Medmenham, making our tenure in Kent seem strangely temporary. Which it was, I suppose. We had been living in Buckinghamshire, and moved there three months before the Bowie broadcast, in April 1972. It was not the happiest of homes. My mother's mother had had a stroke, and as her husband had just died, she moved in with us, and slept upstairs, slowly dying. Neither my brother nor I can remember exactly why my parents chose Deal. My father said it was probably because our grandmother hailed from Romney Marsh, and that moving there was a little like going home. Her presence was certainly the defining aspect of the house, as it appeared to be the sole reason we'd moved, so my mother could care for her and, until she was taken to a nursing home near Dover, Orchard Avenue felt a little like a suburban nursing home. To say this cast a deathly pall over the household would be an exaggeration, although Granny's room was one we tended to avoid, and it became an un-room, a part of the house that just didn't exist for us boys. Most of what we saw in the room was our mother leaving it, having pulled up the bedclothes over her mother's flannelled form. There was just a quietness about the house that I don't remember about anywhere else we ever lived, a constant awareness of any noise, and the dampening of anything loud. This obviously made music even more important than it normally would have been; records had to be played quietly and surreptitiously, radios would have to be listened to under the covers. In our house, listening to music was almost as difficult as accessing pornography.

Deal wasn't Dickensian; it wasn't nearly as violent as Dover or Margate, and in places was actually rather gentrified, especially towards Walmer (residents of Walmer had the same affliction that residents of Hove had, and whenever someone would suggest that they lived in Deal, they'd come back with, 'Walmer, actually') yet there was a definite sense of displacement. Our neighbour worked on the Dover–Calais ferries, and there was always an abundance of contraband. Cheap cigarettes. Free booze. Deal was an odd mix of Fifties gentrification and feral anarchy. Sleepy, yet squalid in pockets. We still had a rag and bone man, who chanted 'Any old iron' as he pushed his horse and cart in front of the cinema; we still had a three-wheeler ice-cream van, and on Fridays, door-to-door toffee apple salesmen. As it was an Edwardian house, the lead pipes eventually went kaput, and we spent three months with the floorboards up, staring at the grime, giving our lives even more of an umbilical cord to the past. I would spend Sundays with my father, chasing driftwood along the front, laughing in the face of the wind and the rain, enjoying the sensation of being exotic and moribund at the same time; to live on the south coast of England was to enjoy both. When we eventually lost whatever log it was we were chasing, Dad would climb back into his rented Ford Escort (soon to be replaced by the ochre Morris Marina estate – 'One of the worst decisions I ever made,' he would say), and drive back to London.

As soon as we moved to Deal I sensed that the south coast was where you moved if your life was going in the wrong direction, if decline and fall were a *fait accompli*. Charles Hawtrey, the Carry On star, had moved there, and my brother and I were always cautioned if we were going into town alone, lest he caught us and attempted to 'fiddle'. (The novelist Simon Raven lived there, too; my mother bought some furniture from him once.) When Kenneth Williams once visited Hawtrey, he found a drunk in loud clothes, anxious and eager to ingratiate himself with the locals; knowing that when he sobered up he would be only too aware – yet again – of his diminished circumstances. Like many who had moved to the coast, Hawtrey immediately realised he had been given a sentence that was unlikely to ever be commuted. You just couldn't get back.

This wasn't London, and no one had access to Shelley's shoes or feather scarves from Chelsea Girl. Hot pants might have hit the high street, and it may have been easy for the girls at school to buy white frosted eyeshadow and stick-on stars for their foreheads, but it was almost impossible for boys to approximate the T. Rex or Ziggy look (there wasn't an abundance of purple boas or silver jumpsuits in the high streets of Sandwich or Dover).

The coast wasn't liberating; far from it. The town felt claustrophobic, close, hemmed in by the sea. There wasn't a great Mediterranean vista in front of me, only a big wall of grey, stretching from the pavement to the sky. Stare at the Pacific, the Med, or the Indian Ocean, and you picture promise, escape, boundless adventure, exponential fun. When I stared at the Channel all I saw was a force-field the colour of wet cardboard. The swell was made all the more oppressive by its proximity to the town; the beach, such as it was, was no deeper than your average cul-de-sac; you couldn't run into the sea as you couldn't get up enough speed, not even at low tide. This was the edge of nowhere, although not in any glamorous way. There were no stevedores down by the docks, we weren't walking to school under the girders of some gargantuan bridge that had been built by Irish and Indians. No *nostalgie de la boue* here. Only ice-cream vans, half-timbered chip shops, and front rooms turned into teashops (along the front you could get 'luncheon' for 75p, afternoon tea for 25p, and dinner for the grand sum of £1.25), half-hearted tourist shops for half-hearted tourists. You didn't visit Deal, you ended up here by mistake. Which is obviously why we were there.

I remember three blindingly hot days there, one of which I spent in the back garden lying on my back, staring at the clouds and listening to a tape I'd made of an old Cat Stevens single I'd found in a junk shop in town ('A Bad Night' coupled with 'The Laughing Apple'), and another which was spent on the dunes flanking the golf club in Sandwich. The other memory involves me cycling back from the cinema on my Raleigh having seen *Diamonds Are Forever*, although even this makes me think the sun only felt more intense because I'd been in the dark for two-and-a-half hours.

Three years previously, I remember being hauled out of our sunny Norfolk garden – forces families lived everywhere, moving every twelve months by instinct as much as decree – to see the recording of something or other that had happened with Apollo 11. When I was nine, it used to be sunny all the time, I was sure of it. Summers were hot and balmy, so hot your bike tyres sank into the road. Now we lived on a tatty Kent verge, where the summer looked out of place. When the sun shone, the town felt confused, almost as though it didn't quite know how to cope with the heat. It was much happier being grey, morose, chilly. Me, I liked to see the ribbons of lights around the pubs flare up at dusk, with the black blinking water roiling under the pier; this meant it was time to go inside and stop worrying why the town looked so depressed. If melancholia slows down time, for me, life in Deal seemed interminable.

Yet the coast appealed to my adolescent sense of self-absorption, or, more likely, encouraged and facilitated it. Mooching along the pebble beach looking for driftwood – a sixteen-foot pine plank found one slate-toned Sunday, soon to be sawn in two! – cycling back from *Flash Gordon* on Saturday morning alone, sending myself to sleep listening to Radio Luxembourg under the nylon sheets. I had only been in town a few months and had not made friends. I was thin, geeky, inclined to stammer, finding myself gravitating towards the nerdier end of class simply because the other end could find no use for me. Sunlight didn't appeal to me – not at that age, anyway – and the gunmetal sky and cloud that enclosed and constrained Deal seemed completely appropriate for a mindset mired in alienation. Sunlight meant physicality, participation, social interaction with girls. How much easier it was to commune with a sagacious (Bowie was in his twenties), otherworldly being, a benign iconoclast who appeared to know exactly what I was going through, even if he was being rather oblique about it. In my corner of my rain-lashed town on the rain-lashed island that was early Seventies Britain, I had found a kind of sanctuary, I suppose, not one I really understood, although certainly one I would enjoy exploring. Ziggy Stardust's testimony wasn't especially revealing, yet its artifice was completely compelling.

In hindsight, my interest in David Bowie could be seen as embarrassingly predictable – as I was at that age when cult heroes traditionally begin replacing your parents – but at the time (which, as someone else said about another epiphany, is the only time that matters when it comes to the transfiguring moment that divides before and after), he was most of what I could see. Looking around me, I couldn't see beyond the town's small rituals. There was bound to be decadence, not that I cared. My ill-formed ideas of debauchery were based around what I imagined were the glamorous extravagances of the fashionable exotics of the world. As far as I could see – which, with the mist and the rain, was often not very far at all – Deal was a town without exclamation marks, so I had to look for them elsewhere.

David Bowie meant a world far away from this dreary domesticity, a small world littered with tiny wicker wastebaskets, lavender soap, and what I was beginning to understand was entry-level food. Bowie represented the dream of a world that was clean and starry and rich and smart. Someone else's world, not mine.

*   *   *

IF THE PAST IS ALWAYS ANOTHER COUNTRY, by 1972 we were all so obsessed by space travel that the past felt like another planet. Throughout the Sixties and for much of the early Seventies, astronauts were our own twentieth-century conquistadors, turned by the media into living gods. From

John Glenn, who in 1962 became the first American to orbit the Earth, to Neil Armstrong, who on 20 July 1969 became the first man to walk on the moon, these were virtual supermen.

The entire world was captivated by the lunar missions of the *Apollo* astronauts. After eight days in space, when Neil Armstrong, Edwin 'Buzz' Aldrin, and Michael Collins splashed down in the Pacific Ocean to a presidential greeting aboard the recovery carrier, the USS *Hornet*, they were the heroes of the nation, and of the world. They became the personification of post-war imperialism, conquering what we knew of space, and carrying hope, goodness, and moral enlightenment with them, in little silver packages. One fifteen-year-old US schoolboy was quoted in the early Sixties as saying, 'John Glenn's an astronaut, and a baseball player ain't *nothing*.'

If you didn't wear a silver jumpsuit for a uniform then you may as well have been a postman. As turmoil became the world's chosen state, so these were the harbingers of change – men who were stepping out into the future, and taking pop culture with them. In America you could buy freeze-dried food, silver college jackets inspired by the Apollo spacesuits, while G.I. Joe (the US Action Man) even got his own astronaut outfit. Barbie was given a 'Miss Astronaut' outfit made out of a metallic silver fabric and which came with gold buckles, zip boots, a white plastic helmet (*so* Op-Art), and a miniature American flag. Cereal manufacturers produced everything from cardboard board games and multicoloured rubber aliens to toy guns and white plastic space visors. A toy wasn't a toy unless it glowed in the dark. A pen wasn't worth the ink inside it unless it was some sort of space pen, and wrote upside down. Magazine publishers found dozens of reasons to produce special commemorative editions, while if you were *Time*, *Life*, or *Newsweek*, astronaut covers were apparently compulsory. When the Italian company Ledragomma invented a large orange rubber ball in 1968, the obvious thing to do was to call it a Space Hopper. There were even baby rockets themselves, like the Valkyrie 2 Rocket ('Liquid gas propellant sends your Valkyrie 2 Rocket up to 1000 feet and an automatic parachute brings it safely back to Earth'). On TV, we had *The Jetsons*, *The Twilight Zone*, *My Favorite Martian*, Larry Hagman starred as an astronaut in the comedy *I Dream Of Jeannie*, *Star Trek* made household names of William Shatner and Leonard Nimoy, and the charts were full of novelty space acts (the Astronauts, the Tornadoes, etc.). Gerry Anderson was a one-man futuristic animation industry, and every one of his shows, from *Supercar* and *Fireball XL5* to *Joe 90* and *UFO* was immersed in alternative worlds seemingly inspired by current events. He wasn't alone. Immediately after Armstrong's landing, hotel magnate Barron Hilton revealed plans for the 'Lunar Hilton', to be constructed underneath the surface of the moon, and Pan Am announced it had accepted nearly 100,000 civilian reservations for tickets to the moon (returns, ha!), in anticipation of a round-trip service. It may have sounded fanciful, and it may have sounded daft, but no one was complaining. The future was now a real possibility. Space was now a legitimate strand of the entertainment industry. On the night of the moon landing itself, Ray Bradbury, the author of *Fahrenheit 451*, stormed out of David Frost's *Moon Party*, a hastily assembled TV talk show counter-pointing the news coverage with everything from a performance by Englebert Humperdinck to a discussion on the ethics of the lunar landing involving A. J. P. Taylor and Sammy Davis, Jr. Bradbury was so incensed by the irreverence of Frost's show, he jumped spaceship.

John Updike also referenced the moon landing, although not in any great celebratory way, using it as a theme in his 1971 novel *Rabbit Redux*. Updike's protagonist finds the moon shot fairly underwhelming, thinking it a political and technological stunt meant to distract us all from the social disorder down here on Earth. Television dominates the book's narrative, and in particular television coverage of the space mission, which is effectively treated as pointless and worthless.

The history of the future always looks quaint in hindsight. In the mid-twentieth century, literary historians were convinced we would all end up as Rodchenko's children, wearing futuristic versions of the Russian constructivist's anti-decorational work suits, complete with tightly fitting collars, elasticated cuffs, and overall-type trousers with dozens of self-adhesive fastenings and patch pockets. Science fiction novels of the time were full of characters wearing this sort of space-age boiler suit, as back then the future was always going to be peopled by hordes of Orwellian, intergalactic worker bees.

Until the Sixties, that is, when the future reinvented itself. Visually, the Swinging Sixties would not have happened were it not for the various fashion designers' obsessions with modernism and futurism, not least Mary Quant and Pierre Cardin, although fashion sociologists always cite Courrèges' 1964 collection with its short dresses, calf-length square-toed boots, and large, helmet-shaped hats – all in white – as the real kicker.

For the next few years, the look of the future became the domain of Hollywood costume designers, who spruced up everything from *Star Trek* to *Barbarella*. Ziggy Stardust, however, arrived from a galactic dust bowl with a look that had little to do with white, reflective, NASA-issue spacesuits, or indeed with the leather and denim sartorial orthodoxy popular in the rock clubs of West London, Sunset Boulevard, and the Lower East Side.

Space was all over the place. Jonathan King, like David Bowie, at the time just another singer-songwriter trying desperately to make it in the music industry, was actually able to get a tape of his single 'Everyone's Gone To The Moon' on board *Apollo 11*, not that anyone heard it. 'I managed to get it onto the actual spaceship on the tape that was going to the moon,' King said in 1972. 'They went up there and stood on the fucking thing, and as he got off and said one giant step for mankind and all that crap I thought, don't bother with all these awful truisms, play my fucking record, I want a plug. And they never did.' It was hardly surprising as the record was already four years old.

1972 also saw the release of one of the era's defining science-fiction films, the environmentally themed low-budget masterpiece, *Silent Running*, directed by the twenty-eight-year-old Douglas Trumbull (who had previously worked as a special effects supervisor on *2001: A Space Odyssey* and *The Andromeda Strain*), written by Steven Bochco (who would go on to help develop *Hill Street Blues*, *L.A. Law*, and *NYPD Blue*), and starring the incomparable Bruce Dern. He plays a space forest ranger in charge of a spacecraft carrying a greenhouse containing the last plant life from Earth. His staff includes three humans, as well as a trio of Lilliputian robots, who he nicknames Huey, Dewey, and Louie (inspiring George Lucas's R2-D2 character in *Star Wars*). When word arrives that the greenhouse is to be destroyed, Dern ignores the order and goes it alone, becoming an eco-hero in the process. As many critics pointed out, if the message of *2001* was that man needed more than guidance from beyond, the message of *Silent Running* (symbolically set in the year 2001), is that man has to be his own salvation.*

....

*Duncan Jones (formerly known as Zowie Bowie) is a huge fan of *Silent Running*, and cites it as an influence on his own space movie, his debut, *Moon*. '*Silent Running* is a lot more political than any of the other films on my list [of favourite sci-fi films], or even *Moon* itself, because it's coming out of a real time and place,' he said in

The other big sci-fi movie of 1972 was *Solaris*, a fascinating Russian psychodrama directed by Andrei Tarkovsky involving the mental breakdown of a science crew aboard a space station studying alien life-forms on the planet they're orbiting. The original Polish novel focuses on the inadequacy of communication between human and non-human species, although the film is more of a psychological drama than a traditional western gadget-fest. Tarkovsky was not especially keen on spaceships or realistic zero gravity, being far more interested in more naturalistic narrative drives. The space station 'has an absent-minded neglect about it that could have come straight out of Dostoyevsky's study,' wrote Richard Eder in the *New York Times*. 'There is a suspicion of rust on the pipes, and the furniture would look at home in the Omsk railroad station. One has the feeling that

---

2009, at the time of *Moon*'s release. 'Douglas Trumbull was trying to get a message across about environmental issues. Bruce Dern is fantastic in it and the characters of Huey, Dewey, and Louie are terrific as well. They created them by hiring these guys who were amputees, building costumes for them in which they walked around on their hands. Once you know that, you realise just how clever they were when they made that film. It was just a brilliant use of limited resources, and was very inspiring for *Moon*, which we made for only five million dollars; even today, I'm very willing to accept the effects the way they are if a story is well told. *Silent Running* is a less direct influence on *Moon* than *Outland* but, like Sam Bell in *Moon*, Bruce Dern's character is not necessarily the nicest guy in the world. If you haven't seen the film you have to see what he's capable of doing.'

wrappers of half-eaten sausage are lying just out of sight and that a samovar is at work. Outer space is shabbiness, lots of tea and urgent philosophical discussions that leave no time for shaving. Nothing that's visible matters very much except for nature – shots of a pond of waterweeds or a running horse – and life's surface is quite unimportant. Because of it, the blockish camera work, the egg-like colours, and the general visual poverty are almost irrelevant. What matters is the conversations, the problems they raise, the faces that reflect them, seen blurrily as if at the end of an all-night session.'

As soon as George Lucas unveiled *Star Wars* in 1977, Hollywood-science fiction movies would all become high-gloss space westerns, often with an undercurrent of self-parody, but films like *Solaris*, *Silent Running*, 1973's *Soylent Green* and John Carpenter's black comedy *Dark Star* from the same year, along with – how could any of us ever forget? – the surreal image-fest that was *The Man Who Fell To Earth* (1976), were proof that the spirit of independent cinema could reach the furthest reaches of the galaxy. (Bowie's appearance in Nic Roeg's film totally affected the film offers he got for years afterwards. 'I get offered so many bad movies,' he said in 1983. 'And [my parts] are all raging queens or transvestites or Martians.')

It's difficult to imagine this from a distance of over forty years, but as a leitmotif 'space' was as ubiquitous in the Sixties and Seventies as the threat of nuclear war was in the Eighties. In some respects it defined our lives, at least in terms of its juxtaposition with what was happening down here on Earth: no matter how bad things were on terra firma, up there in space, the human race was pushing hard into a bright and prosperous new future. Space was sexy, and space was modern, and it infected everything from architecture, fashion, and interior design to cinema, automotive design, and pop music, particularly the type made by David Bowie.

In this respect it had all started way back in the late Fifties, when space-age pop emerged as a way to show off fancy new hi-fi equipment, when technology provided record companies with a showcase for the pan-galactic spectrum of audio reproduction. This echoed the Populuxe mid-century modern designs affecting architecture, automobiles, furniture, and retail environments all over the US. Space-age designs emphasised motion, using boomerangs, flying saucers, atoms, upswept roofs, curvaceous, geometric shapes, and bold, extreme use of glass, steel and neon. Populuxe evoked a sense of futurism and luxury, and – coupled with a suburban fascination for all things Polynesian – created a fantasy world eagerly fed by the entertainment industry. Music and movies became passports to paradise – in split-screen Technicolor, in a Maserati, accompanied by glockenspiel, clave, and marimba. At the cocktail party of our dreams, in our own exotic ranch-style space-place – reachable only by a two-door supersonic Firedrome convertible or a Skyway jet, Danny Williams was rarely off the turntable, Esquivel rarely off the piano; Dean Martin held court by a kidney-shaped pool as Walter Wanderley and Burt Bacharach attempted the perfect Martini. Here in our Polynesian Populuxe dreamworld high above the city, prosperity and convenience surrounded us ('Jeez, this chaise longue has tail-fin arms!'), as did the stabbing saxophones, angular banjos, swirling Moogs, giddy basslines, and gorgeous intrusions of massed violins. Here, in our faux-frontier fantasyland, night closed in, the moon cast extravagant shadows on the street below, and the robotic fizz of laughter crawled from the TV.

Here in the UK this seemed all the more exotic. To teenagers, even those vaguely aware of things like Vietnam, America was still enormously cool. America was young. 'America used to be the big youth place in everybody's imagination,' said John Lennon in an interview in 1966. 'America had teenagers and everywhere else just had people.'

Americana loomed large in my life in 1972, as, like Ziggy Stardust, it meant escapism, and the only other things that captured my imagination at the time were Joseph Heller's *Catch-22*, and, a little while later, George Lucas's *American Graffiti*. Set in California in 1962 – and, from what I could gather at the time, reproduced rather accurately – Lucas's nostalgic coming-of-age movie was full to the flat-tops with the very best music from that era. It was only a decade away, a blink by modern standards, but back then 1962 felt as though it came from a different century. The confluence of brash truck-stop imagery, over-designed automobiles, and the kind of teenage fashions that were by then almost comically generic, still seemed almost transcendentally exotic. The Cleftones' 'Heart And Soul', 'A Thousand Miles Away' by the Heartbeats, 'Party Doll' by Buddy Knox, 'See You In September' by the Tempos, and everything else on the *American Graffiti* soundtrack sounded as if it had been made by intuitive cavemen, at least compared to the kind of records that were common currency in 1972 and 1973. It was a retro-neon micro-climate, both literally (the film was set in Modesto, in California, and for reasons of cost mostly shot at night) and figuratively, signifying a desire to live in the past rather than the present. There was an urgent sense of authenticity about the film, one sadly missing from all the faux Fifties music cluttering up the British charts at the time.

The Fifties were still everywhere. One of the big British films being made in 1972 was *That'll Be The Day*. Ostensibly a vehicle for the young, pretty-boy pop star David Essex, it turned out to be a classic example of Britrock *cinéma-vérité*, one that expertly summed up the drabness and poverty of the post-war years, a small sepia world of coffee bars, ducktails, jukeboxes, and squalid sex. Unlike the dawn of pop in the US, which was glamorous almost beyond belief, the early rock and roll years in the UK revolved around holiday camps and funfairs, full of frustrated ambition and class hatred. Rock and roll was barely fifteen years old, and already it was being celebrated as a golden period, even if the British version was a little tatty around the edges, perhaps because it was a safe place to revisit after all the turmoil of the Sixties. Certainly the pop charts were full of the chugga-chugga twelve-bar swagger of rock and roll; T. Rex, Slade, and Mud based many of their biggest hits on old-fashioned rock, and few people seemed to either care or notice.

The same year, even one of rock 'n' roll's most cele-brated legends was experiencing a comeback as he hit the revival circuit, appealing to all those ageing British teds who had wilfully refused to engage with any form of music since the Beatles decided to comb their hair down instead of up. Chuck Berry had been booked to play at Coventry Univer-sity's Lanchester Arts Festival, supporting Billy Preston, Slade, and Pink Floyd ('One of the most adventurous bills ever,' suggested the *NME*, and they weren't wrong). Using a local pick-up band (Berry was famous for always travelling alone, demanding cash before he went on stage, rarely acknowledging whoever had been hired to back him), Berry rattled through 'Roll Over Beethoven', 'School Day', 'Back In The USA', 'Maybellene', and a long, vulgar version of 'Reelin' And Rockin'', which then turned into 'Fuck Around The Clock', followed by an audience-response song that had become one of the mainstays of Berry's act, the appalling 'My Ding-A-Ling'. The gig was recorded, Berry's reductive sing-along was released as a single, and one of the inventors of rock 'n' roll had his biggest ever British hit.

In 1972 many of us were living in the past, even those like me who didn't really have much of one. It was only eight years since the release of *A Hard Day's Night* (to the day, actually: it premiered on 6 July 1964), seven years since the death of Churchill, barely six since the death of Buster

Keaton. In January, Rose Hamilton had become the first female judge to officiate at the Old Bailey and the same month British miners had gone on strike for the first time since 1926. We were still only months away from Nixon's massive 'Christian bombing' raids on Hanoi, while Vietnam remained the most popular backdrop for counter-cultural insurrection. The previous year, the former world heavy-weight champion, Sonny Liston, was found dead at his home in Las Vegas.

Sometimes the world we know today can appear strikingly similar to the one we inhabited in 1972, not least because of the linear nature of the entertainment industry, and the way in which the Seventies are still heavily referenced today. I always imagine the passage of time, in decades, as an arc rising from left to right (whereas the months of the current year move round the clock anti-clockwise, with December sitting between midnight and five past), and the distance between 1972 and 2012 looks ridiculously short (in my head no more than six inches), hardly equivalent to how forty years ought to look. If you were famous in 1972, there's a good chance you are still famous now. David Bowie is and forever will be.

Yet the distance from 1932 through to 1972 seems unimaginably long, via a world war, Korea and Vietnam, the East/West divide, JFK, MLK, the space race, the cultural and class emancipation of the Sixties, attrition in the Middle East, and the unanticipated explosion of pop culture. Stop, though, and look again, and the distance between 1972 and

2012 was just as long, as demonstrated by the nature of fame. These days, using the ever-increasing channels of social media, it is possible to communicate personally on a global scale equipped with only a mobile telephone and a point of view. In 2012, celebrity was only a tweet or a poke away. In 1972, the distance between David Bowie and myself was little different than the distance between Deal and Mars, or wherever else it was Bowie playfully imagined Ziggy had come from. To a generation of pasty, bum-fluffed school-boys, and over-excited, under-confident schoolgirls, Ziggy Stardust was the most exotic thing we had ever seen. And he was talking directly to us, the intergalactic gypsy queen beaming straight to every secondary-modern, grammar, and crammer of early Seventies Britain.

By 1972, Britain had more than anyone's fair share of teenagers, and they were ripe for exploitation. David Bowie had already tried. In 1968, inspired by a combination of the Apollo missions and seeing Stanley Kubrick's *2001: A Space Odyssey*, he recorded a song called 'Space Oddity'. He saw the film three times, at London's Casino Cinerama, which had a huge 70mm screen. 'It was the sense of isolation I related to,' Bowie said, in early 2012, forty years after first seeing the film. 'I found the whole thing amazing. I was out of my gourd, very stoned when I went to see it – several times – and it was really a revelation to me. It got the song flowing.'

Considering that up until this point Bowie was thought

to be something of an unsuccessful novelty act, the record was actually quite sophisticated. 'Space Oddity' was carefully constructed, with seven distinct sections, one of which – the 'tin can' section – was loosely based on the breezy chords used in Simon & Garfunkel's 'Old Friends' from their *Bookends* album, which Bowie loved. He recorded the demo with John Hutchinson, the guitarist from his old band the Buzz, and if you listen to Bowie's first recording of the song you can hear him singing the first verse. 'The single was going to be by Bowie and Hutch,' says Bowie. 'But then, two or three days before the session, Hutch said that he really didn't think that we were going to make it in rock. He was married, and had a kid up in Yorkshire, and he decided he was going home. So I ended up doing the whole thing myself.' The first proper version of the song appeared in Bowie's promotional film *Love You Till Tuesday* (in an interview a year later Bowie said this original version was a mix of Salvador Dalí, *2001*, and the Bee Gees), while a rerecorded version was rush-released to coincide with the *Apollo 11* moon landing the following summer. It was promoted through advertisements for the Stylophone, which was played by Bowie on the record. The single generated decent enough reviews, but it wasn't until the BBC started using it to accompany their coverage of the US moon landing that it began getting some traction.

'It was picked up by British television and used as the background music for the landing itself,' says Bowie, 'though

I'm sure they really weren't listening to the lyrics *at all*; it wasn't a pleasant thing to juxtapose against a moon landing. Of course, I was overjoyed that they did. Obviously some BBC official said, "Right then. That space song. Major Tom . . ." blah blah blah. "That'll be great." Nobody had the heart to tell the producer, "Um . . . but he gets stranded in space, sir." '

As for Major Tom himself, Bowie got the name from theatre posters he'd seen in Bromley as a boy, advertising a well-known music hall performer, Tom Major, who was actually the father of Prime Minister John Major.

'When I originally wrote about Major Tom,' says Bowie, 'I thought I knew all about the great American dream and where it started and where it should stop. Here was the great blast American technological know-how shoving this guy into space, but once he gets there he's not quite sure why he's there. And that's where I left him.'

To promote 'Space Oddity' Bowie was photographed in the London flat of kinetic sculptor Dante Leonelli, dressed up as a space boy in a silver jumpsuit (his Major Tom suit was made by Dandy Fashions in the King's Road) and generic frizzy hair.

'I suppose it was inspired by the newspaper malarkey about space shots and all that,' Bowie said at the time. 'It just sort of oozed out. There's never any heavy thought behind much of my material. It just finds its way out. I have very few preconceived ideas about what I'm going to write.'

For someone who had been so off-kilter for so much of

his career, 'Space Oddity' came as some surprise, as it was immediately ahead of the curve.*

While 'Space Oddity' was as much of a nod to Stanley Kubrick as to the space race itself, so 'Starman', and indeed the whole Ziggy Stardust project was something of a throwback, another example of Bowie regurgitating old ideas (it had worked once, so why shouldn't it work again? Not only that, but alien life forms obviously manifested themselves in many different ways, so who was to say that this one couldn't have red hair and allude to homosexuality?). For Bowie, the benevolent spaceman

SINCE 1963 HE HAD BUSIED HIMSELF ON THE FRINGES OF THE MUSIC INDUSTRY, POSING IN FASHION SHOOTS, SELLING HIMSELF AS A YOUTH SPOKESMAN, AND MAKING RECORDS IN A VARIETY OF STYLES, FROM R&B AND SOUL, TO MUSIC HALL, AND PROTO-PSYCHEDELICA.

was already something of a trope, so why not go round once more?

....

* His obsession with space flight is ironic when you consider that, ever since a traumatic flight to London from Cyprus after a brief winter holiday with his wife Angie in 1971, Bowie had been petrified of flying.

Up until 'Space Oddity', Bowie had been something of a failure. At school he had shown some flair for art, and though he failed everything except English at O-level, this got him a job as a junior visualiser with the advertising agency Nevendy Hirst in Bond Street for six months: '. . . which I loathed. I had romantic notions of artists' garrets, though I didn't fancy starving. Their main product was Ayds slimming biscuits, and I also remember lots of felt-tip drawings and paste-ups of bloody raincoats. And in the evenings I dodged from one dodgy rock band to another looking for one who'd let me write the songs.' He then moonlighted as a saxophonist for a series of mediocre R&B groups (his sax was plastic), hopping from tinny band to tinny band, buying the instrument after reading Jack Kerouac's *On the Road*. Like many his age at the time, he wanted to be like Sal Paradise and Dean Moriarty, 'And I succeeded, as much as anyone could in a dump like Bromley.'

Since 1963 he had busied himself on the fringes of the music industry, posing in fashion shoots, selling himself as a youth spokesman, and making records in a variety of styles, from R&B, 'mod' and soul, to music hall, and proto-psychedelica. As Jon Savage wrote about the ambitious changeling of this period, 'It was as though the currents of the decade flowed through him.' Or at least the currents as appropriated by advertising campaigns. He had no interest in any Sixties doctrine of revolution. According to his manager at the time, Kenneth Pitt, 'His direction was that in which he happened to be facing in any given week.' From

1964 to 1971 he was fleetingly a member of the Konrads, the Hooker Brothers, the King Bees, the Mannish Boys, the Lower Third, the Buzz, the Riot Squad, Turquoise, Feathers, Arnold Corns and the Hype (he even recorded songs for the *Top Of The Pops* albums, as Elton John also did, memorably covering 'Penny Lane' – on this track, while pretending to be northern when singing the word 'customer', he forgets to do the same with the 'another' that precedes it). Bowie's struggle was an easy one to grasp – it was a struggle against becoming nobody, and then slinking back again to south London. Or worse perhaps, Deal.

In a way, Ziggy Stardust had three births. David Robert Jones was born in Brixton, in south London on 8 January 1947, but he didn't assume his alias until eighteen years later, taking the name of the Arkansas knife in 1965 to avoid being confused with Davy Jones of the Monkees, who were then temporarily challenging the Beatles for pop supremacy – Bowie liked the way Mick Jagger's surname sounded aggressive, like a dagger, and wanted something with similar connotations. Immediately his past had been disappeared.

There was a theatrical seam to his family: his father, Haywood Stenton Jones, enjoyed vaudeville, and had once invested in a theatre troupe, as well as a London piano bar called the Boop-A-Doop, before losing all his money and joining the charity Barnardo's as a promotions director. Bowie's mother, Peggy, was an usherette. There were rumours of mental instability in the family, although Bowie tended to exaggerate them in order to appear more interesting. 'There's a schizoid streak within the family, so I dare say that I'm affected by that,' he said in 1973. 'The majority of the people in my family have been in some kind of mental institution, as for my brother he doesn't want to leave [his]. He likes it very much. My mother signed him in, which is very sad, but she's been in as well. She thought it did her good but it didn't. We had to take her on holiday, we put her out in Cyprus for a while.' Bowie's older half-brother Terry was diagnosed as a manic-depressive and schizophrenic, and was eventually institutionalised. In 1985, he climbed over the wall of a psychiatric hospital in Surrey and walked to the nearby station, where he lay down on the track directly in the path of the oncoming London express train. He was forty-seven.

Bowie didn't attend the funeral, sending roses instead. And a card: 'You've seen more things than we can imagine, but all these moments will be lost, like tears washed away by the rain. God bless you – David.'

It was Terry who first introduced his brother to Jack Kerouac, Nietzsche, and Buddhism, Terry who took him up to London to see the beatniks, who smuggled him into Soho strip-clubs. 'Terry really opened up my mind,' said Bowie. 'He had an innate intelligence, an excitement about the world and an appetite for knowledge. He taught me how to learn things, how to go out of my way to discover things.' As he got older, Terry's schizophrenia would increasingly become a problem, making him angry and distressed. 'He was a big guy, very physical, very violent. He fought with a lot of people.

'I remember once taking him to a Cream concert. The sound level utterly devastated him. On the way home he had a terrible vision that the pavements and the roads were breaking up and fire was coming out of them. He fell down and was calling out to me to help him because he was being sucked into the cracks. It was horrible.' Years later, during the *Let's Dance* period, Bowie would tell an interviewer, 'It is my fault we grew apart, and it is painful.'

Bowie rose up from a world just as invisible as mine, more unknown to the great majority of mankind than a Bantu village or the easternmost reaches of Brooklyn. As Tom Wolfe wrote, Tongaland and the Puerto Rican slums may at least reek, in the imagination, of bloodlust and loins oozing after sundown. The London suburbs, however, like the south-east coast, were empty of fizz, devoid of anything but quiet desperation and the desire to keep up and move on. And David Bowie was born with a need to move on.

Which is more than enough to make a person want to be a pop star.

For a while in the mid-Sixties, Bowie was one of those straight-trousered, straight-haired, bombers-for-breakfast members of Swinging London put through their paces by Wolfe in 'The Noonday Underground', a sixteen-year-old wannabe in a custom-made shirt and a Carnaby Street suit, with a college boy haircut and a general sense of under-achievement: if everyone around him was becoming a copywriter or a model or a designer or a photographer or a set designer or a writer or a film director (better) or a pop star (best), then why not me, he thought? Why not David Jones?

But in those days nothing worked. He could sing about Trafalgar Square and Old Compton Street and the King's Road and Portobello Road – where it was important to wear black velvet trousers, a Regency coat, and big-buckle shoes – but none of it rang true. Bowie's orgy of nostalgia – dressed up as a *Time* article about London's swinging nightlife – was no different from anyone else's. His lyrics at the time were too scattershot, too imprecise. He couldn't even write to order: towards the end of 1967, he was asked to supply some English lyrics to the French song '*Comme d'Habitude*', eventually coming up with 'Even A Fool Learns To Love'. The song was so bad that the publisher opted for Paul Anka's lyrics instead. The song was 'My Way'. (Bowie was so incensed that he adapted the tune's opening chord sequence, and used it for 'Life On Mars', which started life as a parody of the Sinatra recording.)

'Space Oddity' was smart as it jumped ahead on the Monopoly board, bouncing *off* the board, up into space, away from the parochial reality of mods, dollies, and their like. Stylistically, at least, it encouraged him to experiment.

Bowie once said that he found freedom only in the realms of his own eccentricity, referring specifically to his hair and clothes. On the original cover of his 1971 LP, *The Man Who Sold The World*, Bowie was seen reclining in a 'mandress', an ankle-length blue and green silk creation designed by Mr Fish. (He only stopped wearing his smock dresses when he was accosted by a large Texan whilst touring the US.) During his *Hunky Dory* period he wore floppy hats, primary-coloured bellbottoms, and shoes from Terry de Havilland's Cobblers To The World. (De Havilland started life in the East End as plain old Terry Higgins. Like Twiggy's manager Justin de Villeneuve – born Nigel Davies, the photographer David Bailey used to call him 'Justin New Town' – Higgins had decided to give his name a face-lift.) Bowie was so thin he looked as though he'd spent the previous six months existing on a diet of nothing but the juice sucked from a wet mitten. He was audibly wan, his paleness almost looking like a statement of intent. You could hear his whey-facedness as soon as you heard him sing.

Like Katharine Hepburn, Bowie had great cheekbones, although it was difficult to ignore his eyes, one of which had a much larger pupil, due to a childhood accident (contrary to popular belief, he didn't have different coloured eyes, they were both the same colour. It's just that the enlarged pupil – a condition called anisocoria – gave the effect of two different coloured eyes). The pupil stayed permanently open instead of dilating and contracting with the light, and it left him with a wonky sense of perspective. When driving, for instance, cars didn't come towards him, they just got bigger. This made him even more alien, even more intriguing, and an almost perfect advertisement for his narcissism. If – through his constant reinvention – Bowie liked to erase any trace of his true self, that true self always had its own, somewhat quirky, shield (he was legally blind in his damaged eye).

Bowie may have been expedient, but he had a genuine sense of purpose; he *hated* orthodoxy. In March 1973, when he had become a star, he was featured in Andy Warhol's *Interview*, and asked about the state of British culture. 'It's all on a down play,' he said, emphasising its reductive nature. 'You know we've got this thing in England, to be hip is to speak very down – like John Peel. And that just about sums up England. They don't realise when they talk like that, then that is what they represent – absolutely. John underplaying everything like vodka. Totally kind of frustrating within himself I suppose.'

By 1971 he had got the whole reinvention thing down pat. 'I believe in fantasy and star images,' he told the *Cheltenham Chronicle*. 'I am very aware of these kind of people and feel they are very important figures in our society. People like to focus on somebody who they might consider not quite the same as them. Whether it's true or not is immaterial.' Bowie won't have read it, but one of Richard Nixon's aides said a similar thing in a memo to his internal staff during the 1968 election, 'We have to be very clear on this point: that the response is to the image, not to the man, since ninety-nine per cent of the voters have no contact with the man. It's not what's there that counts, it's what's projected.'

1972 would be the year in which Bowie's world finally expanded to his own satisfaction. Compounding his success with Ziggy was his new-found ability to help with heroes and friends alike: Iggy Pop, whom Bowie defined as a nihilistic god; Lou Reed, who with the Velvet Underground was around at rock's alternative Year Zero; and Mott The Hoople, who were the band Bowie may have fronted had he not been blessed with the Spiders. When Bowie threw a welcome party for Iggy at a little vegetarian restaurant just off Westbourne Grove that summer, he was fusing two different worlds; as guests sat on the floor eating lukewarm samosas, Iggy and Ziggy walked amongst the throng, a pair of glam devils. Yet if Iggy Pop was 'strange enough' (to be successful), Bowie had slogged and slogged to get where he was in 1972; even if to most of us he looked fully formed and spontaneous.

TWO

'Lady Stardust Sang His Songs, Of Darkness And Disgrace'

DAVY JONES INVENTS ZIGGY, 1971–1972

'Starman', The Rise And Fall Of Ziggy Stardust
And The Spiders From Mars, *and how a haircut,
some premeditated schizophrenia, and a rivalry
with Marc Bolan begat Glam. 0.2.*

'The four of us were dressed in the height of fashion, which
in those days was a pair of black very tight tights with the
old jelly mould, as we called it, fitting on the crotch
underneath the tights, this being to protect and also a
sort of design you could viddy clear enough in a certain
light, so that I had one in the shape of a spider'
Alex, in Anthony Burgess' *A Clockwork Orange*

BY 1971, David Bowie was almost a has-been. In the two
years since 'Space Oddity' he had wandered back to the
fringes of success, and his albums were gradually pushing him to the margins. Even at the time the creation of

Ziggy seemed unduly calculated, yet somehow the time felt right.

The idea of a larger-than-life rock figure struck Bowie around the end of 1970. The British charts were full of dismal Radio 2 fodder like Shirley Bassey, Lee Marvin, Rolf Harris, and Norman Greenbaum on the one hand, and old Sixties hangovers such as Crosby, Stills and Nash on the other. One of the few records he liked was Free's 'All Right Now', as it had a certain kind of attitude. It spoke of freedom, but without any particular purpose in mind. For Bowie, Britain was turning into denim hell. Street life was long hair, beards, flares, and leftover beads from the Sixties.

The idea for Ziggy was kick-started in January 1971, when Bowie was on a promotional tour of the US. At one point on the tour he was rooming with the record producer Tom Ayers, who at the time was working with the ageing rocker Gene Vincent (Bowie loved old rockers, and had once idolised Billy Fury). One night Vincent and Bowie recorded a song the Brit had just written, 'Hang On To Yourself', and Bowie convinced himself that he could adapt a Vincent-type character and turn him into a vehicle for himself. 'I went on to explain that Ziggy wasn't going to be a real rock star and that I would play him,' said Bowie. 'I think they all thought I was talking in terms of a musical. It's possible I was.'

He was also going to weave in a little Vince Taylor. He was a British rock 'n' roll star brought up in America, who had found some success at the very end of the Fifties, and whose most famous song, 'Brand New Cadillac', was covered by the Clash on *London Calling* in 1979. Vince Taylor wore black leather like Gene Vincent, wore gloves (also inspiring glam-rock throwback Alvin Stardust), sported eyeliner, would chew gum when singing, and demonstrated an ability to celebrate the obvious tropes of early rock 'n' roll, while offering a broadly drawn caricature of how a rock star should look and behave. He embraced booze, LSD, and over the years ever-so-slowly went crazy. Finally, after years of erratic behaviour, he fired his band and went on stage alone one night in a white bedsheet, telling the audience to rejoice, and that he was in fact the living embodiment of the biblical apostle Matthew. Obviously. He was committed to an asylum and ended up working as an aircraft mechanic at Geneva airport, just a short drive from where Bowie would one day live. Bowie had met Taylor a few times in the Sixties, and says he remembers him opening a map outside a Tube station on the Strand, laying it out on the pavement and kneeling over it with a magnifying glass, pointing out all the sites where UFOS were going to land.

'He used to hang out on Tottenham Court Road and I got to know him then,' says Bowie. 'He had these strange plans, showing where there was money buried, that he was going to get together; he was going to create this new Atlantis at one time . . . And he always stayed in my mind as an example of what can happen in rock 'n' roll. I'm not sure if I held him up as an idol or as something not to become. Bit of both probably. There was something very tempting about him going completely off the edge. Especially at my age, then, it seemed very appealing: Oh, I'd love to end up like that, totally nuts. Ha ha! And so he re-emerged in this Ziggy Stardust character.'

So he was added to the pot.

The character had other, more fundamental, influences, too, namely the exoticism and the theatrics he experienced at his local church when he was a boy. 'My mother really was in love with the ritual of the Catholic church,' says Bowie. 'I remember the look of pure devotion on her face as I stood beside her. I'd never seen her as moved, as trusting, as that. Yet I felt somehow that she was falling for something, that it was all really a kind of scam.'

The real origins of Ziggy, however, date back to an earlier date in 1970, when he had made a pilgrimage to New York to see the Velvet Underground. After their set, Bowie pushed his way backstage, knocked on their dressing room door, and asked to speak to Lou Reed. To his obvious delight – and, it has to be said, surprise – the band's singer came out to talk to him. 'I went back home, telling everyone, "Wow! I actually met Lou Reed." Then one of my friends said, "You can't have. Lou left the band a year ago." '

' "But it was Lou Reed," I said. "He looked like Lou Reed. He talked to me as Lou Reed." In fact it was the guy who'd replaced Lou in the band [Doug Yule] and who looked just like him. That got my mind really working. About a rock star who wasn't real but in whom the audience – me – totally believed. I think that was probably the real beginning of Ziggy Stardust.'

Ziggy was broadly sketched as a benevolent and sexually ambivalent folk hero. Yet he wasn't born in a vacuum, and the musical and theatrical themes were cherry-picked from the Velvet Underground, Iggy Pop, Lindsay Kemp, Marc Bolan, and all the darker and sexually aggressive elements of garage rock, glam rock, and what was already being called punk. Ziggy was a composite of everything that Bowie found intriguing about rock 'n' roll, some of which had been sourced by his manager at the time, Ken Pitt, who in 1967 had come from America with a copy of the first Velvet Underground album. 'I'd been in New York [and had] met Andy Warhol and the people from the Factory and I knew everything about them would appeal to David,' said Pitt. 'So I brought their album back for him. He was living in my flat at the time. He put it on, listened to part of it, turned round and said, "I'm going to pinch that."'

Bowie's world was one he wanted full of drag queens, transsexuals, and pin-eyed pop-tarts. He may have started the decade looking like a renegade – if snaggle toothed – Hollywood siren (Lauren Bacall was often mentioned), but he wanted nothing to do with those awful singer-songwriters now, with their sagging denim and naval-gazing dirges. Oh no, not them. Bowie had a new-found confidence bolstered by new management, a pushy wife (Angie), and a genuine belief in himself as an *übermensch*, a 'homo superior', a leader of men. With his seemingly immobile short, spiky hair, his wink, and his Nietzschean PR spiel, he was finally ready for the Seventies.

And we, the Seventies, were ready for him. Empowered by the belief that we really were the children of the revolution, and not really wanting to have anything to do with the revolution itself, who better to lead the charge over the hill than an imperious chisel-cheeked spaceman?

The ingredients for his version of high-glam were dizzyingly disparate (it was almost as if he created Ziggy at a granular level), from the droogs in *A Clockwork Orange*, Lindsay Kemp, Kansai Yamamoto, and Fritz Lang, to Luke Reinhart, Andy Warhol, and Colin Wilson. Oh, and rather a lot of Iggy Pop. There was some Marc Bolan in there, some Legendary Stardust Cowboy, and Nik Cohn's 1967 novel, *I Am Still The Greatest Says Johnny Angelo* (a book about a messianic rock star).

The Legendary Stardust Cowboy was an eccentric American country and western singer called Norman Carl Odom, who was on the Mercury label with Bowie in 1969. He was a one-hit wonder, the hit being a novelty song called 'Paralyzed' which reached the Billboard Top 200 the same year. He once appeared on the US TV show *Rowan & Martin's Laugh-In* but when the audience collapsed in laughter, he stormed off, devastated.

'He's the guy I got the name from, [and I] just liked the Stardust bit because it was so silly,' said Bowie. 'It's the original outsider music, music by people probably not playing with a full deck. He played guitar, and he had a drummer and a one-legged trumpet player. They assembled their music without any awareness that there are supposed to be rules to follow. And so they go in directions that wouldn't occur to even a semi-trained musician. And it's such a freeing exercise, listening to them commit to those performances with full integrity, knowing they're not joking. When I first joined Mercury Records in the late Sixties, he was one of the only other artists they had. They gave me his entire catalogue, which at the time was three singles. I immediately fell in love with his music. Well actually, the idea of his music. As the music itself wasn't recognisable as being such.' (Bowie later recorded Odom's 'I Took A Trip On A Gemini Spacecraft' for his *Heathen* album, and actually made a fair fist of it; the original is almost unlistenable.)

Visually, Bowie's idea was to hit a look somewhere between Gene Vincent, Vince Taylor, and Malcolm McDowell, the star of *A Clockwork Orange*, with his one mascaraed eye, and the feel of *The Wild Boys* by William Burroughs – a marauding gang who all had Bowie knives ('That wasn't lost on me,' said Bowie). The band also had to have an arachnoid feel – they weren't called the Spiders by accident.

The name Ziggy actually came from a tailor's shop called 'Ziggy's' that he passed one day on a train through London's East End. He liked it as it reminded him of Iggy, and, 'as it was a tailor's shop I thought, well, this whole thing is gonna be about clothes, so it was my own little joke.'*

---

*Bowie would eventually come clean about all his influences, something not all musicians are so keen to do. Managers tend to fess up to their strategies as it makes them sound like cynical

Bowie and Ziggy were not only conflated to great effect, but Bowie had become transformative. Whereas rock was the music of rebellion, encouraging you to kick that silly old tin can down the road as far as you liked, this was the music of transformation, which also held the promise of trans-formation. Although the whole idea was essentially an attempt to revive his flagging career, Bowie ended up creating one of the most durable pop stars of all time. It was all about the quality, and in this he was relentless, monomaniacal and unbending in his focus.

Bowie was always an expert magpie, and would steal anything from anyone if he thought he could use it (lyrical themes, Gene Vincent's stage technique, guitar riffs . . .). Ziggy was an agglomeration of everything that Bowie had soaked up through a decade in the entertainment industry; it was as if it had all been braided, with great attention to detail, with exacting standards. Ziggy Stardust was a total construct. This was an enigma built in a laboratory, one that fed off thirty years of qualitative research.

---

impresarios (Malcolm McLaren promoting outrage with the Sex Pistols, or Bernie Rhodes encouraging the Clash to write polemical lyrics), but rarely the talent. Others are brazen: David Byrne dropped out of Rhode Island School Of Design to form a band – Talking Heads – that sounded as though all the members were technical drawing students, until Byrne went native and performed a spectacular volte face. Having been introduced to the rhythms of Fela Kuti, he quietly became obsessed: 'The grooves were so intense, trance inducing almost. I couldn't wait to steal that sound.'

'For me the transformation happened over a period of time, so it wasn't any great surprise,' says Ken Scott, who produced *Ziggy Stardust*. 'I didn't really notice it was going on because it was so gradual. I was seeing David fairly regularly, and the character just got further and further evolved. It's like your kids: when you see them every day you don't really think they're changing, you don't realise how much they've grown until their grandparents come over and say, "Oh God, they got so big." It was that kind of situation.'

Ziggy's clothes were flamboyantly ambitious. Before Ziggy Stardust, Bowie had always been some way behind the curve, rather too eager to keep up with those ahead of him. In photographs from the Sixties he mostly looks average, knowing which sort of jacket to wear, how thin his trousers and ties should be, but never looking transcendent – with Ziggy he was so far ahead of everyone else, he may as well have not been in the race (and it was always a race). The first Ziggy outfits were put together by Bowie's designer friend, Freddie Buretti, in January 1972, riffing on luxury and opulence. The singer was encouraged to wear extravagantly proportioned jackets, jumpsuits, kimonos, dresses, loincloths, you name it. 'When I first started wearing dresses there was a big outcry about them,' Bowie told the readers of *Mirabelle* magazine, revving them up a little, 'which I really couldn't understand. There doesn't seem to be anything wrong to me in any guy wearing something which is both comfortable and fashionable.' He'd worn eyeshadow as a mod, knew that Elvis had worn it, too, and so started using make-up in a way no pop star had ever done before – no male star, anyway. Some of the other glam rock groups may have worn cheek glitter before him, but Bowie did it with so much more panache. Up until Ziggy, only women were allowed to have legs, not men. Ziggy showed his – clean-shaven, apparently elongated, pushed tightly into platforms. Everything helped: Bowie's Sixties friend Calvin Mark Lee used to wear a small, diamond-shaped, reflective forehead decoration, and Bowie expanded on the idea, changing the size and shape. Fashion designer Ossie Clark was so impressed he even launched a 'Ziggy' dress. Many years later Bowie would tell me that for him, dressing is all about performance, and that clothing only accentuated his characters. With Ziggy, a twenty-four/seven character, he had a twenty-four/seven wardrobe, and costume was essential to the showmanship.

Clothes, though vital to the success of Ziggy, were nothing compared to the influence of the haircut. For the cover of the *Ziggy Stardust* LP Bowie's hair had been cut into a blond crop, and though it was a complete change from the long locks seen on the Garboesque cover of *Hunky Dory* (his previous LP), it was not the definitive Ziggy. The Ziggy cut was done by Suzy Fussey in February 1972, not long after Bowie's appearance on *The Old Grey Whistle Test.** Suzy

....

*If the Spiders' performance on *Top Of The Pops* was epochal, their appearance on *The Old Grey Whistle Test* was actually far more exhilarating. They played three songs, the best of which was worked at the Evelyn Paget hair salon in Beckenham, south London, close to where Bowie and Angie spent most of their time, at a place called Haddon Hall where they rented rooms. She used to cut Bowie's mother's hair, who then introduced her to Angie. 'I did Angela's hair a couple of times and suddenly she asked me to come to Haddon Hall and meet David, and have a look at his hair,' says Suzy. Angie's hair had already been cut by Suzy (and subsequently dyed red, white, and blue).

'David came in and asked me what I'd do with his hair,' says Suzy. 'At the time it was all Marc Bolan, and long hair was prevalent. I said, I'd cut it off. He had a great face, you see. And his body was odd; kind of girlish. He seemed excited

---

'Queen Bitch' (a song written about Lou Reed), from *Hunky Dory*, with Bowie sashaying like a hula-hula girl on speed. He looks off his chops, dancing on the spot, swinging his guitar, and giving the most salacious looks to the camera. This was just before the Suzy session, and the hair was still short and spiky, Mia Farrow after a nasty shock, the haircut that John Lydon first wore when he became Johnny Rotten. Honestly, if you ever doubt the ability of rock 'n' roll to imbue you with a sense of invincibility, watch this. Of course, not everyone was impressed. Nick Kent, writing in *Oz*, said that in concert, Bowie was an 'almost grotesque parody of early Elvis Presley complete with outrageously tasteless costume, butch hairstyle, and calculated effeminate gestures.' And it had been difficult for Bowie and the band to get on the show, as they had enormous resistance from the BBC. The producer Mike Appleton didn't appear to want them, but eventually some of the people on his staff persuaded him to relent after one of the scheduled acts cancelled at the last minute.

about that. They had all these fashion magazines I'd never seen, and we came up with a combination of three hairstyles from them.'

Between the three of them they fashioned the Ziggy Stardust haircut, both the cut and the colour copied from a Kansai Yamamoto model on the cover of *Honey* ('Definitely not *Vogue*,' said David), and using a potent German dye called Red Hot Red, Fantasy Colours by Schwarzkopf, liberal amounts of peroxide, and a formidable setting lotion called Guard (actually a dandruff treatment). After two days of trial and error, Suzy Fussey's Ziggy Stardust haircut was born: a scarlet rooster cut with a blow-dried puffball front and a razored back. (When Bowie's manager Tony Defries first saw Ziggy's hair he reputedly dreamed up a scheme for marketing Ziggy Stardust dolls with day-glo hair, which sang 'Wham Bam Thank You Ma'am!') Bowie was so happy with the outcome that he later employed Fussey as the Spiders' full-time personal hairdresser.

The Ziggy haircut epitomised the androgyny of glam rock and, copied by both boys and girls, became the hit of 1972. Not only was the Ziggy Stardust persona influential during the heady days of that year, but throughout the late Seventies and early Eighties the image of the day-glo rock 'n' roll messiah was abused by countless new pop mannequins, including Toyah, Richard Butler (the Psychedelic Furs), Siouxsie Sioux, Gary Numan, Steve Strange, John Foxx (Ultravox), and Peter Murphy from Bauhaus, who even covered the song 'Ziggy Stardust' with surprising chart success in the early Eighties. (Even though Ziggy Stardust was a self-confessed 'plastic' pop star, next to him the others who came in his wake – which, written down, actually looks rather transgressive itself – looked like they were made out of balsa.)

Wherever David Bowie looked in 1972, his haircut went with him. If he looked up at you, he'd be seeing an ocean of orange. If he looked straight ahead, the undercarriage of his hot red puffball bounced in front of him like an embarrassed silhouette on a cinema screen. If he turned sideways, his long feather cut would brush the top of whatever it was he was wearing around his neck. When he walked into his dressing room, the first question – rhetorical, obviously – to Angie or one of his bandmates, would always be the same: 'How does my hair look?'

DURING HIS FIRST TOUR OF AMERICA, HIS MANAGEMENT DECIDED THAT AS BOWIE EARNED OVER £1,000 AN HOUR FOR PERFORMING, JOURNALISTS SHOULD EXPECT TO PAY HIM AT THE SAME RATE. THEY TRIED TO EXERCISE SIMILAR CONTROL OVER PHOTOGRAPHERS.

Bowie's sales pitch to the people waiting out front – the ones who had sat through Roxy Music or one of his other support acts, who had looked keenly at the stage as the music from *A Clockwork Orange* started filtering through the speakers – was a simple one: You want me.

There was such interest in Ziggy that, in November 1973, Bowie even shared his beauty secrets with *Music Scene* magazine. To wit: 'In his last few English concerts, Bowie painted tiny lightning streaks on his cheek and upper leg. Once in a while he uses pearlised gloss on his lips in a tan/pink that comes across like a white-silver highlight. And – a warning! He doesn't use glitter too much, because it falls into his eyes when he's performing and it just isn't soft looking enough, he feels. Sometimes he will outline that gold circle in tiny gold rhinestones, stuck on with eye-lash glue.'

Who knew? With his Japanese hair, his panstick, and his jumpsuits, he was off.

Tony Defries, Bowie's new manager, shared his charge's ambitions, and was intent on making Bowie a 'real star' which, as he pointed out, was not a Rod Stewart or a Cat Stevens-type star but a James Dean or a Marlon Brando-type star. Stuart George, who was Bowie's bodyguard at the time, told the writer Steve Turner about a meeting that took place in a restaurant in the King's Road at which this whole operation was discussed. Defries apparently turned to Bowie and said, 'Do you want to be a star, or do you want to be famous, or do you want to be rich, famous and a star?' Bowie opted for the third alternative.

Both Bowie and Defries knew that in order to be a cult

figure you had to recognise the need that people have for such a person and then fill it.

Dai Davis, a former music journalist, had been brought in to handle PR. 'The general idea was that Bowie was a phenomenon rather than a pop star,' he said. 'After a while it became a question of controlling the press coverage so that we could have prestige magazines and large spaces. You had to ration it out in order to get more.' During his first tour of America, his management decided that as Bowie earned over a £1,000 an hour for performing, journalists should expect to pay him at the same rate, though there is no evidence of any publication ever doing so. Management tried to exercise similar control over photographers, issuing the following instructions: 'There shall be no still, cinema, television, video, or other cameras in the auditorium during the performance, except those authorised by MainMan.'

All pictures were tightly edited, not least as Bowie's look was constantly evolving. In America he shaved off his eyebrows, adopted different disguises, and ended up with a chandelier earring hanging from his left ear.

'Another important characteristic of the cult figure must be his aloofness,' wrote Turner. 'In 1971 Bowie explained this to his music publisher and close confidant Bob Grace. He said that he would have to become elusive. He said it was terribly important.' By the end of that same year Grace couldn't contact him by phone and even his mother's number had been changed. He went to one of his first concerts only to find him protected by bodyguards and whisked off by a chauffeur after the show. 'It was that whole image thing,' recalls Grace. 'With all this protection and transport it was obviously costing them a lot more to put concerts on than they were getting at the time, but that was the whole style of it – the Greta Garbo bit.

'Most rock groups tour the States two or three times before they take top billing. Bowie headlined on his first tour. With him were an entourage of twenty-four, including three bodyguards, a hairdresser, a publicity designer, two photographers, a wardrobe mistress, and a press officer. In order to become successful he was acting the part already. Photographs were released of the product walking towards the stage flanked by two burly bodyguards – the sort of treatment one associates with Presley. Attention begets attention.'

Sean Mayes toured with Bowie several times during the Seventies, both as a member of Fumble, one of Bowie's support acts during the Ziggy tours, and also as a member of his backing band on the 1978 tour. 'His appearance then was bizarre even offstage. His white skin had a waxy translucence and his eyebrows were plucked right off. He looked as if the blood had fled his face into that alien hair. His clothes were that pre-punk style he created with a sidelong glance at the Fifties – tight fitting, black and savage colours, more plastic than glitter – the glitter was in his eyes, unnaturally bright.'

In the world of the music press, Bowie was already something of a cause célèbre, having admitted in an interview with

Michael Watts, published in *Melody Maker* on 22 January, that he was gay. Not bisexual, not bi-curious, but *gay*. In a world that was besieged by the glam-rock fripperies of Marc Bolan, Gary Glitter, Sweet, Alice Cooper, and Slade (with all their silks and taffeta, velvet and lace, silver and gold), this was big news, and in the space of a few paragraphs Bowie somersaulted over all of them in terms of his media profile. His peers were furious: how dare he steal their thunder – he wasn't even famous!

In the piece, entitled OH YOU PRETTY THING, Watts wrote the following:

'David's present image is to come on like a swishy queen, a gorgeously effeminate boy. He's as camp as a row of tents, with his limp hand and trolling vocabulary' – love that – ' "I'm gay," he says, "and always have been, even when I was David Jones." But there's a sly jollity about how he says it, a secret smile at the corners of his mouth. He knows that in these times it's permissible to act like a male tart, and that to shock and outrage, which pop has always striven to do throughout its history, is a balls-breaking experience.

'And if he's not outrageous, he is, at least, an amusement. The expression of his sexual ambivalence establishes a fascinating game: is he or isn't he? In a period of conflicting sexual identity he shrewdly exploits the confusion surrounding the male and female roles. "Why aren't you wearing your girl's dress today?" I said to him (he has no monopoly on tongue-in-cheek humour). "Oh dear," he replied, "you must understand that it's not a woman's. It's a man's dress." '

Bowie admitted years later that this admission was somewhat expedient, and that it was said to drive publicity rather than anything else. To a British media whose idea of exotic sex was the familiar tableau of soft-core pornography – jardinières, art nouveau lamps, and high Victorian camp – this was gravy.

Just weeks later he was denying it. In one interview he burst out laughing when the journalist mentioned what a furore it had caused. 'That was hilarious,' Bowie gasped. 'I didn't have a reaction. It was quite a good article. We drew bigger audiences than we had ever drawn!' He laughed again and then decided to turn serious. 'I get floored when people ask if I'm straight or gay or whatever. I don't want to recognise those categories. I refuse to. I will not be tied down by those kinds of things. I am drawn to those people with whom I have a sexual empathy even though I still do not think that everybody has to go out and say who exactly they're laying and why they're laying them if they did lay them and why they didn't enjoy it if they didn't.'

The freshly minted rock star scowled. 'I don't know,' he barked. 'I can't tell you. I wouldn't tell you. Ziggy is a conglomerate, a conglomerate rock star. He just doesn't exist for the moment.'

He was prodded some more, but to little avail. 'Please don't ask me to theorise on Ziggy,' he pleaded. 'Having written it down, there are some things in it that are so personal that I find the whole thing has become a monster on me and there are some things I never dreamed that I would have put in it.' Bowie wasn't gay, although he was certainly bisexual, often sharing lovers with his wife Angie. He'd had an affair with the mime artist Lindsay Kemp (who accused Bowie of stealing all his ideas about presentation, dress, and make-up), and picked up boys with the same gay abandon he picked up girls. 'He was a right stud,' said his wife at the time. 'A stallion. He could poke a hole in the wall.'

In the *Melody Maker* interview he also anticipated the second half of his career: 'I'm going to be huge,' he said to Watts, 'and it's quite frightening in a way.'

It was an extraordinary thing to say, but then there was so much about Ziggy Stardust that was extraordinary.

John Lydon, who in 1976 would find fame if not fortune as Johnny Rotten in the Sex Pistols, admired Bowie for his integrity, and his balls. 'Around *Ziggy Stardust*, Dave Bowie was an absolute full-on "I'm a homosexual". That was his image. And it was as challenging to the world as you could ever hope to be at this point, and that was a damn brave statement to make. And yobs, hooligans, basically working-class [guys] really liked him for the bravery, for the front of it. It was taking on the world, going *that's what I am and fuck you!* A very, very good thing.'

'We took a risk,' says Watts. 'We put him on the cover when no one had heard of him. We had letters in saying "Who is David Bowie?" I'm sure he did [the gay quote] for publicity. I think that he sensed that it was becoming vogue-ish, that the permissive was becoming permissible.'

However, when Bowie 'owned up' to Michael Watts,

the rather more traditional Spiders were the ones who suffered – guitarist Mick Ronson, bass player Trevor Bolder, and drummer Woody Woodmansey, all formerly in a band called the Rats, and all hailing from Hull, and none of whom had a penchant for glitter socks.

'At the time when that story came out, my family in Hull took a lot of flak about it because they'd never even heard about it up there,' said Mick Ronson. 'It came like throwing paint over the car and paint up the front door and stuff like that, which really annoyed me. It's pretty sad. Some people thought I was gay. I wasn't gay and when some-body asked me I'd say, "No I'm not," which was the truth. That's what I had to say about it. If somebody doesn't like the truth then it's too bad. It was a bit of a pain for a couple of weeks. It was very short-lived but at the time it was a bit of a shock. It wasn't a shock amongst ourselves – it was more of a shock from other people's reactions. For instance, throw-ing paint over the car and my mother going through it. People were really annoyed up north. That was something at the time that I felt I didn't really need myself.'

Ronson was doubly insecure, as he hadn't really made it as a guitarist yet. And here he was, being painted a freak by the very person who employed him.

'I wanted to be known as a musician rather than some other phenomenon, and I think that had an effect on me too. Maybe other people were seeing me as something other than what I wanted to be naturally. Audiences like to see a bit of theatrics here and there. They like to be able to go to a show and to be able to see something that they don't see in their everyday lives.'

'Well, you got accused of being the same as Bowie, which was unfair, because we weren't,' says Trevor Bolder. 'We were just a band going along with his idea of how to be big. I mean, it was a big issue for Mick, because Mick being the blond guitar player, he was like David's sidekick, I suppose he got more people thinking he was like David than we got. But it was a bit of an issue when you came back to Hull. Because people get jealous, don't they? So you'd come back to your hometown and all the people who were your mates, or you thought were your mates, turned out to be not your mates, because they put you down all the time. But we didn't get a lot of it, but you did get that sort of thing happening just because you were associated with David.'

'[They were] the stuff of legend, rock 'n' roll style,' said Mick Rock, who spent much of the early part of the Seventies photographing Bowie. 'Nothing as worldly as the Crickets or the Beatles [but] these insects were from Mars. After recording the album it was decided that to promote the record these three should be dubbed The Spiders From Mars. Thus they were restyled, from head to toe, and the illusion was complete ... Weird and Gilly – Trevor and Woody. Not as noticeable as the multi-talented Ronno, but an essential part of the drama. And they knew how to play. The hard thing for Trevor and Woody was all the attention devoted to Bowie and Ronno, of which they got to share little ...'

All the band had something going for them. Lloyd Watson, a half-Jamaican singer-songwriter from Peterborough, who was the winner of a *Melody Maker* folk-rock competition, and who supported Roxy Music and Bowie at the famous Rainbow gig in Finsbury Park that August, said, 'I remember walking into the Rainbow and Bowie's band were all standing around up onstage wearing this really weird attire. I actually thought Woody Woodmansey was Bowie [as] he looked the weirdest.'

Ronson was the blond axeman who could easily have fitted into Slade (he was described by one critic as being 'so sexy he crackles'), Woodmansey could easily have been cast as a droog by Stanley Kubrick, and Bolder? Well, it was often said of the Who's John Entwistle that he looked as though he'd walked onstage as if he were looking for his dog. Bolder was a tad more animated, but not much. In the words of Mark Radcliffe, he looked like a Dickensian Dandy from the future.

They all had trouble with the clothes at first, though, and boy, could the Spiders look uncomfortable ('I don't think we're in Hull any more, Toto,' observed the *NME*'s Charles Shaar Murray). Their costumes were all put together by Bowie, who dressed them in calf-length lace-up boots, Lurex breeches, glittering sequinned zip-up bomber jackets, spangly platforms, and make-up. 'I like to keep my band always well dressed,' said Bowie, finally using prescience in a way in which he would become an expert. 'I'm out all the time to entertain. I'm the last person to pretend I'm a radio.

I'd rather go out and be a colour television set.' Many said that Ronson was a lot less convincingly androgynous than his flame-haired cohort, but to my eyes he was still astonishing – apart from anything else he appeared to be largely responsible for the extraordinary noise emanating from his guitar.

In truth, Bowie's sartorial instructions were straightforward. He simply took them to see *A Clockwork Orange*.

'When he wanted to describe exactly how he wanted us to look, he took us to see the film,' says Trevor Bolder. 'The whole Ziggy thing is based on *A Clockwork Orange* – the costumes, everything. A lot of people thought it was *Star Trek* but it wasn't, it was totally based on the characters in *A Clockwork Orange*. And we just dressed up. It was the make-up thing that was the big deal; I remember that. Ronson was definitely against it, but then when we started using it, it wasn't that bad because we didn't use that much. It was more theatre make-up than anything glammy or anything. He just wanted us to stand out. Whereas if you go onstage and you look normal, there's nothing different. So he wanted us to wear this make-up, which wasn't a lot but it made your features and your face look different, and it made you stand out. We went along with it; of course, everybody took to that, and all the girls liked it that we met, so it was all right after that. It was good.'

Forgetting all his protestations about the clothes they were being asked to wear – 'I'm not wearing that!' was initially a common refrain heard within the dressing room – Bolder was enormously proud of what Bowie had achieved on their behalf, saying it was like reaching the summit of Everest. 'If he'd pushed it at us, we might have pulled away, thinking, "What's he trying to do?"' says Trevor Bolder. 'He just slowly did it for us.'

'Oh, he protested at the beginning,' says the producer Tony Visconti, about Ronson. 'At the start it was as if this blues band from Hull, the Rats, moved down one by one and became the Spiders From Mars. And Bowie often says that in the beginning they all protested – no glitter, no platform shoes. But once they were getting the girls – who were going nuts over them – then they'd be arguing backstage: "Can I use your lipstick? Can I use your eyeshadow?" So all of a sudden this was a very masculine thing, it was something that the girls were into. It was very, very odd.

'Bowie said in a 1994 interview that Mick was the perfect foil for the Ziggy character. He was very much a salt-of-the-earth type, the blunt northerner with a defiantly masculine personality, so that what you got was the old-fashioned Yin and Yang thing. As a rock duo, Bowie believed they were every bit as good as Mick and Keith, or Axl and Slash. Ziggy and Mick were the personification of that rock 'n' roll dualism.'

Back in the dressing room, Ronson would always reveal himself as a pragmatist. 'At one time I was worried that the gay image might overtake the music. Our act is quite natural. It's not sex or anything, although some of the movements are exaggerated. Homosexuality has been going on for centuries. At the moment having a gay image is the "in" thing, just like a few years ago it was trendy to walk around in a long grey coat with a Led Zeppelin album under your arm.

'I'm gay in as much as I wear girls' shoes and have bangles on my wrist, but I was doing that before I met David.' And then, just in case he felt he'd gone too far off message, he finished his pitch with, 'I get offers, but I don't accept them.' Bless.

'I ain't gonna go on the stage in the silk tights,' he said, talking about his impending first solo tour. 'Against David's lightness I was always the heavy one.

'I always believed that when I started out that Ziggy for me was what it was all about. I said it with Ziggy . . . and I believe that you can go up or come down or be carried along by the tide for a few years. The only thing to do, if you want to contribute to culture, or politics, or music, or whatever, is to utilise your own persona rather than just music. The best way to do this is to diversify and become a nuisance everywhere.'

'We were a gang, I suppose,' says Bolder. 'But by the time we started in the Spiders we'd been together for a couple of years, playing together, all from Hull, and we'd known each other for years and years, since we were kids, really. And I think David was quite lucky to get us as a band, really, in that we slotted quite quickly into being the Spiders and it worked so well. I don't know if he'd have got that with individual musicians. I think he tried it with individual musicians earlier on but it didn't work. But us as a band, we'd been playing together as a band, we were all best friends; I mean Mick Ronson was the best man at my wedding. And me and Woody were great friends. And I think that's why we were like a gang.'

Ronson would later turn up on Bob Dylan's Rolling Thunder Review in 1975, and as Sam Shepard noted in his diary, it was Ronson who was the chief instigator of the 'make-up' craze that swept through the tour like brush fire. 'Da da!' Ronson would also fix certain members' hair, using a blow dryer and hairspray.

And the music? What about the music?

Listening to *The Rise And Fall Of Ziggy Stardust And The Spiders From Mars* for the first time, you could almost feel the warp drive in Bowie's brain accelerate, and although the concept album as a precept would go on to be much derided, this is one of the most thrilling, as well as one of the most convincing comments any rock artist has ever made on his own art form. Ziggy is the human manifestation of a benign alien attempting to present humanity with a message of hope, five years before Armageddon. He comes in peace, yet is destroyed by his own excesses, and the fans he inspired. As *Rolling Stone* said, this was the story of an alien who fell to Earth, and who lost everything but left a legacy. The narrative arc is condensed into eleven chapters (ten if you discount the Ron Davies cover, 'It Ain't Easy', a leftover from the *Hunky Dory* sessions that Bowie insisted on including), yet the script is so precise that only by being successful would Bowie have made the whole thing work. If Bowie's impersonation of Ziggy Stardust had been unsuccessful then the record would have been meaningless. Tired of allowing other people to determine his success, with Ziggy, Bowie decided to take his career into his own hands, and by becoming a star, Bowie validated the idea completely.

An easily digestible concept album, *Ziggy Stardust* contained Bowie's most cogent songs so far, custom-built melodramatic vignettes that were brash and dynamic and full of great hooks. In truth, the record sounded like a soundtrack album to an imaginary film. There was a high finish to the record, one that offset the odd nature of the lyrics. Released on 6 June, just a month before the *Top Of The Pops* performance, it was instantly fêted. It confused many – *Cashbox* magazine called it 'an electric age nightmare' – but then that was the point.

'The thing that surprised me most about the record originally was the fact that David thought I wouldn't like it,' says Ken Scott. 'We'd finished *Hunky Dory*, and it was only a very short time later that I saw David and he said we've got to start making another record. *Hunky Dory* hadn't even come out yet, but his management wanted him to do another album, so that's what we did. And he said, "I don't think you're going to like this one. It's going to be a lot more rock 'n' roll." I can't remember if he said it was going to sound like the Velvet Underground or Iggy Pop, but as I didn't know of either band at the time, it didn't really make much difference. And he was completely wrong, as I loved every second of the album. I think my greatest achievement with the record was making an album that the five of us were happy with.'

The songs on the record were so efficient in creating a constituency that they supplied – as Pete Hamill once wrote about Sinatra – a partial response to the urging of E. M. Forster: 'Only connect'. It is unlikely that Bowie possessed anything like Forster's humanistic impulses, though; he was simply trying to produce something that gave the impression of being important.

Which, obviously, is very appealing to a twelve-year-old boy living on the metaphorical edge of society, and on the verge of adulthood.

When discussing Bowie's Seventies records – which, despite his protestations, account for most of his 'canon' – it is mandatory to chronicle the way in which his various personas were responsible for their creative narrative; with *Ziggy*, the narrative is delivered fully formed. It's a concept album, plain and straight, with finite parameters. All we had to do was buy into it.

Which we did, in huge numbers.

The album was so bright, so full of spin and sparkle, grit and glitter. Cleanly produced, and with the vocals mixed unusually high (what would be the point of having a narrative if you couldn't hear it?), the album is actually rather sparse, and in parts sounds not unlike the *John Lennon/Plastic Ono Band* album from 1970. Recorded at Trident Studios in Soho, in London, the drums crack like bullets, Mick Ronson's guitar bursts out of the speakers as though it can't wait to get home, while the piano – the same sonorous piano the Beatles used on 'Hey Jude' – casts a spell over the whole record.

And what songs. Over the years, many songs have become my equivalent of Proust's *petite madeleine*, from Jackie Trent's 'Where Are You Now' and the Union Gap's 'Young Girl', to the Beatles' 'Revolution' and Rod Stewart's 'Wear It Well'; nothing, though, has the accumulative power of the *Ziggy Stardust* album, with all its nooks and crannies, its hooks and pulls, to spin me to the past with such intensity. For me, the album unfolds in a purposefully urgent manner, pushing the narrative along like a ticker tape. It begins slowly, with 'Five Years', Woody Woodmansey's drums announcing Bowie's first soliloquy as though they're on parade (if Bob Dylan's 'Like A Rolling Stone' begins with a drum beat like a pistol shot, 'Five Years' starts and finishes in military style). Setting the scene, 'Five Years' heralds the end of the world, and after a soothing 'Soul Love', 'Moonage Daydream' introduces Bowie's space invader, jump-starting a series of energetic, if clipped rock songs that scrunch the messiah fable into short, sonic newsreels. There is the homoerotic rockabilly sleaze of 'Hang On To Yourself', the portentous campfire camp of 'Lady Stardust', the progressive glam of 'Suffragette City', and so on, and so on. Ascent, descent, and eventually a rock and roll suicide, a climax of bathetic proportions. When Bowie played 'Rock 'n' Roll Suicide' live, he extended his reach to the crowd, as he sang, 'Give me your hands, because you're wonderful, Oh, give me your hands . . .' 'It was a loving moment, and a political one,' says critic Mikal Gilmore. 'It was the offering of unashamed embrace and encouragement. Quite a gesture for a man who denied he had any warmth inside him.' (As I listened to 'Five Years', I would practise my drumming – I wanted to be a sticksman – by slapping my thighs, and tapping on the coffee table, my right hand acting like the bass drum, my left the snare.)

It's often said that Ziggy Stardust is one of the most influential albums of the Seventies, whereas in reality it is anything but. Bands such as Led Zeppelin and Bad Company were more influential as many more people copied them. Ziggy was actually *sui generis*, and existed in a world of its own. The idea of Ziggy was copied relentlessly – the alien theme, the existential pop star stuff, the make-up (although not the quilted jumpsuits) – but the music itself was so self-contained and so particular that it didn't inspire a host of imitators.

'As soon as we recorded "Moonage Daydream" I knew something was going to happen,' says Trevor Bolder. 'After listening to the guitar solo, I just thought, "This is going to be amazing, this is going to go somewhere. This is special." And then it did, you know. That was the point when I knew, "Hang on, there's something special here. This is going to be really, *really* good."'

In a *Rolling Stone* interview with William Burroughs, Bowie expanded on the *Ziggy Stardust* story: 'The time is five years to go before the end of the Earth. It has been announced that the world will end because of a lack of natural resources. Ziggy is in a position where all the kids have access to things that they thought they wanted. The older people have lost all touch with reality and the kids are left on their own to plunder anything. Ziggy was in a rock and roll band and the kids no longer want rock and roll. There's no electricity to play it. Ziggy's adviser tells him to collect news and sing it, 'cause there is no news. So Ziggy does this and there is terrible news. "All The Young Dudes" is a song about this news. It's no hymn to the youth as people thought. It is completely the opposite.[*]

'The end comes when the infinites arrive. They really are a black hole, but I've made them people because it would be very hard to explain a black hole onstage.

'Ziggy is advised in a dream by the infinites to write the coming of a starman, so he writes "Starman", which is the first news of hope that the people have heard. So they latch on to it immediately . . . The starmen that he is talking about are called the infinites, and they are black hole jumpers. Ziggy has been talking about this amazing spaceman who

....

[*]When Bowie offered Mott The Hoople's Ian Hunter 'All The Young Dudes' he didn't know Bowie had intended to use the song on *Ziggy Stardust*. Years passed before Bowie revealed that the line 'All the young dudes carry the news' refers to a point in the Ziggy story when, with no electricity left in the world, Ziggy uses songs to spread the news. ' "All the Young Dudes" is a song about this news,' Bowie explained. 'It's not a hymn to the youth, as people thought. It is completely the opposite.'

will be coming down to save the Earth. [The starmen] arrive somewhere in Greenwich Village. They don't have a care in the world and are of no possible use to us. They just happened to stumble into our universe by black hole jumping. Their whole life is travelling from universe to universe. In the stage show, one of them resembles Brando, another one is a black New Yorker. I even have one called Queenie, the Infinite Fox . . . Now Ziggy starts to believe in all this himself and thinks himself a prophet of the future starmen. He takes himself up to the incredible spiritual heights and is kept alive by his disciples. When the infinites arrive, they take bits of Ziggy to make them real because in their original state they are anti-matter and cannot exist in our world. And they tear him to pieces on stage during the song "Rock 'n' Roll Suicide". As soon as Ziggy dies onstage the infinites take his elements and make themselves visible.'

Phew! All this and tunes too?

RCA put a lot of muscle behind the record, taking various full-page ads in all the music papers. My favourite is the ad that uses a blurred black and white photograph of Bowie, on which small stars and planets have been superimposed. A circle sits at the bottom of the image, containing the copy: 'Wherein Ziggy Stardust makes himself manifest to all.' Then in smaller type: 'Ah, Ziggy. The rock & roll technocrat, the space-age androgyne and soul plunderer. David Bowie *is* Ziggy Stardust on this his newest album, off on a transgalactic musical tailwind to the tune of some very shiny and hard-edged rock music indeed . . .'

'It was the perfect team, and there was a great sense of camaraderie when we were making the record,' says Ken Scott. 'We started on *Hunky Dory*, and got so close that we could almost finish each other's sentences. It had almost reached that point. We were making records for ourselves, and if other people happened to like them then that was great.' The band all wore jeans and T-shirts when they were making the record. Bowie was slightly more flamboyant, but the recording was incredibly relaxed. From *Aladdin Sane* onwards he would begin to record in full character dress, but for *Ziggy Stardust* he wore what he might wear when he got up in the morning.

'Starman', the song that Bowie would perform on the BBC on 6 July, was the first single from *Ziggy Stardust*, yet it's the least representative song on the album. While issued as the album's first single, the song itself was a late addition, having been written and recorded on 4 February at Trident Studios after the rest of the album was finished, and only replacing Chuck Berry's 'Round and Round' and Jacques Brel's 'Amsterdam' on the album in March (both would be released as B-sides, on the flip of 'Drive In Saturday' and 'Sorrow' respectively). Nothing else on the record was considered commercial enough to launch the album, hence this song, almost written to order (as would happen to Bruce Springsteen a decade later, when he was told *Born In The USA* needed a radio-friendly single, resulting in 'Dancing In The Dark'). It was included on the album at the suggestion of Dennis Katz, the A&R man from RCA's New York office, who had actually signed Bowie to the label. (Katz wanted RCA to be more than a distributor for Elvis Presley and Jefferson Airplane records, and in the space of nine months signed Lou Reed, the Kinks, and Bowie to the label in an attempt to make it trendy.) Bowie had wanted to release it as his next single, but had never intended for it to be on the album, even though it encapsulated the LP's conceit perfectly.

'RCA told us *Ziggy Stardust* was great, but we needed a single, something they could pull straight off the album,' says Bowie's sound engineer at the time, Robin Mayhew. 'So David went off and wrote what he called "Somewhere Over The Rainbow". His "Starman" song.'

Starting with acoustic dreamy chords, echoing his only hit to date, 'Space Oddity', it soon turns into a galloping frenzy of a pop record – Judy Garland's 'Somewhere Over The Rainbow' with staccato guitars and faux-cockney pronunciation. It was perfectly constructed, and probably the most commercial record Bowie had yet made, even if he hadn't yet thrown off all his camp trappings (much has been made of the octave jump in the chorus: 'Star*man*' echoing Garland's 'Some*where* Over The Rainbow'; he would even weave the tune into 'Starman' onstage).* So overtly commercial was it that Marc Bolan would later claim elements of

....

*In 1898, when the American author Frank Baum was writing *The Wonderful Wizard Of Oz*, he couldn't think of a name for the magical land where little Dorothy ends up. One day, as he was peering at the two-drawer filing cabinet in his office, lost in it had been borrowed from T. Rex's 1971 hit 'Hot Love' ('Let all the children boogie', is pure Bolan). In a way the song offered deliverance, although when Bowie sings, 'There's a Starman waiting in the sky, He'd like to come and meet us but he thinks he'll blow our minds', he's really talking about himself. When Bowie sings, 'Hey that's far out, so you heard him too,' he's inadvertently commemorating his own success. In short, it's little but a well-executed messianic rant: 'He's told us not to blow it, 'Cause he knows it's all worthwhile.'

'Starman' offers redemption, as it's actually a pop song about pop, as Bowie's alter ego appears only as a voice on the radio. 'He's basically a cosmic DJ,' said one critic, 'whispering secrets to a teenager listening late at night – it's how pop

---

thought, he noticed that the top drawer was labeled A-N, and the bottom drawer O-Z. Suddenly, he had his name. It seems hard to believe now, but 'Somewhere Over The Rainbow' was twice deleted from *The Wizard Of Oz* before the film was released, as MGM thought the movie was too long. Once reinstated, it quickly became Judy Garland's defining song, as well as one of Hollywood's most enduring standards. 'In Dorothy's journey to the other side of her rainbow there were echoes of a thousand brave adventurous travels, from ancient Greek classics through to modern science-fiction,' wrote Max Cryer in *Love Me Tender: The Stories Behind The World's Best-Loved Songs*. 'People everywhere could identify with the girl whose life was "grey" and who dreamed of a distant life where dreams come true. And yet there was also a comforting hint of realism in Dorothy's story. She was Cinderella in reverse: the girl who went to a vivid Technicolor ball but when she got home realised that home was best.'

music can instantly create secret societies, break up the tedium of your life, liberate you from your parents.'

'The song tells the story of an extraterrestrial contacting the youth of the doomed Earth through the medium of radio,' Bowie said at the time, painting his Starman as a benign spirit. 'The extraterrestrial promises salvation but is weary of his impact on the planet. [It] can be taken at the immediate level of "There's a Starman in the sky saying Boogie Children", but the theme of it is that the idea of things in the sky is really quite human and real and we should be a bit happier about the prospect of meeting people.' The song also accurately predicted the plotline of *Close Encounters Of The Third Kind.*

As well as the nod to Garland, the Morse code link between the verses and the chorus was a direct steal from the guitar refrain in 'You Keep Me Hanging On' by the Supremes, while the guitar riff also owes more than a little to 'I Hear You Knockin'' by Dave Edmunds. Ken Scott says the Morse code sound that introduced the chorus was a piano and guitar mixed together and put through a Countryman phaser ('I can't remember if it was two guitars and one piano or the other way round,' he told me, 'but that was the idea'). Then Mick Ronson's solo swirls manically off into the air. '[It's] a perfect example of how to build a strong, memorable melodic line over a simple IV-I-V-I progression (Bb-F-C-F),' says Jesse Gress, the author of *Ten Things You Gotta Do To Play Like Mick Ronson.* 'The idea is to target the three of each chord on every downbeat and connect them with adjacent F major scale tones, while "playing" the strategically placed rests and making the melody more guitar-y by adding bends and finger vibrato.'

Almost all the vocals on the album were captured immediately, including 'Starman'. 'They were first takes! And then he would go, "OK, I'll double it",' says Woody Woodmansey. 'I'd worked with other singers before, and I'd never met any singers who could sing the same thing again so you couldn't tell they were double-tracking it.' Woodmansey also remembers working with producer Ken Scott to arrive at the song's unique drum sound: 'Ken would sometimes get me tuning a tom-tom for an hour, so that when it came up through the desk, it was right. On some tracks, he would have the snare tuned so flat and dead that it was like hitting a potato chip bag. It was just soggy and the sound in the drum booth was horrible. But what Ken was able to do with it when he brought it up through the [mixing] desk . . .'

The bass line on 'Starman' was very simple. 'We recorded it very quickly,' says Trevor Bolder. 'Everything we did with David was like one take. He learned it and away we went, and that was the finished product. But it's a pretty simple bass line to play. I just used to play whatever came into my head that felt good, really.'

'RCA had said they needed a single so we went and made one,' says Ken Scott. 'It was as simple as that. I like it, and it's a cute record. I didn't notice the Judy Garland reference at the time, but when I made "My Sweet Lord" for George Harrison

I didn't realise that it sounded a bit like "He's So Fine" by the Chiffons. When you're working on records you just don't hear anything other than what you're making at the time.'

BOWIE ATTENDANTS THE WORLD OVER WOULD FLOCK TO HEDDON STREET IN MUCH THE SAME WAY THAT DICKENS STUDENTS WOULD TRACE THE OLIVER TWIST WALK, FROM SMITHFIELD MARKET TO NEWGATE PRISON VIA CLERKENWELL GREEN, HATTON GARDEN AND SAFFRON HILL.

The single was released on 14 April, and like the album it came from (which would be released on 6 June), 'Starman' was reviewed enthusiastically. 'David Bowie is, with Kevin Ayers, the most important, underacknowledged innovator in contemporary popular music in Britain,' said John Peel, writing in *Disc & Music Echo*, 'and if this record is overlooked it will be nothing less than stark tragedy.'

Strangely, the song that made Bowie a star was treated as an orphan by its parent. No sooner had he become famous than Bowie dropped the song from his live set, unable to acknowledge the fact that it had been responsible for his success; admitting that the meticulously contrived 'Starman' enabled him to skip over the velvet rope meant accepting that for much of the last nine years he had been on the wrong side of it.

The *Ziggy Stardust* album cover was shot by Bowie and the photographer Brian Ward outside Ward's studio in London's Heddon Street, just off Regent Street, on a rainy January night. Bowie is photographed alone, although only because the rest of the Spiders thought it too cold and declined to join him for the picture. Originally shot in black and white, Ward commissioned the artist Terry Pastor to hand-tint the pictures to give them more of an otherworldly feel (he had also hand-tinted the *Hunky Dory* cover). As *Time Out* magazine once pointed out, the graffiti on the wall behind the phone box (a K2 1927 version) that featured on the back cover bore testimony to its status as third only to the Tardis and Clark Kent's changing room in space-age phone booth mythology. When Bowie revisited the renovated site in 1993, a woman walking by said to him, with a genial smile, 'They took your phone box away – isn't it terrible?' (Ziggy wasn't hurtling towards Earth at twice the speed of a shooting star, he was standing nonchalantly inside a phone box in Mayfair.)

Bowie attendants the world over would flock to Heddon Street in much the same way that Dickens students would trace the Oliver Twist walk, from Smithfield Market to Newgate Prison via Clerkenwell Green, Hatton Garden and Saffron Hill. The individual black and white photographs on the inner sleeve were done in a style aping *A Clockwork Orange*, making the band look as sinister as possible. On the cover, Bowie is dressed in a turquoise circuit-board jumpsuit open almost to the navel, the same one he would wear the following month on *The Old Grey Whistle Test*. On the back, Bowie has been photographed in a phone booth and he looks as if he is waiting for an obscene proposition from anyone who might happen to wander by. One hand rests inertly on his hip, and there is a languorous and lascivious expression on his face. (The signs on the door to Number 23, the building next to him, are: Top sign, Paquarette Dresses 4th floor; Second sign, Ramar Dresses Ltd 3rd Floor; Third sign, International Wool Secretariat; Fourth sign, Cravats Ltd, main entrance, T H Ferris 2nd floor.)*

'He always comes to you with a definite idea of what he wants but he also respects what you're doing and leaves you a lot of room to work,' said Brian Ward. For the *Hunky Dory* cover session Bowie arrived at Ward's studio with a book on Marlene Dietrich and pointed out a particular photograph he wanted imitated. For *Ziggy Stardust* he phoned Ward up and asked him to check out a location for what he described

....

*The yellow K. WEST sign on the cover belonged to the Henry Konn furriers ('West' indicated the West End), and soon became part of the whole Ziggy legacy. Although the owners initially weren't thrilled about being associated with the idea. Within a month of the album's release, K. West's solicitors contacted RCA: 'Our clients are Furriers of high repute who deal with a clientele generally far removed from the pop music world. Our clients certainly have no wish to be associated with Mr Bowie or this record as it might be assumed that there was some connection between our client's firm and Mr Bowie, which is certainly not the case.'

as 'a Brooklyn alley scene' where he'd appear alone like some alien being. 'He was playing on this man from Mars thing,' said Ward. 'He wanted to come over like a real stranger, like a science-fiction movie.'

At the time the photographer Mick Rock regarded Bowie as one of the first rock performers to understand how important photography was to the creation of image. 'He understood in an intelligent way what pictures could do. It was a refreshing change for me to be involved with someone who saw things in this way. An image in photography is a difficult thing to portray. You're basically dealing with a body and yet it's somehow got to be more than that. What you have to do is to try and distil some of the mystery behind it. You can create a feeling of inaccessibility in that you can build an aura by lighting, angle, and just the kind of sympathy you can elicit from your subject.'

Bowie's image on *Ziggy Stardust* was transfixing, so different was it from the image of any of his peers. In the Fifties, Roland Barthes went to a revival of Greta Garbo's early films in Paris, and his experience mirrored that of those who fell under Bowie's spell: 'Garbo still belongs to that moment in cinema when capturing the human face still plunged audiences into the deepest ecstasy, when one literally lost oneself in a human image as one would in a philtre, when the face represented a kind of absolute state of the flesh, which could be neither reached nor renounced.' And Barthes was not a man prone to exaggeration.

I pulled the album out the other night, as I was trying

to finish this chapter, and I looked at the inner sleeve. In the space between the first column of songs ('Five Years', 'Soul Love', and 'Moonage Daydream') and the second, I'd drawn an upright box in blue, green, and red biro, detailing the length of each side: Side 1, 15.54 minutes, Side 2, 18.25 minutes. Up until recently, the sleeve was stuffed with photographs of Bowie I'd torn from the pages of pop magazines of the time. They're all now in a drawer, with all my other Bowie paraphernalia – the album reviews, posters, Polaroids, postcards, and the like. I also appear to have thirty-seven books on Bowie, which to the layman might seem a tad excessive, but probably not to those who got the bug back when I did.

Before Bowie came careering along, in his boas and boots, most glam-rock bands looked as though they'd be far more comfortable knocking about on children's television, singing to a man in an oversized bear outfit, say, or dancing merrily in a multicoloured plastic playground surrounded by foam palm trees. By dint of its immediacy and its novelty (especially its novelty), all pop was interesting, but until Bowie's performance on 6 July, not much of it in the early Seventies looked particularly dangerous. Until Ziggy came along, the Seventies was the sort of decade that tucked its shirt into its underpants. Compared to Bowie, the rest of the glam-rock crowd was full of window dressers.

I was at the age when I was looking for meaning – or the absence of it – in everyone and everything around me, and there wasn't much meaning to be had in 'Wig Wam

Bam' or 'Rock 'n' Roll Part Two', none that I could see, at least. Was there any difference between Mud and the Wombles? Well, the Wombles certainly had better dress sense. What Bowie did was introduce a postmodern pop icon into a small world of novelty acts and teenybop make-weights, an exquisitely dressed, razor-boned fashion plate at a party full of podgy boys and girls with blue eyeshadow and ginger flick hair.

Slade were the bad boys on the corner, the lowest common denominator, and it was easy to make fun of them, easy to mock. Easy to laugh at their trash terrace aesthetic, their twelve-bar oikishness, and the ridiculous mirrored top hats. With seventeen consecutive Top Twenty hits and six number ones between 1970 and 1975, Slade were the *lingua franca* of glam, the reductive end of androgyny, the hapless beneficiaries of a nation with more sentimentality than taste (their almost subliminally popular holiday anthem 'Merry Christmas Everybody' has been on sale continuously since it was released in 1973). Slade equalled music for yobs, silly haircuts, and chain-store platforms. They were what you listened to at the rugby club on a Saturday night, before you had a bust-up with your ex's ex, and the inevitable fight outside the chip shop. Hod-carriers in eyeliner, they were the acceptable face of glam, much to the annoyance of those like Roxy Music, Lou Reed, and David Bowie, who tended to take themselves rather more seriously.

Yet they connected. Dovetail tight. Mott The Hoople's Ian Hunter said once that when his band were deep into glam he felt like a 'brickie in gilt', and yet Slade just thought it was a way of securing success. Smack on a bit of glitter – who cares? During 1972 and 1973 Slade were so big, so enormously popular, that even the combined panstick of Marc Bolan and David Bowie found it hard to match them. T. Rex appealed to the young girls, Bowie to the aesthetes, and Slade, well Slade appealed to anyone who turned up – a packet of Bensons pushed up into the shoulder of their T-shirt, a pint on the bar, and a girl on the dance floor (with whom said Slade fan would arrive and leave, ignoring at every opportunity in between).

Up until 6 July, the Sun King of glam was Marc Bolan; as soon as the camera panned back to Tony Blackburn after the Spiders finished 'Starman' that night – himself rather nonplussed by the performance – Bolan was making his way down the hierarchy. 'It wasn't enough that he was Marc Bolan of T. Rex,' said Tony Visconti, who produced them both. 'He seethed with contempt for David when he came up with Ziggy Stardust. When Bowie's album came out he made some very petty and nasty comments.'

For a while Bolan and Bowie despised each other, circling one another as if they were out-of-favour courtiers, fighting for a chance to impress the king, each thinking the other was stepping on his razzle-dazzle moon boots. Bolan thought space was his domain, having spent the back end of the Sixties wittering on about mystical goblins, cosmic rays, and the rejuvenating qualities of moonlight. Bowie saw a chancer, like himself, a Tin Pan Alley spiv in funny trousers and the latest shirt – not an ambulance chaser as such, but as near as dammit.

I knew what he was thinking. When I was thirteen or fourteen, my mother said, apropos of what I'm not really sure, 'Everyone will hate you when you grow up because you're middle class. You might not like it, but it's true. The upper class will hate you because you're encroaching upon them; the working class will hate you because you're trying to leave them behind; and the middle class will hate you because they see themselves in you, and don't want to be reminded of where they came from.' This is how Bowie and Bolan felt about each other.

They'd first met around seven or eight years previously. 'We were just two nothing kids with huge ambitions,' says Bowie. 'We both had the same manager at the time, and we met the first time painting the wall of our then manager's office. "Hello, who are you?" "I'm Marc, man." "Oh, what do you do?" "I'm a singer." "Oh yeah, so am I. You a mod?" "Yeah. I'm King mod. Your shoes are crap." "Well, you're short." So we became really close friends. Marc took me dustbin shopping. At that time Carnaby Street was going through a period of incredible wealth, and rather than replace buttons on their shirts or zippers on their trousers, at the end of the day they'd just throw it all away, in the dustbins. So we used to go up and down Carnaby Street and go through all the dustbins about nine, ten o'clock at night, and get our wardrobes together.'

Bowie says that Bolan ('the little imp') opened the

door, but, 'What was so great, however, was that we knew he hadn't got it quite right. Sort of Glam 1.0. We were straining in the wings with versions 1.01 and 1.02, while Marc was still struggling with satin. But boy, he really rocked. He did, y'know?'

Bowie was constantly keeping an eye on Bolan's activity, but towards the end of 1972 and through into 1973, started to wonder whether or not his oppo had the capacity to change; Bolan's records were good and they were successful, but they didn't evolve. Bowie had a history of evolving, and perhaps one of the strangest things about his success with Ziggy Stardust was his eagerness to move on so quickly when he was done with it. Many who had struggled for so long would have been tempted to milk Ziggy for all it was worth.

If Bolan could traffic brash twelve-bar rock songs dressed up as teenage anthems, then Bowie could move several stages further, by adding lyrical ambition and his innate sense of unorthodox melodies. He wanted to prove that he could go back to the future better than anyone.

Anyone who watched *Top Of The Pops* could reproduce Bolan's glitter, or Sweet's mock-Cherokee make-up after a visit to Woolworth's. 'Bowie once described the Ziggy Stardust look as being "Nijinsky meets Woolworth's", as effective a summary of glam's clumsy genius as any,' writes Peter Doggett in *The Man Who Sold The World: David Bowie and the 1970s*.

Glam's essence was entertainment, and that was both

its appeal and for many of its protagonists, its curse. By 1973, Marc Bolan was declaring, 'I don't want to go on the road for fear of being involved in the dying embers of glam rock. I don't feel involved in it, even though I started it!'

Bowie was always aware of the vagaries of fashion, as he had largely spent the previous ten years being the victim of it. He was already pushing to move on, folding new ideas into old, world-weary ones. Bolan had nothing else up his velvet cape sleeve; unable to repeat his earlier success, he descended into parody, committing the cardinal pop sin in the process: he got fat. Bolan's claim to have 'invented' glam rock should be treated with caution, too. The leitmotifs and trends in fashion and music – what would soon become known forever more as the zeitgeist – were already on the churn by the time Bolan decided to wear a bit of sparkle. More men were wearing make-up (ever since the mid-Sixties, festival-goers had painted their faces), adult cartoons were becoming popular, the rainbow had been co-opted as a symbol of a benign counterculture, Biba was seriously influencing the high street, and in London (as well as New York, LA, and San Francisco) the idea of using bisexuality as a style was gaining considerable traction.

What was salient about Ziggy was the devotion to inauthenticity. Bowie didn't have to worry about his newfound fame meaning millions of people suddenly having the wrong idea of who he was, because Ziggy wasn't who he said he was in the first place. The Sixties had all been about expression, emancipation, and the struggle for some kind of truth.

Ziggy wasn't interested in truth; artifice was all, and all was artifice. Mick Rock used to enjoy using a J. K. Huysmans quote about his friend, and it was perfectly apt: 'Tired of artificial flowers aping real ones, he wanted some natural flowers that looked like fakes.'

No, Bowie wasn't into altruism, he was into narcissism. He wasn't kicking against any crypto-fascist regime, he was kicking against failure.

If a lot of rock music concerned itself with escape, both physically and emotionally, from family ties, traditions, and the narrow confines of possibilities and expectation, Bowie's transgressions took that several stages further – not to the next big town on the map, not to the metropolis, nor to the star-studded cocoon of genuine fame, but to the stars. Ziggy Stardust was science-fiction, a primitive form of escape, and in musical form one complete without any kind of romantic existentialism. Yet if you narrowed your eyes at the concept, you could see it was more pulp fiction than science-fiction. It was thin, it was manufactured, yet it reinvented the idea of teenage rebellion for a generation that was following in the footsteps of a generation that had actually been involved in the transformation of itself as well as society. Ziggy Stardust was actually a far more conservative construct, even though it was modern, although being modern is sometimes just good enough.

Like any fan, even though I knew I wasn't alone in my appreciation, I was conceited enough to assume that I had docked in a way no one else had. Being a boy somewhat prone to melancholia, Bowie's music offered plenty of drama without much self-analysis. There was glamour, and there was a hint of danger, and he certainly appeared to have a whole bunch of problems; however they were problems you could share, rather than problems you had to carry around yourself. Ziggy's world was one we could dip into without fear of worrying too much about what was going on in our real lives. The whole point of Ziggy Stardust was that it wasn't real at all.

One of the things that had an obvious appeal for us was the knowledge that Bowie wasn't just dressing up for work, that he wasn't just donning glamorous garb for his stage work; what he wore onstage were costumes, but he was just as strangely fashionable in real life. His mufti was like no one else's. Soon magazines and newspapers would be full of photographs of Bowie, and the off-duty pictures were often more intriguing than the on-duty ones. Bowie was properly fashionable, in a way that perhaps only Mick Jagger had been before.

There is one image of Bowie which I love from this period, taken by his friend and backing singer Geoff MacCormack when they were visiting Moscow in 1973, having travelled there, en route to Paris on the Trans-Siberian Express.* He is walking through the famous Gum

* Bowie's persona only faltered when he crossed borders, and had to show his passport: the photograph was taken circa 'Space Oddity', when he had a late Sixties perm.

department store (to open another parenthesis: Mac-Cormack was acutely unimpressed with the place, 'It looked a bit like London's famous Crystal Palace. After it burned down'), and in amongst the fairly drab-looking Moscovites is a tall man with flame-red spiky hair wearing a blindingly luminous yellow zip-up jacket, a bright yellow scarf, billowing flared orange trousers, three-inch heels, and a camp, floppy hat. 'We were every inch the freakiest show in town,' said MacCormack. 'I was his poor understudy in a dark-blue version of his jacket and a mere two-inches of heel – though my boots were bright red. Everywhere we went people stared in amazement but few had the courage to approach us. Those who did were kids. They asked for chewing gum and gave us badges with patriotic designs on.'

Exactly ten years later I had a similar experience in Moscow, at the airport, flying back to Heathrow from Tokyo, where some friends and I had been guests of the fashion designer Takeo Kikuchi from Men's Bigi. One of our party was the former Blitz Kid, the British designer Stephen Linard, who walked across the airport concourse wearing a combination of gold lamé and distressed denim, carrying a bright pink plastic ghetto-blaster the size of an industrial sink, pumping out French hip-hop. Like Bowie, he was showing off, although if you had asked Stephen where he'd found the gumption to act in such a way, or indeed if you had asked the same thing of any of us who had our heads turned by Bowie, and who had grown up through punk, the Blitz, and the already burgeoning club culture of early

Eighties London, we all would have mentioned that sum-mer's day in 1972 when the world suddenly went from black and white to colour, when we passed from childhood to ado-lescence, almost as if we'd slipped through the wardrobe into Narnia.

'I suppose the greatest part was in the very early days, before we made it, when we all lived at Haddon Hall with David and we were putting it all together,' says Trevor Bolder. 'It was so much fun, you know? Writing the songs up and going in the studio together, it was real fun. That's my fond-est memory, even though there are great memories from after, when we made it really big, but it was the early days of no pressure on us. We just had a lot of fun. We went down the pub together; nobody knew who we were. We went into the studio and there was no pressure. David wrote his songs and we played along, and then they were put together. *Top Of The Pops* changed all that.'

'Starman' entered the charts at number 49 on 24 June. The following week the band was invited to appear on *Top Of The Pops*, and the Seventies would finally begin.

THREE

'Let All
The Children Boogie'

TOP OF THE POPS, 6 JULY 1972

*The day my world turned day-glo. When Bowie appeared on
TV on a warm summer's evening, a generation awoke from
its black and white slumber. Oh no love! You're not alone.*

'When we made the film forty years ago, we made it
as a comedy, albeit a very black one. There was a lot
of humour, but when it came out, because it was so
startling and shocking, people just sat there dead
silent. At the end they didn't move out of their seats'
Malcolm McDowell, talking about *A Clockwork Orange*

BY APRIL, 1972 was already turning out to be a tumultuous
year. In February the British government had declared a
state of emergency over the miners' strike, five women and
an army priest were murdered in an IRA bomb attack on
the 16th Parachute Brigade headquarters at Aldershot, the
British Army had killed twelve unarmed nationalist civil
rights marchers in Derry in Northern Ireland, and Pakistan
had withdrawn from the Commonwealth of Nations.

But in Oxfordshire, the New Year didn't really shock itself into life until April. That month a sixteen-year-old grammar school boy pummelled an Irish sexagenarian down-and-out to death, mirroring a scene in Stanley Kubrick's adaptation of Anthony Burgess's *A Clockwork Orange*, where Alex – the book's generic delinquent hero – attacks a vagrant. At the trial, the boy's QC argued in his defence that he'd been so influenced by the film ('Being the adventure of a young man whose principal interests are rape, ultra-violence, and Beethoven') that he had re-enacted one of its most horrific scenes, even though he'd only heard about the film through his friends. This was hardly an isolated incident: not only did a pensioner die of a heart attack after being badly beaten up by another youth immediately after he'd seen the film, but a Dutch girl on a camping holiday in Lancashire was also raped by a gang singing 'Singin' In The Rain', another echo from the film. And there were many more examples.

David Bowie had shoe-horned the film into his performances at the very start of the year, after seeing it just after Christmas, introducing the Walter Carlos theme music from the film, having it played loudly over the public address system before he appeared on stage. This would then segue nicely into Beethoven's Ninth, also from the film, as huge amounts of swirling dry ice quickly enveloped the stage. This wasn't just stagecraft, it was a deliberate attempt to click with the zeitgeist, co-opting the fashion and design tropes of the film, and inadvertently the media furore sur-rounding the copycat crimes in the process (for Bowie the connotations were perfect: in London, 'He's as queer as a clockwork orange' had been a popular colloquial term since the Second World War). For Bowie, Kubrick had already kick-started the twenty-first century, pulling together all the unarticulated loose ends of the previous five years into a desire of unstoppable momentum. He thought that both *A Clockwork Orange* and *2001* provoked one major theme: that there was no linear line in the lives that any of us were lead-ing. We were not evolving, merely surviving. And the clothes were pretty fab, too: *2001* with its Courrèges-like leisure suits, and *Clockwork*'s droogs in their functional-chic out-fits, dressed to kill, quite literally.

Kubrick wasn't the first person to see the potential in Burgess's book. Back in the mid-Sixties the photographer David Bailey tried to get the project off the ground as his dir-ectorial debut. He wanted to cast Mick Jagger and Andy Warhol. 'Mick and Andy and the rest of the Stones were going to be the gang,' says Bailey. 'I thought it would be funny if the Stones were the only men in the film, and all the other gangs were women. Andy was going to make these huge silk-screen sets, mirroring what he was doing with his portraits at the time. But nobody in the film world really knew who the Stones were at the time so investors weren't exactly biting my hand off. Plus, Andrew Oldham, their manager, wanted more money for the Stones than had been budgeted for the whole film, so it died on the vine. In the end the owners sold the rights for $7,000 dollars to a property developer who eventually sold them to Kubrick.'

Burgess's book was published in 1962, and was based partly on a new-found obsession with the teddy boys he'd seen in London coffee bars, youths dressed smartly in neo-Edwardian suits with heavily soled boots and distinctive coiffures. 'They seemed too elegant to be greatly given to violence, but they were widely feared by the faint-hearted,' wrote Burgess. 'They were a personification of the zeitgeist in that they seemed to express a brutal disappointment with Britain's post-war decline as a world power and evoked the age of Edwardian expansion in the clothes if nothing else. They had originally been called Edwardian Strutters.'

The teds were followed by mods and rockers, who in Burgess's eyes were rebelling against the same things, only this time they were taking it out on one another. 'These young people seemed to love aggression for its own sake,' he said.

Burgess decided to set the novel in the future, in 1970, during a time when youthful aggression had reached so frightful a pitch that the government would try to eradicate it with brutal Pavlovian techniques. As this was science-fiction, he invented his own slang, and the vocabulary of his space-age hooligans was a mixture of Russian and demotic English, seasoned with rhyming slang. The Russian suffix for teen was nadsat, and that became the name of the teenage dialect spoken by drugi or the droogs, the friends of violence. The hooligans' social centre is the Korova Milk Bar, which in Kubrick's mind became a ridiculously modern nightclub; his ideas for the place were so particular that he commissioned the British pop artist Allen Jones to produce coffee tables and waitresses' uniforms based on work the artist had already produced. The director had seen an exhibition in which Jones had shown some extraordinary and disturbing pieces of sculpture. '[For Kubrick] I conceived a waitress's dress that was totally clinical – the first useful rubber dress,' says Jones. The idea was that however attractive the waitress might be, as soon as she turned around, and the customer was exposed to the bare bottom contained within Jones' rubber dress, the whole conceit was flipped. 'When approaching she was functional,' says Jones. 'And when retreating she was decorative.' The problem was, Kubrick thought Jones would design his sets for a credit instead of a fee, and told him so by phone. According to Jones, Kubrick said, 'I'm a very famous film director, this will be seen all over the world and your name will be known.' Jones held the phone away from his ear, 'I was just staggered anyone would say that. It showed an ego that dwarfed that of any artist I've known.'

Allen consoled himself by designing a poster for the 1972 Munich Olympic Games.

There ended up being two versions of *A Clockwork Orange*: the original, in which the book's antihero eventually denounces violence, and the American version in which the ending is rather more open-ended (the US publishers basically lopping off the final chapter). This is the version that Kubrick read and eventually filmed, which is one of the reasons there was such a critical and public outcry when it was eventually released, ten years after the novel was published.

The *New Yorker*'s Pauline Kael hated the film, calling it cruel and amoral. 'The movie's confusing – and, finally, corrupt,' she wrote. 'Morality is not, however, what makes it such an abhorrent viewing experience. It is offensive long before one perceives where it is heading, because it has no shadings. Kubrick, a director with an arctic spirit, is determined to be pornographic, and he has no talent for it. In *Los Olvidados*, Buñuel showed teenagers committing horrible brutalities, and even though you had no illusions about their victims – one, in particular, was a foul old lecher – you were appalled. Buñuel makes you understand the pornography of brutality: the pornography is in what human beings are capable of doing to other human beings. Kubrick has always been one of the least sensual and least erotic of directors, and his attempts here at phallic humour are like a professor's lead balloons. He tries to work up kicky violent scenes, carefully estranging you from the victims so that you can enjoy the rapes and beatings. But I think one is more likely to feel cold antipathy toward the movie than horror at the violence – or enjoyment of it, either.'

Kael did acknowledge that it was prophetically accurate, as did its director. Bludgeoned by the media furore surrounding the copycat crimes, Kubrick withdrew it from circulation, and until his death in 1999, the film was only available as a bootleg. 'He felt maligned,' said Kubrick's widow, Christiane. 'He felt that it was unfair to suddenly blame every crime on him. He did not feel guilty. He felt frightened. He didn't like the sudden storm. Who would?'

Even before Kubrick withdrew it, the film had become something of a cult, a glossy B-movie to be debated rather than enjoyed. Along with Sam Peckinpah's *Straw Dogs*, Michael Winner's *Death Wish*, and Ken Russell's *The Devils*, it was seen as another example of Hollywood's attempt to pander to an audience who were no longer interested in the blockbusters that had served the industry so well, and who wanted more entertainment in the vein of *Easy Rider*. Whether the film was deliberately exploitative, or simply rather cack-handed – and opinion largely favoured the latter – for a while it became cinema's bête noire, paraded as empirical evidence that society was going to the dogs (or at least the droogs), in a spiralling debate over sexual politics, graphic violence, excessive profanity, and the elasticated boundaries of censorship.

During filming, the matter of Allen Jones' fee came up, a disagreeable matter that had Kubrick screaming at Jones, treating him like a subordinate, and repeatedly telling him that 'things were going to be OK'. Unsurprisingly, the rest of the world refused to take any notice.

There were some who just loved it.

'In no other movie did actors talk like this, nor did any previous movie look or sound like this,' wrote Howard

Sounes in his book, *Seventies*. 'Nadsat gave the film dialogue a unique quality. Wendy Carlos' music [she was billed as Walter as this was before her sex change later the same year] was not the normal nature sounds of movie soundtracks – wind over reeds, vibrating gut string – but an oscillating brrrrrrrr of electricity. As arranged by Carlos, Beethoven's Ninth took on an alarming new life, and Purcell's "Music For The Funeral Of Queen Mary" was wondrous strange indeed. From the pop-art opening titles, *A Clockwork Orange* was linguistically and sonically amazing, mind-expanding, eye-popping cinema, demonstrating that Kubrick was a superlative filmmaker not only of the Sixties, but as he moved into middle age, also of the Seventies.'

Still, Anthony Burgess remained fuming, although in one respect he would get his own back, although unwittingly. 'The essence of pop stardom is immaturity,' he wrote, unaware that David Bowie had used his book to create a world-beating pop icon. 'A wretched little pseudo-musical gift, a development of the capacity to shock, a short-lived notoriety, extreme depression, a yielding to the suicidal impulse.' Just like Ziggy, in other words.

The *Ziggy Stardust* tour was starting to kick up dust all over the country, yet the set didn't exactly include a cavalcade of hits; Bowie was playing highlights from his last three albums, only one of which contained an actual hit record ('Space Oddity'). Which, as his management and record company quickly realised when they listened to the *Ziggy Stardust* album for the first time, meant Bowie needed a hit.

Hence the hasty recording of 'Starman', and the need to get it onto *Top Of The Pops*. RCA pluggers were relentless in their attempts to get the record onto the Radio 1 playlist, and even more insistent when it came to its appearance on the BBC's only commercial pop programme.

As ever, Bowie appeared to be cocky, and a few days before the taping of *Top Of The Pops*, was bragging about what he thought was a foregone conclusion. Who was going to challenge his pandrogynous fiction? Mud, Wizzard, Sweet? Sweet did transgressive about as well as Roger Moore did sincere. You could imagine the thought bubble arrogantly hovering above Bowie's head: 'Watch yourselves, nascent glam-rock kings – I wear the strangely patterned brightly coloured trousers in this house.'

For those of us in the cheap seats, those of us sitting on the beige plastic pouf, or lying on the oblong purple fire hazard in front of the television, it was difficult not to feel patronised when you were presented with the likes of Suzi Quatro, Alvin Stardust, Showaddywaddy, or the Glitter Band. Who were these bozos? Where was my youth when I expected it? Glam rock in the Seventies wasn't anything at all like its airbrushed Eighties new pop counterpart (the one that came complete with clipped fingernails and hospital corners). Honestly, Slade's Noddy Holder may have been the voice of the people, but his guitarist Dave Hill looked like a metal nun. In this company, Bowie should have been confident, but he'd been convinced of his brilliance time and time again, and hardly ever with great success.

Sure, he had his innate arrogance, but this was a real test.

Three weeks earlier, on 15 June, 'Starman' had been performed by the band on Granada's *Lift Off With Ayshea*, a teatime children's show that showed Bowie and the Spiders filmed against a background of cheap coloured stars. Broadcast on 21 June, this was the first time that Ziggy had been foisted on the TV public. But *Top Of The Pops* was the Big Time.

Duran Duran's Nick Rhodes was one of those who saw *Lift Off*. He was at home in his parents' bungalow in suburban Hollywood, on the outskirts of Birmingham, the same town that the band's bassist, John Taylor, grew up in. He was ten years old and besotted. *Ziggy Stardust* was the first album he ever bought, and the whole period still has enormous significance for him.

He was sitting in the living room, 'Which was very *Abigail's Party*, with a little more sophistication, but not that much.' The furniture was brown, with a round glass G-Plan table in the middle of the room, and a huge colour television with the smallest of screens. His parents had bought it for the moon landings, failing to realise that all the transmissions would be in black and white. 'Thinking back now the TV looked like a piece of conceptual art. It was just this enormous cathode ray monstrosity, but it did the trick because David Bowie pumped out of it.'

Hosted by the singer Ayshea Brough (along with an owl puppet called Ollie Beak), the show that week featured Tony Christie, Hello, and a South African performer called Emil Dean Zoghby, as well as Bowie.

'*Lift Off* was a teatime show, and we watched it when we got home from school. She was a groovy-looking chick in white zippy outfits and there was always music on it,' says Rhodes. Bowie was wearing the jumpsuit he would wear on *Top Of The Pops*, but played an ordinary, unlacquered acoustic guitar. Woody Woodmansey had yet to bleach his hair. 'We already knew who Bowie was, because we liked the record as we'd heard it on the radio, people at school [Silvermead School in Wythall] were talking about him, and we'd seen his pictures in magazines. So we raced home from school that day as we knew he was on. He was a phenomenon in the same way the Sex Pistols were a few years later.'

'I remember eating beans on toast watching [*Lift Off*] and nearly spilling my dinner,' says ABC's Martin Fry, who was living in Sheffield at the time. 'It was [then] that I realised that I was a square peg in a round hole.'

BBC broadcaster Marc Riley, formerly of the Fall, also saw the show:

'I'll never forget the moment my friendly little mate Ollie left the screen and on came this ... thing with his weird mates. I was absolutely gobsmacked. My gran was shouting insults at the TV (which she usually saved for Labour Party Political Broadcasts), and I just sat there agog. I was experiencing a life-changing moment. I know it sounds ridiculous – but it really did knock me for six. It was three weeks later when he popped up again on *Top Of The Pops* . . . and for the second time in my life I was transfixed by a bloke in a quilted jumpsuit and red leather wrestler's boots! There's no doubt that Bowie's appearance on *Top Of The Pops* was a pivotal moment in British musical history. Like the Sex Pistols at the Lesser Free Trade Hall in Manchester in '76 – his performance lit the touchpaper for thousands of kids who up till then had struggled to find a catalyst for their lives. And through him we discovered Lou Reed, Iggy Pop, the Velvet Underground, and everyone else. Bowie encouraged you to have a broader interest in pop culture, not that it was called that back then.'

Top Of The Pops was recorded the day before broadcast, on the Wednesday, at BBC TV Centre in Wood Lane, just a few hundred yards from Shepherd's Bush, the area that had been so important to Bowie during his mod days six years earlier. Though he had a habit of appearing cocky, on the day of the recording, Bowie was understandably nervous. This was the first prime-time outing for Ziggy, and although the Spiders had appeared on *Lift Off* in Manchester, and while they'd previously played *The Old Grey Whistle Test*, today's programme was a huge opportunity. Get this right, make this work, and the Ziggy project would be properly launched. If he blew it, all Bowie would have to look forward to was yet more flip-flopping from the critics in the boulevard press.

Which wasn't really the point. In order for Ziggy Stardust

to be successful, he needed to be famous. Properly famous. Household name famous.

So *Top Of The Pops* needed to work.

In order to convince the BBC executives, they had been encouraged to come and watch the Spiders play a gig at The Croydon Greyhound the week before. Even though there were barely fifty people in the audience (the bar was so empty that Bowie actually performed a part of the set down in the crowd), they were suitably impressed, and booked the band there and then.

As with all 'live' performances on *Top Of The Pops*, the record had to be rerecorded, in order to suit the Musicians Union, although this in itself was always something of a farce. 'The way we used to rerecord the songs for *Top Of The Pops* in those days was very simple,' says Ken Scott. 'Because of the Musicians Union every song that appeared on the show had to be rerecorded, but all we did was this: because they forced us to rerecord them, we'd go into the studio and then invite the MU representative down to witness it. Then you'd set up as if you were going to rerecord, and then someone from the record company would come down and take the MU rep down to the nearest pub. And by the time he came back from the pub, we had miraculously rerecorded it. This is how it happened, time and time again. And all we'd done was mix the backing track from the original version, and this is what we handed over to the rep.'

On 5 June, the day of the *Top Of The Pops* recording, the entire band felt elated. By eleven o'clock, as they climbed into the limo outside Haddon Hall (their management had decided that they should do the trip in style), it was already a hot day. The band's stage clothes were all on hangers laid out in the boot, along with two bags of shoes. It wasn't quite the hottest day of the month, but it was hot enough for the band to pile into the car in their shirtsleeves, with no jackets. From being kids they'd all watched *Top Of The Pops*, and seen all these monstrously successful bands on the show and never really thought they'd get there. 'To actually be there and play on it was a thrill,' says Trevor Bolder. 'I actually achieved a goal in that way.' As they were miming, they were a lot more nervous than they ought to have been.

It was just before midday when they arrived, the time they'd been told to turn up (this was no occasion to be fashionably late). They climbed out of the limo, and then ambled into the Stage Door reception, all the while being monitored by the crowd of young autograph hunters lying in wait in the lobby. They walked by the famous T. B. Huxley-Jones sculpture of Helios, the Greek god of the sun, by the concave, stone, spaceship-shaped edifice in the central courtyard, and then through the two sets of glass double doors, across the diamond-patterned linoleum, past the bronze Richard Dimbleby wall plaque, across the lobby, past Security, past the marble-set lifts, and down the criss-cross corridors into Studio 8. First right, then right again, and then left under the stairs, and there it was, just fifty yards from the reception. Hallowed ground. Studio 8, where the magic happened. The red 'KEEP OUT' sign had yet to be illuminated, although the blue 'REHEARSAL' sign was fully lit. They arrived at Studio 8 around 12.15, went to their dressing room, hung around for a bit, playing cards and gossiping about the other acts on the show, and then went to the BBC bar.

Gary Glitter was the first act to rehearse, at noon sharp. Bowie and the Spiders were next, at 12.50, before Pan's People (2.30), Sweet (3.00), and finally Lulu, at 4.30. At that time, all the acts rehearsed in their street clothes, allowing the cameramen to set up their shots for the recording (street clothes for Bowie didn't mean the jeans and T-shirts worn by the others, but rather a red bomber jacket, black tailored trousers, and a white chiffon shirt). When the crew were happy with Bowie's performance (or at least their understanding of it), they all walked back to their dressing room, where they opened some syrupy white wine, and climbed into their Ziggy costumes, steaming their satin tops, and checking that nothing visible was stained (the recent gigs had often resulted in drunks in the audience flinging plastic cups of beer at them). Bowie commandeered the dressing table, checking his make-up and attending to his hair. Before a show, Bowie could spend up to an hour in front of the mirror, not in an especially narcissistic way, but just to make sure he looked as perfect as possible. He had to check for stubble, not just on his chin, but above the eyes, too, as he so frequently plucked his eyebrows (he would first shave them on the next tour of America, which made him look even more of a freak). Bowie's hair was naturally springy, and whether he needed it up in an Afro – during the 'Space

Oddity' years, for instance – or fulsome and laying on his shoulders (*The Man Who Sold The World*), it was compliant. The new Ziggy haircut was bedding in, however, and so the singer always had a sports bag full of hairspray, just in case the TV make-up artists and hairdressers weren't fully equipped. This afternoon he sprayed so much of it that the rest of the band started barracking him about it, asking him to take it outside and spray himself in the corridor. He had got used to his hair's aerodynamicity, and the way it made him feel was something he'd never really felt before. When he had long hair, he was one of a gang, with a generational agenda. With his red shag, he looked like no one on Earth, and its power was extraordinary. Not only did people respond to him differently, he felt different himself, almost as though he had dyed his skin. This wasn't a hat he could simply put on and take off, this was part of his body now.

The dressing room was only about twelve feet by ten, and, as they always did just before and after a gig, they felt like a gang, the four musketeers, out for glory, gold, and girls. Bowie may have been d'Artagnan, but Athos, Porthos, and Aramis still lived by the motto: '*Tous pour un, un pour tous.*'

Slender-limbed, his legs crossed girlishly, Bowie dabbed away at his face, painting dust on skin and bone, the light bulbs surrounding the mirror making his work look even more theatrical. The lights were so strong it felt like being on the tiniest of football pitches as the floodlights covered everyone in a white heat. The tiniest of football pitches, or one of the white rooms in Kubrick's *2001*, a hermetically sealed, temperature-controlled, airless white womb, waiting to be filled with life. There was not one bead of sweat on his face. Inside the flaps of his partially undone jumpsuit you could see Bowie's ridiculously concave chest, the whitest European body you'd ever see (he almost looked Japanese). Not that anyone would ever see it like this, as the whole point of Ziggy was to watch him onstage, under the red and yellow plastic filters, as he was gliding around and about like a tiger on Vaseline.

As Bowie continued to dab away at his face, he started singing the chorus of 'Starman', deliberately catching himself in the mirror as he did so. Having finished with 'Let all the children boogie', he smiled and shuffled in his seat, turning to smile at Woody, the first of many conspiratorial glances that evening. Uncharacteristically, Woody winked back in acknowledgement – intimate, rather than presumptive. They all knew how important tonight was. Ronson and Bolder, now fully dressed in their costumes, were both sitting on metal chairs, staring at the black and white TV bolted high on the wall, watching a trailer for a weekend show, not that they were really concentrating. All they were concentrating on was what was going to happen in a few minutes' time; everything before it, and – they suspected, having done a little TV before – after it, was just killing time. Everything that wasn't performing was something done to kill time, even, sometimes, recording.

They absent-mindedly picked at some finely cut

sandwiches on the table behind them, which was covered in plates, beer bottles, wine, and a circular tin ashtray. Most of the cigarettes in it were Bowie's, as he hadn't stopped smoking since arriving at the BBC. The grey wall-to-wall carpet – it had the texture of underfelt – around the dressing table was covered in ash, almost as though someone had spilled grey flour on it. Someone mentioned the other bands on the show that night, and someone else again mentioned Sweet, causing Bowie to laugh theatrically. He, like the rest of the band, thought they were preposterous, a reductive noise when no noise would have been preferable. They chatted about the Who, Family, Mott The Hoople, and other bands they respected. Kudos was everything. Always was. Bowie reached down into his bag – an old cloth Biba holdall that Angie had bought for him years ago – and he pulled out a bronze can. He sprayed his hair some more – was this the fourth or fifth time he'd done this? – and flicked the fringe a few times, as though he was trying to flip it to the other side of the dressing room by bouncing it off the mirror. His hair looked OK, he thought, good enough, at least, for the twelve or fifteen or so million people who might be watching him tonight. If he had stopped for a while to think about the numbers, their accumulation may have scared him, but that was how many people watched *Top Of The Pops*. Frankly, that was how many people watched television.

The production team kept popping in, checking none of the band had wandered off – they had famously lost a member of the Faces once – and regularly apprising them of the schedule, one that was so obviously written in stone, but yet was apparently so fluid that it appeared to change every ten minutes. For the band, the experience wasn't so different from being backstage at a festival, where every band was subservient to the process, to the schedule; you simply went on when you were told to, and where diva-ish behaviour wasn't just frowned upon, it was demonised. But they weren't going anywhere, and didn't fancy squandering the opportunity. Later, some autograph hunters knocked and came in, flattered by the band's charm and attention. Some of the BBC researchers were talking about the closure on Broadway of *Fiddler On The Roof* after a record 3,242 performances, a few lamenting the fact they'd never seen it. News was also coming in from San Francisco, concerning a team of FBI agents who had stormed a hijacked Pacific Southwest Airlines jet, killing the two men who had been holding eighty-six people hostage on board Flight 710. One passenger was killed in the crossfire and two other men were wounded, including the actor Victor Sen Yung, who played Hop Sing in the TV series *Bonanza*.

A little after four o'clock, Bowie and the Spiders were called back to the studio for the full dress rehearsal, and as they left the dressing room, Bowie actually pinched himself, threw back his head, and then laughed at the ceiling. 'Ha!' None of them could believe their luck, and none more so than Bowie. As he stepped out into the winding hall (Television Centre was built in a circle, it was said, so that the buck couldn't ever stop), and as he looked at the rest of the band slowly walking towards the studio like gunslingers, his mouth went dry. He had butterflies in his stomach that had turned into bats driven mad by cheap BBC white wine. Was this going to be another false start, like 'Space Oddity'? Or was this really the start of something big, something important, something that was actually going to change his life? His manager believed in Ziggy, his wife believed in Ziggy, and Lord knows Bowie himself believed in Ziggy, but were the public going to buy into him in any serious way? He thought back to his days with Lindsay Kemp, thought back to those evenings waiting in the wings at tawdry little arts clubs, as twenty or thirty people shuffled in their seats out front, wanting diversion but not expecting to have their worlds shifted.* Would anyone's world shift tonight, would anyone believe in this ridiculous dream enough to actually embrace it?

After Studio 1, Studio 8 was the biggest studio in the building, measuring over six thousand square feet. Opened in 1967, at the behest of producers who wanted a studio large

....

* Bowie used to tell a story about playing the working men's clubs up north, when he was just starting out as Ziggy, although to my mind it sounds apocryphal, to say the least (and I'm fairly sure I've heard it before): 'I was in the dressing room at one club, and I said to the manager, "Could you show me where the lavatory is, please?" and he said, "Aye, look up that corridor, and you see the sink attached to the wall at the end, there you go." I tottered briefly on my stack-heeled boots and said, "My dear man, I'm not pissing in a sink." He said, "Look son, if it's good enough for Shirley Bassey, it's good enough for you."'

enough for a live audience, it soon became the home of BBC sitcoms, as well as *Top Of The Pops*. For those acts that had never been on television before, it could also be fantastically imposing.

The band did a full run-through in stage clothes, and then hit the bar. And as they were still in their stage clothes, sipping their white wine and beer, people kept coming up to them, intrigued, asking if they were in *Doctor Who*. This is where Bowie met Lulu, who was also appearing on the show, and they hit it off; so much so that they ended up having an affair, while Bowie would produce, sing, and play saxophone on her versions of two of his songs, 'The Man Who Sold The World' and 'Watch That Man'.

They were back in the dressing room by nine, finishing off the wine. Twenty minutes later a researcher knocked at the door and said they were ready to film. Bowie's heart leaped and seized. This was it. Finally, an audience with the audience, the largest audience it was possible to have. Who needed a Hammersmith Odeon when you could spend four minutes in the company of twelve million? Thirteen million? Fifteen million? He stood up, stared once more in the mirror, his feet splayed like a ballerina, as he flicked his hair one last time.

'David was always in character, but we just dressed up for live shows or TV,' says Bolder. 'Once, when we were in America, staying at the Beverly Hills Hotel, these kids knocked on our door. We had just come offstage, and were all dressed in jeans and T-shirts, but the kids were there dressed up in these weird outfits and stuff. They said, "Geez, you guys are really weird." And we thought, "Have you looked in the mirror?" They were living what we were doing onstage, but we were walking away from it once we'd finished onstage.'

1972 was an odd year for music in Britain, as the momentum of pop continued to move from the single to the album, stumbling on its platform heels as it went. The big British LPs of the year were *Exile On Main Street* by the Rolling Stones, *Close To The Edge* by Yes, *Never A Dull Moment* by Rod Stewart, *Machine Head* by Deep Purple, *The Slider* by T. Rex, *Argus* by Wishbone Ash, *Honky Château* by Elton John, *Seventh Sojourn* by the Moody Blues, *Catch Bull At Four* by Cat Stevens, and Lindisfarne's *Fog On The Tyne*. In retrospect, one would no doubt add the likes of Nick Drake's *Pink Moon* and the first Roxy Music album, but at the time, these were the records we bought and enjoyed. And while the US may have been responsible for a greater proportion of classic records that year – Neil Young's *Harvest*, Lou Reed's *Transformer*, Stevie Wonder's *Talking Book*, Steely Dan's *Can't Buy A Thrill*, Big Star's *#1 Record*, Tim Buckley's *Greetings From L.A.*, Curtis Mayfield's *Super Fly*, Todd Rundgren's *Something/Anything* to name only a very few – the British music scene felt fairly robust.

In the same way that revisionists like to say that punk emerged in something of a musical vacuum, where the only acts filling the void were bombastic American rockers and excessive British prog-rock groups, so it's easy to look quickly at the music scene in the early Seventies and say it was lumpen and dull. Both opinions are woefully wide of the mark. There were so many great albums released in 1976 that it was almost a banner year for music – Stevie Wonder's *Songs In The Key Of Life*, Bob Dylan's *Desire*, Tom Waits' *Small Change*, Steely Dan's *The Royal Scam*, Joni Mitchell's *Hejira*, Bob Marley's *Rastaman Vibration*, Marvin Gaye's *I Want You*, The Steve Miller Band's *Fly Like An Eagle*, J. J. Cale's *Troubadour*, Tom Petty And The Heartbreakers' first record, Dr Buzzard's Original Savannah Band, Blue Oyster Cult's *Agents Of Fortune*, the Eagles' *Hotel California*, Jackson Browne's *The Pretender*, Nils Lofgren's *Cry Tough* for instance – but they were all of American provenance. What there wasn't was anything British, nothing capturing the zeitgeist – largely because there was no zeitgeist to capture. Likewise there was a lot going on in 1972, and the music scene was actually extremely rich, just a little aimless. There were classic singles from Neil Young ('Heart Of Gold'), Family ('Burlesque'), Free ('A Little Bit Of Love'), The Temptations ('Papa Was A Rolling Stone'), Lou Reed ('Walk On The Wild Side', produced by Bowie),[*] Mott The Hoople ('All The Young Dudes', written by Bowie), Roxy Music

---

[*] Having worked out that the only people occupying the end of the market Ziggy was aimed at were Lou Reed and Iggy Pop, Bowie co-opted both of them, bigging them up in interviews, and rather brilliantly managing to take them under his wing, even though they had already had considerable success in their own right.

('Virginia Plain'), Yes ('Roundabout'), Steely Dan ('Do It Again'), Roberta Flack ('The First Time Ever I Saw Your Face'), Thin Lizzy ('Whiskey In The Jar'), Elton John ('Tiny Dancer'), Timmy Thomas ('Why Can't We Live Together'), Curtis Mayfield ('Superfly'), Carly Simon ('You're So Vain'), Billy Paul ('Me And Mrs Jones'), Alice Cooper ('School's Out'), the Spinners ('I'll Be Around'), and the Kinks ('Celluloid Heroes'). Nearly half of these were British, proving that the art of making classic singles was still being practised with the same attention to detail as it had been five years previously, when the competition to keep up with the Beatles put their peers under an increasingly unreasonable amount of pressure. But what there wasn't was any great sense of purpose, what there wasn't was any sense of momentum.

It's possible that 1971 was a better year for the album, producing the likes of Jethro Tull's *Aqualung*, David Crosby's *If I Could Only Remember My Name*, Sly And The Family Stone's *There's A Riot Going On*, Marvin Gaye's *What's Going On*, *Who's Next* by the Who, *Tapestry* by Carole King, *Shaft* by Isaac Hayes, *Imagine* by John Lennon, *Teenage Head* by the Flamin' Groovies, *A Nod Is As Good As A Wink . . . To A Blind Horse* by the Faces, *Blue* by Joni Mitchell, *Songs Of Love And Hate* by Leonard Cohen, *Every Picture Tells A Story* by Rod Stewart, Elton John's *Madman Across The Water*, *Surf's Up* by the Beach Boys, *Electric Warrior* by T. Rex, *Sticky Fingers* by the Rolling Stones, *At Fillmore East* by the Allman Brothers Band, and Bowie's own *Hunky Dory*. These albums were as diverse as they were rich, and amongst critics there was a sense that perhaps rock had already reached its apotheosis. After all, if the Beatles, the Rolling Stones, and Bob Dylan really were the rock trinity of the Sixties, by 1972 the lovable Mop-Tops were no more, Bob Dylan was still in semi-retirement, and the Stones – while still making great music – had the look of a band about to slip into self-parody.

You certainly didn't get a sense of great quality by watching *Top Of The Pops*, and the biggest single hits of the year were hardly vintage, giving the impression that – much like appearing on *Top Of The Pops* itself – if you were given enough exposure then you might be in with a chance of success. Unlike the album charts, which were a genuine reflection of the spirit of the times, the singles charts were a bag of Woolworth's pick and mix: old rock 'n' roll stars and keen-eyed hippies dressed up in glitter in the hope of resurrecting their careers (twenty-eight-year-old Gary Glitter at one end, twenty-five-year-old Marc Bolan at the other), novelty records, gimmicky light entertainers, boogie bands, and insipid soul singers. During this period it became a weigh station for musical clowns, 'a harlequinade of sequin-spangled concave chests'. Never has there been a better example of democracy at work than the British singles charts of 1972.

Yet these preposterous figures were becoming big stars. This was the era when the close-up was coming into its own, and new TV cameras made it easier to focus at close range. Television now looked like the movies.

The year's best-selling single was a tartan-by-numbers

version of 'Amazing Grace' by the Royal Scots Dragoon Guards, closely followed by a novelty pub-rock anthem, 'Mouldy Old Dough' by Lieutenant Pigeon. The rest of that year's Top Ten was made up of such anodyne nonsense as Little Jimmy Osmond's 'Long Haired Lover From Liverpool', 'Son Of My Father' by Chicory Tip, 'Mother Of Mine' by Neil Reid, and 'I'd Like To Teach The World To Sing' by the New Seekers (which started life as a Coca-Cola ad). The only singles possessing any teenage chutzpah were 'Metal Guru' by T. Rex and Gary Glitter's debut single, 'Rock & Roll Part 2'. The only best-selling singles in the UK that year to still have any traction forty years later on the radio are 'American Pie' by Don MacLean and 'Without You' by Nilson, two songs that could have been written and recorded at nearly any point in the early Seventies.

There were seventeen number ones that year, while the song that was at number one in the week that Bowie appeared on *Top Of The Pops* was 'Puppy Love' by Donny Osmond, a saccharine cover of the Paul Anka hit from 1960. This also spent five weeks at number one, as a wave of Osmond-mania swept the country. The rest of the chart looked like this: 2: 'Rock & Roll Part 2' by Gary Glitter; 3: 'Take Me Back 'Ome' by Slade; 4: 'Little Willy' by Sweet; 5: 'Vincent' by Don MacLean; 6: 'Circles' by the New Seekers; 7: 'Rockin' Robin' by Michael Jackson; 8: 'Ooh-Wakka-Doo-Wakka-Day' by Gilbert O'Sullivan; 9: 'An American Trilogy' by Elvis Presley; 10: 'California Man' by the Move. I would hazard a guess that none of them had been recorded with any great sense that by doing so their creators were somehow achieving immortality (they may as well have been Pickettywitch, Edison Lighthouse, Love Affair, or Middle Of The Road). Bowie didn't think he was cheating death either, but in 'Starman' he was fairly certain he had a hit.

With the almost immortal words, 'It's number one, it's *Top Of The Pops!*', Britain's foremost music programme made its debut on New Year's Day 1964, just eight years before Bowie appeared playing 'Starman'. Initially scheduled to run for six weeks only, it lasted until July 2006. In 1972, as in most other years, the continuity announcer would look at his cue card and say, in the manner of a benevolent uncle or a form teacher who was trying to sound disapproving but so obviously wasn't, 'Now on BBC One, it's time to hear about the latest developments in the pop charts from Jimmy Savile and Tony Blackburn.' Then the theme song, CCS's thunderous version of Led Zeppelin's 'Whole Lotta Love', would begin percolating, and we were cooking.

Savile would begin gesticulating wildly with his unlit cigar – 'Hey, hey!' he'd say, as if to calm down the studio audience, and then Blackburn would crack his Cheshire Cat grin and introduce the first act of the evening, almost certainly using his favourite adjective, sensational (which to my knowledge only caused a problem once, when he had to introduce The Sensational Alex Harvey Band). The show was presented by a revolving team of jocular and profoundly strange TV light entertainers: as well as Savile (memorably described by the *Daily Telegraph* as 'an improbable figure with a helmet of platinum hair, dressed in a lurid tracksuit and bedecked in ostentatious jewellery') and Blackburn ('There is an opinion that I'm a complete idiot and that I've never had sex. That's not true!'), there were Alan Freeman, Dave Lee Travis, and Noel Edmunds. A litany of loons, big on gurning. Of course what we didn't know at the time was that Jimmy Savile was one of Britain's most prolific sex offenders, Gary Glitter had a predilection for young girls, and that Dave Lee Travis would one day be found guilty of indecent assault.

There were no autocues in those days, at least Blackburn didn't use them. 'I was a bingo-caller more than anything,' he says. 'I just had to introduce the acts. You had to try and make sure that everything was perfect, because if you had to do a retake, it cost so much money. Video was so big and so expensive in those days that you were encouraged to get it right first time. I loved the glam-rock era because it was so much fun, what with everyone dressing up. It was a real performance. All of the acts could be guaranteed to put on a show. It was almost like music hall.' Blackburn tended to hang out with the soul stars who appeared on the programme, as this was the music he liked, although he does remember one conversation he had with Bowie, about a year later. 'I told him that I loved "The Laughing Gnome", not meaning anything by it, and he turned and very gently said, "Oh, that's not me," and walked off.'

In the Eighties the studio set resembled a nightclub,

with girls in cages, fluorescent tube lighting, mammoth amounts of dry ice, and post-apocalyptic backdrops; in the Seventies the sets of TV pop shows tended to look terribly generic, and had a style all their own – there would be huge palms, some neon, ridiculously bright, overhead lighting, and in the BBC's case, usually some kind of convoluted and contractually unfinished stage design involving whatever bits of plastic the *Doctor Who* set builders hadn't used that week. Huge hexagonal, pentagonal, and octagonal shapes would regularly descend from the rafters, almost as if they had been delivered by mistake from the *Tomorrow's World* studio.

TOP OF THE POPS WAS A GENUINELY INCLUSIVE FAMILY MOMENT. IF YOU WANTED TO WATCH SOMETHING ON TELEVISION YOU HAD TO WATCH IT IN REAL TIME, HUDDLED AROUND A LARGE UGLY BOX IN THE CORNER OF THE ROOM, THE WAY THE PREVIOUS GENERATION HAD CROWDED AROUND THE WIRELESS.

There was a variety show side to *Top Of The Pops*, one that steadily intensified during the Seventies. This didn't always appeal to some of the less knockabout stars who appeared on it. When the country music singer Tammy Wynette turned up to play her follow-up to 'Stand By Your Man', 'D.I.V.O.R.C.E.', she was sandwiched between the Goodies, play-acting through 'Black Pudding Bertha', and the Wombles, wombling through 'Wombling White Tie And Tails (Foxtrot)', before being surrounded by the *Top Of The Pops* dancers Pan's People, covered entirely in fairy lights. The jet-lagged star could take no more, screaming, 'I thought this was a music programme but it's a goddamn freak show!' before rushing back to the relative safety of her dressing room.

So much pop in the early Seventies had a whiff of bierkeller oom-pah-pah about it, as perfectly evinced by ABBA – a song such as 'Take A Chance On Me' sounds as though it could just as easily be performed by a bunch of giddy grandmas around an upright piano in an East End pub. Look at YouTube clips of *Top Of The Pops* performances now and, compared to Bowie, most of the other acts look as though they're in panto. With the other glam acts, there is a premium on showmanship, a general sense that the audience is in charge, demanding satisfaction. Nuance is nowhere to be seen, as Gary Glitter, Mud, and all the others scuffle about as if in the playground, physically painting their garish pictures with the very broadest of brushstrokes, hamming it up as if they were in the recreation room, re-enacting what they had seen on television the night before. Bowie could never have been in the audience, even though that's desperately where we wanted him to be. Bowie was simply too perfect a creation to walk among us.

Top Of The Pops was a genuinely inclusive family moment; no one had televisions in their bedrooms, and there were no laptops, handhelds, or tablets. If you wanted to watch something on television you had to watch it in real time, huddled around a large ugly box in the corner of the room, the way the previous generation had crowded around the wireless, listening to new Olympic records, regenerated music hall stars, or the outbreak of war. This was how we all watched the trip to the moon landing in 1969. I remember being dragged in front of the television countless times and told these were the most momentous events I'd ever see on TV; but then my parents didn't know that three years later – in our fourth house since Neil Armstrong went walkabout – I'd be watching David Bowie on BBC One.

Television was the quintessential communal experience of the decade, in which all members of the family were forced to consume each other's culture. It was like a cathode version of the Sunday newspaper – current affairs for Dad, *Upstairs Downstairs* for Mum, *Top Of The Pops* mostly for teens, and *The Two Ronnies* for everyone.

Top Of The Pops wasn't trendy or narrowly targeted, as that wasn't really the point. The show was inclusive, it was mass. 'It wasn't cool, because most people aren't cool,' said John Peel, not long before he died. 'There was something attractively provincial about it. The fashions weren't hard-nosed and the dancing wasn't particularly good. If you watched it you wouldn't feel excluded. If you watched similar things now you'd think that unless you were fantastically good looking [or] were prepared to wear virtually no clothing then you could barely exist as a human being.'

'I think people have forgotten the significance that *Top Of The Pops* had throughout the Seventies,' says Nick Rhodes. 'It really focused the entire nation, every Thursday night for half an hour, on music, on what was going on. Sometimes the groups could be absolutely horrendous, and other times they were just brilliant. And either way it didn't matter if you had to watch a lot of gimmick acts as you knew you were going to get Roxy Music, or David Bowie, or Cockney Rebel, or Sparks, or any other number of oddities. Everybody watched it. It was a family event. You knew there would be novelty acts like Mud and Showaddywaddy, but I even had a soft spot for Sweet, as I loved "Ballroom Blitz".'

The show was recorded every Wednesday at Television Centre (nicknamed the 'Electric Doughnut' and now part of Nick Jones's Soho House empire) in Wood Lane, in London's Shepherd's Bush, and then broadcast twenty-four hours later. (The charts were announced on Tuesday lunchtime, giving the *Top Of The Pops* producers time to collate the show.) So every Wednesday the TV studios would be besieged by dozens of proper, above-the-line famous pop stars, which inevitably produced an atmosphere of Top Trumps hysteria and farce. There were often so many screaming dervishes outside that it was difficult for anyone else working at the BBC to actually get into the building.

'We were at *Top Of The Pops* with T. Rex once and our drummer, Don Powell, had parked his white Bentley next to

Marc Bolan's white Bentley,' says Noddy Holder. 'We all left together by the back door. There were hundreds of fans waiting there. We made a run for it, jumped in the car and slammed the doors, then looked out to see Bolan banging on the window. We had jumped in his motor by mistake and locked him out. The kids tore him to pieces – scratched his shirt off his back and ripped ringlets out of his hair.'

The dress rehearsal tended to start around 4.15, and then after the final timings of the live performances were calibrated, the video elements were mixed in, up in the control room. There was a break at 6 p.m., when the floor crew, the presenters, and the performers all disappeared to the canteen or the BBC bar, the pub or their dressing rooms. The toilets adjacent to the BBC bar were not exactly fit for *Blue Peter*, as wisps of marijuana squeezed their way through the cracks of the lavatory doors, the remnants of hastily chopped speed and cocaine left lying on the lid of the cistern. During the run-through there were often problems with the smoke guns, which were as temperamental as some of the performers.

It's all very well saying that television is a medium only because it is neither rare nor well done, but I miss it, miss it in the way it was able to bring us all together in the pursuit of temporary enlightenment. We still have event TV (sports, royal weddings, riots), although appointment TV has all but disappeared. When television started overhauling our domestic habits in the Fifties and Sixties, we were repeatedly told that it was destroying family life, whereas in some ways it actually improved it, forcing us to come together as a group around our big teak box in the corner of the room.

Top Of The Pops forced you to have an opinion on the charts whether you wanted one or not, forced families to warily consider each other's chosen brand of entertainment at close quarters. We would sit and fawn and mock in equal measure, proud of our choices, curious but inevitably embarrassed about everyone else's. Now that I have teenage daughters, I would love to be able to sit myself down in front of the flatscreen every Thursday evening and devour the generation gap. They are at the age that I was when I first saw 'Starman' on *Top Of The Pops*, and I'd like to watch their faces for signs of their own little epiphanies.

As it is, I usually have to wait until we sit down for breakfast or Sunday lunch to be told about whatever it is they've just seen on YouTube. Their experiences are now a perplexing oil-and-vinegar mix of the viral and the bespoke (behavioural retargeting, social media marketing, and location-based advertising having become so sophisticated it will soon be possible to target every person in the world individually), which pushes them further and further away from any truly collective experience.

Mark Cooper, the BBC's Creative Head of Music Entertainment, was Executive Producer of *Top Of The Pops* when it was cancelled. He lobbied to keep it, but the ratings were falling so sharply that its death was unavoidable. 'It's been especially hard for me, as no one from the BBC will talk

THREE

about it,' he says. 'So the person who ends up speaking about it is the person who made and loved the show. Me. The idea that I've become the spokesman for its demise when I was actually making the show is ridiculous. If a show doesn't have the support of the controller, then there's no hope. Lorraine Heggessey [the former controller of BBC One] was here for five years, and *Top Of The Pops* was one of the last things to come on to her radar. She looked at the declining figures, and asked if this was the best way to serve the audience. She decided it wasn't.'

The show was doomed the day in the mid-Nineties when it was decided that Radio 1 should stop being a station for everyone from the postman to the midwife and become instead a station for 'youth'. After this, *Top Of The Pops* was never going to survive, and so having become a programme for the young instead of a programme for everyone ('*Top Of The Pops* was never a music programme,' says Cooper, 'it was an entertainment show'), the death knell had sounded. This was one of the most symbolic acts of sabotage the BBC has ever been responsible for. When Radio 1 ceased to be the nation's radio station, *Top Of The Pops* ceased to be the nation's guilty pleasure. The whole nature of pop changed then, as it ceased being a national glue; the postman couldn't whistle the latest number one because the postman hadn't heard it. It was no longer a public service.

YouTube may have made valiant efforts to build a mass audience for long-form shows online, but the culture since the dawn of the Noughties has been all about narrow-casting – albeit narrowcasting down tunnels littered with user-generated obstacles.

David Frost once said that television is an invention that permits you to be entertained in your living room by people you wouldn't have in your home; as soon as I saw Ziggy, I would have loved the idea of him deciding to perform an impromptu gig in the back garden. At that age, the celebrity fantasy almost always involved the celebrity somehow interacting with our world, rather than us entering theirs. It meant much more to me to imagine that David Bowie might play a gig in the Assembly Hall at school, having asked me to introduce him, rather than me maybe meeting him in his dressing room or being invited onto the tour. We wanted celebrity to elevate and enhance our lives, to help us show off in front of our friends; becoming a part of their world wouldn't have meant much to us as we would have had no frame of reference. It would have all been far too abstract. No, if we were going to enter the orbit of celebrity, it had to flatter us.

Watching *Top Of The Pops* at my age in 1972 was compulsory, something you simply could not miss. It was appointment TV. 'It was like a religious experience,' says Def Leppard's Joe Elliott. 'I would be thinking about *Top Of The Pops* for three days before it came on, and I would be so excited,' says Glenn Tilbrook from Squeeze. Noddy Holder spent much of the first half of the Seventies on the programme, but was an avid viewer during the Sixties, 'The only reason I'd miss it was if I was playing a gig.'

In the early Seventies, the show was crucially entwined with many bands' careers, and their relative fortunes. It needed to be treated with respect, as did the DJs. 'The presenters had huge egos; these guys were opening supermarkets for thousands and were even bigger stars than the bands,' says Slade's Jim Lea. 'Then you'd see Pan's People looking bedraggled in the morning and the sets all held together with sticky tape, and it demystified it.'

Peer pressure at school was so intense that if, for whatever bizarre reason, you had actually missed it, then the simplest thing to do was to lie – after all, how incendiary could a performance of Slade or the Jackson 5 be? Not that you'd want to miss it, not when the sense of anticipation was so high, when it was possible to go dry in the mouth just thinking about how exciting it would be when it was on. Apart from the radio, there was almost no other way to hear new music, let alone see it.

All you had to do the following day in the playground was nod and say, 'Yeah, great', and move on. No detail was necessary, just an acknowledgement that you had actually been where you ought to have been. Which was at home in front of your television, having just had your tea and having avoided your homework (you had obviously given it a cursory glance although there was obviously no need to admit that to anyone but yourself). Because to have been anywhere else would have been weird. Why would you miss *Top Of The Pops*? You were a twelve-year-old boy with the social life of a twelve-year-old boy, so how complicated would your day have had to be in order for you to miss one of the few shows on television aimed at teenagers? As we all got older, we embraced the ever-expanding litany of acceptable excuses as to why we hadn't seen it, as these obviously highlighted our ascent into adulthood: we were down the pub, at the club, on our way to a gig, or – the holy grail, this, and I have to say one I didn't achieve until I was much older – with a girl (there would be some boys who would attempt to use a roughly cali-brated combination of these excuses, although apart from two or three of them, they were always lying through their teeth). But at the age of twelve the only acceptable reason for not watching *Top Of The Pops* was football practice or a ser-ious injury (and even the latter was debatable).

It was an uncharacteristic evening on television that night of 6 July, as much of the BBC's programming that week was taken up with the Wimbledon tennis finals. BBC One's afternoon outside broadcast finished at 4.50, with commentators Harry Carpenter and David Vine passing over to themselves on BBC Two, and handing the channel over to the children of the house – *The Magic Roundabout*, *Top Cat* (ignorantly branded *Boss Cat* in the UK, in case any under-tens might be persuaded to badger their parents into buying Top Cat meat chunks for their pet moggy), a fairly turgid buy-in called *Barrier Reef* (which, unlike *Boss Cat*, did what it said on the tin), and then *The Adventures of*

Parsley, before the national news and the current affairs/life-style show, *Nationwide*.

I probably plonked myself down when *Nationwide* was on, and sat through that before suffering a bit more Wimbledon, waiting for *Top Of The Pops* to start at 7.25. At the time I could never understand why the show was thirty-five minutes long, before making way for *The Goodies* at 8 p.m. It was so precise, so preternatural, and it lent the BBC an omnipotent Orwellian swagger, as though the corporation controlled time itself (earlier that day, the 'For Schools, Colleges' strand had started at exactly 11.18, before the channel closed down ten minutes later, rearing itself into action again at 12.55 for a programme in Welsh).

The rest of the evening rolled along with warm predictability. After *The Goodies* at 8.30 was *The Burke Report*, which even to my callow eyes looked like one of those programmes given to presenters – in this case *Tomorrow's World*'s James Burke – who the BBC didn't want to leave but whom they didn't really know what to do with. Burke seemed determined to exploit the growing interest in the 'white heat of technology', the experimental products that appeared to be the result of the colossal investment in space technology. On his show, extravagant household appliances would be revealed, almost as if they had magic powers; he would proudly unveil robots that were meant to do away with household chores; and volunteers would be summoned, seemingly at will, from the studio audience and then unceremoniously strapped to infallible lie-detector machines. Here was the Fifties all over again, pandering to the insecure house-wife, and even exploiting that decade's security neuroses and political paranoia: in one programme Burke introduced one of the world's first computer hackers, who showed the watching millions how to break into the Inland Revenue's computer system.

Then it was time for *The Nine O'Clock News*, followed by a repeat at 9.20 of the rather magnificent *Elizabeth R*, starring Glenda Jackson as the eponymous monarch. If this televisual bath wasn't quite warm enough for you, over on the other side BBC Two was showing a repeat of *Morecambe And Wise*, this week starring John Mills, Mrs Mills (no rela-tion), and Kenny Ball and his Jazzmen. (In one scene, Morecambe, Wise, and John Mills are playing army officers during the war. Mills looks at a message on a piece of paper before saying, '. . . signed Adolph Hitler, boss of Germany . . . This note will never fool the Germans.' To which Ernie Wise's response is, 'Of course not. Hitler wouldn't use a pen-cil.') And just in case your day was not finely calibrated enough, Eric and Ernie also started at 9.20. I would have been kicked upstairs between ten and eleven, not that there would have been much to watch if I'd stayed downstairs. After the weather, the channel shut down at midnight sharp, unless you were watching some impenetrable foreign film on BBC Two, in which case the station stayed up until 12.25. On 6 July 1972, the treat on offer was a 1931 epic directed by the Austrian auteur, Georg W. Pabst, concerning German miners going to the aid of their French colleagues, and while

Philip Jenkinson extolled the film's virtues in that week's *Radio Times* (Robert Powell was on the cover, puffing his performance in *Shelley*, which was being shown on the Wednesday), in hindsight it looks as though it had been scheduled only because it was cheap, or, more likely, free. (Looking through that week's *Radio Times*, one of the idiosyncrasies which strikes me more than many others, is the word 'Colour' written in italics just by the broadcast time, a public service announcement deemed necessary in case you had recently bought a colour television only to turn it on and find – *Zut alors! Gott in Himmel!* – some French or German film made back when God was a boy. On 26 August that year, the American listings magazine *TV Guide* discontinued the practice of using a 'C' to indicate colour programmes, and instead started using a 'BW' for monochrome, as at the time about half of the TV households in the US had colour sets.)

In some ways this was the golden age of British television, and on the BBC alone that week you could watch *Parkinson*, *Doctor Who*, *Omnibus* (Frank Muir was in discussion with Groucho Marx), *Panorama*, *Film Night*, *Grandstand*, *Horizon*, *Late Night Line Up*, *Man Alive*, *Dave Allen At Large*, *Kenneth Clark's Civilisation*, and this during the summer season, when it was assumed that no one would be watching television anyway.

Look at the scheduling for Saturday night, though, embedded deep into the evening's entertainment at 8.25, and you see a cultural anomaly that shows not just how backward light entertainment still was, but also, judging

from the uncharacteristically commercial plug in paren-
theses at the foot of the *Radio Times* entry – advertising the
Black & White Minstrels' appearance at shows in Victoria,
Scarborough and Paington – how the troupe were an
engrained part of British life.

Elsewhere in the *Radio Times* you had a column written by the presenter of *The Old Grey Whistle Test*, Richard
Williams, which illustrated the attritional nature of the programme's relationship with *Top Of The Pops*. Describing
Saturday's edition of *In Concert*, he writes, 'How good it is to
see a group of Argent's calibre succeeding on a mass scale,
topping the charts amongst the morass of rubbish.' (That
week on *The Old Grey Whistle Test* there was Todd Rundgren, the Impressions, 'and any guests who may drop in.')
Bowie was one of the few artists to appear on both shows.
('We did that in an afternoon in a tiny little studio with one
camera,' says Trevor Bolder. 'You were so enclosed, you
couldn't move or go anywhere or do anything. And it was
just us, there were no other bands in there, it was just us on
our own, the Spiders. I remember watching it the following
week on TV and we were all sitting around in Haddon Hall
slapping each other on the back for being on TV. It was
marvellous.')

Judging by photographs taken at the time, I'd guess
our television was a Rediffusion, being a fairly standard box
with a coffee-table magazine shelf underneath it. I would
have been lying down on the green vinyl sofa (actually a set-
tee), button-backed with winged corners, with my feet up

on the actual coffee table, on top of which would have been the *Daily Mail*, that week's issue of the *Radio Times*, and an ashtray. We had previously been a *Daily Express* family, but changed to the *Mail* when it went tabloid, a year earlier, in May 1971. There would also have been that month's copy of *Cosmopolitan*. The British edition of the magazine had launched in March, just a few months earlier, and I can still remember the shock I felt looking at Burt Reynolds' naked body, the first of their male centrefolds. My mother loved the magazine, and it gave me something of a thrill to think that she was getting so trendy. It probably gave her a thrill, too, although I can't remember her buying many more issues after the first two or three. The TV commercial was certainly memorable: 'A sensational new magazine for women who are interested in men, love, fashion, food, men, travel, films, beauty, and themselves . . . and men.'

Behind the sofa was the drinks trolley, proudly advertising my parents' penchant for advocaat, Campari, Gordon's Gin, and – inexplicably – crème de menthe. The one defining object that made this home was an oval, gilt-effect wall mirror, which moved from house to house like our cat – if we had moved to a new house and the mirror had not travelled with us, my suspicion would have been that the whole thing was a dream. Sadly, this was probably the mirror I stood in front of playing air guitar with Mick Ronson as Tony Blackburn top-and-tailed 'Starman'.

Apart from the kitchen and the downstairs loo, this was the only room on the ground floor, and so had been bisected by a glass partition, with an inexpertly cut wooden door in the middle. The front part of the room housed the dining table, a chest of drawers, and the stereogram, and the sitting room at the back had the TV and the soft furniture. Designed this way to give a greater sense of space, it only succeeded in making the room feel extremely cramped, as though there was simply too much going on in it.

An Axminster filled the back half of the room, another by-product of the Jones travelling circus, a carpet that moved with us every year – as my father was in the Air Force we were never anywhere longer than twelve months – and which may as well have come with its own press release: 'No matter where you move, and no matter what size your living room, I am superior in every respect. Tread with care!' The television was always covered with hard cards; we weren't a mantelpiece family, so any invitations or cards celebrating an anniversary or party were paraded on the TV, and this meant that when David Bowie appeared he was framed by a small potted Yucca, three wooden figures my father brought back from his posting in Kenya, and half a dozen cards congratulating my brother on reaching his seventh birthday.

Presented by an incongruously attired Tony Blackburn,[*] the edition of *Top Of The Pops* that summer night

....

[*]That summer Blackburn was also hosting the Radio 1 breakfast show, followed throughout the day by Jimmy Young, Dave Lee Travis, Johnnie Walker, Alan Freeman, Noel Edmonds, and finally John Peel.

was its usual collection of bubblegum pop, plodding nascent glam rockers (some of whom – particularly in the case of Sweet – looked like they had been hod-carrying the week previously), and parochial soul stars.

And then there was David Bowie, the low-tech uber-freak with the mismatched pupils. This was Bowie's third appearance on the show (the previous two had been for 'Space Oddity'), but this was the one that properly resonated with its audience, the one that would go on to cause such a shift in the zeitgeist. With his tall, flame-orange cockade quiff, lavishly applied make-up, white nail polish, wearing a multicoloured, quilted jumpsuit that looked as though it were made from fluorescent fish skin (chosen by Ziggy co-shaper, the designer Freddie Buretti), and with his blue, twelve-string acoustic guitar slung across his pelvis, a bone thin Bowie appeared not so much as a pop singer, but rather as some sort of heavily made-up stick insect, a concept helped along by the provocative appearance of his guitarist, the chicken-headed Mick Ronson, who was also dressed in a tight-fitting jumpsuit (his made of gold satin), with both of them unapologetically sporting knee-length patent leather wrestler's boots (Bowie's were red). 'Most people are scared of colour,' Bowie said later. 'Their lives are built up in shades of grey. It doesn't matter how straight the style is, make it brightly coloured material and everyone starts acting weird.' Oh my word. (A few months later, Status Quo, the bastions of generic twelve-bar boogie, were waiting on the *Top Of The Pops* set, as they were due to perform straight after the

Spiders. Francis Rossi, who, like the rest of the band, was dressed head-to-toe in their trademark denim, turned to Woody Woodmansey, the Spiders' drummer, and said, 'Shit, you make us feel old.')

'Starman' didn't feel any less calculated than anything else on *Top Of The Pops* that night, however, it had a kind of arrogant elegance about it that was impossible to ignore. The band all stood there, looking like cabaret storm troopers, as obviously ill-at-ease studio dancers in tank tops shuffled about behind them as though they were at a school disco. Of course the whole charade was premeditated, yet Bowie wasn't certain it was going to work, and looking at the clip now on YouTube, it's odd to see how embarrassed they all look, even Bowie, as though he was still unsure if the whole Ziggy construct would appeal to people in sufficient numbers (at one minute thirty-six seconds, when he sings the line, 'I had to phone someone so I picked on you', he points a wiggling finger at the screen, hoping to connect with someone, anyone). After all, he'd been trying to be a star for a decade, so why was it going to be any different now? He'd had a false start with 'Space Oddity' three years previously, but since then he'd been a cult artist who didn't look as though he was ever going to be anything but.

Seven twenty-five . . .

'Now on BBC One, it's time to hear about the latest developments in the pop charts from Tony Blackburn.'

The theme tune. The neon logo. The introduction from Tony. The show.

This edition of *Top Of The Pops* is one that the BBC, in their finite wisdom, decided to wipe, and the only broadcast-quality clip left is the clip of the Spiders themselves. The typed running order remains, two sheets of ring-bound A4 origin-ally dictated in the office of Johnnie Stewart. This particular show was being presented by Blackburn ('Disc Jockey', it says on the notes, helpfully). Along with Pan's People (Babs, Ruth, Dee Dee, Louise, Andrea, the US choreographer Flick Colby and, later, Cherry and Sue, started their reign in 1967, and were the programme's resident dancers until 1976), appearing live that evening were the Ladybirds (the female vocal har-mony trio who provided backing vocals for any band that needed them), Sweet (all four of them, playing 'Little Willy'), Gary Glitter (plus six), Lulu accompanied by the *Top Of The Pops* orchestra conducted by Johnny Pearson ('Even If I Could Change'), and Bowie ('with four musicians'). Interspersed with them were filmed sequences featuring Dr Hook ('Sylvia's Mother'), Love Unlimited ('Walkin' In The Rain'), and Donny Osmond, along with playbacks of the New Seekers, the Who ('Join Together'), Frederick Knight ('I've Been Lonely For So Long'), and the Partridge Family ('Breaking Up Is Hard To Do', the old Neil Sedaka hit).

Tony Blackburn's introduction to 'Starman' was as anodyne as any other he'd made on the programme over the years, no more, no less – 'And now it's David Bowie with

"Starman" at number 29!' – and I can't remember having any great sense of anticipation, or indeed expectation. You were always intrigued to see someone on the show you hadn't seen before, though Bowie was a special case, as he'd been around for a while, and so expectations were limited. In a way I probably felt a little like the media did when it was announced that Richard Attenborough had decided to cast Robert Downey Junior as Charlie Chaplin in the biopic he started filming in 1991; the consensus was that we would have preferred either an unknown, or someone monumentally famous. Downey at the time was something of a makeweight, and I suppose Bowie was thought to be the same. At least by those who hadn't yet seen him in concert.

And so at a little after seven forty that night, David Bowie and the Spiders from Mars walked into our living rooms, and into our lives.

It was hardly an auspicious entrance. The show had started with the Who and Sweet, followed by Love Unlimited, the New Seekers, Lulu, and then Dr Hook. As the film of Dr Hook playing 'Sylvia's Mother' is faded out, Tony Blackburn blithely introduces 'Starman'. And as the applause dies down, all we see is a pale hand strumming a bright blue twelve-string (the same guitar he'd used to play 'Queen Bitch' earlier in the year on *The Old Grey Whistle Test*), before we see Bowie's face, carrying a smile that says, 'I can't believe we're actually here' (this look was conspiratorial, which shows how early this phase was in Ziggy Stardust's development, as he soon wouldn't need his band's validation for anything). Then the camera pans out, allowing us to see for the first time what he is wearing: a full-length, multicoloured, quilted jumpsuit.

As the camera continues to move in reverse, we hear Bowie reference Marc Bolan when he sings, 'Some cat was laying down some get it on rock 'n' roll . . .', before we're greeted by the sight of Woody Woodmansey playing his drums, sporting an identical haircut (his was bleached), and wearing a shimmering pink, satiny two-piece. When Bowie sings, 'I had to phone someone so I picked on you', he points a wiggling finger at the screen, almost as though he is trying to talk to all of us at once, individually. Having pointed at the camera, he starts to raise his eyebrows, beginning to understand the importance of what he's doing. He then self-consciously grabs his right shoulder with his left hand before turning it to the audience and waving it in the air. The hands go everywhere – on his hips, swaying in time to the chords, pointing in front of him, clutching his chest, clutching his guitar strap, tapping conspiratorially at Ronson, pointing again to the audience, occasionally strumming his guitar, and clapping in time to the coda.

Crucially, Bowie is shot from below, making him appear imperious and starry. In contrast, when Ronson and Bolder are caught chatting to each other during the second verse, they look not so much like gladiators as shifty-looking waiters at an Elizabethan banquet. Having had two rehearsals, Bowie knows exactly where the cameras are going to be, knows exactly what he is going to do when they are trained on him. When he points at Camera 2, reaching out to what he hopes is soon going to be his constituency, the camera is complicit in every way. He knows the cameras will disappear during the middle of the song, and try to capture some virtuosity, yet for the first minute and a half, he has them, knows what they are going to do and where they are going to be.

After some obligatory cutaways involving some spectacularly naff *Top Of The Pops* coloured lights, the camera pulls back again, this time to show Bowie pushing his guitar up forcefully in the air before launching into the first chorus, as he languidly curls his arm around the shoulders of his guitarist, a peroxided Mick Ronson, who has just walked into shot, dressed in something equally shiny (this time, pale yellow). This is the moment that everyone who saw it remembers so well, the public display of affection, the draping of the arm, the proud way in which Bowie casually touches his friend. Why did he have his arm around him? Seriously, why?

As Bowie and Ronson huddle-in for the chorus, Bowie twists his guitar around behind his back, carrying it now like a rifle, with its machine head pointing to the floor. When he sings 'waiting in the sky' he pronounces 'waiting' using the same mockney intonation he had used throughout much of the Sixties, a voice that would soon become synonymous with Bowie in the way it had previously with Mick Jagger. He takes great care with his enunciation, moving his jaw in a way that betrayed all those hours spent working on his theatrics. This was a stage play if it was anything, and you could tell from the way Bowie moved his head, his jaw, his whole body, that he had been trained in the art of playing to the gallery as well as to the camera.

'The thing that interests me is intentionality,' says Mark Cooper, discussing the 'moment'. 'I might be completely wrong, and I know that Bowie was a careerist and was capable of being completely calculated about these things, and I always thought the moment he told Michael Watts he was gay was calculated, but there's something completely natural about the way he puts his arm around Mick Ronson's shoulders. In hindsight we assume that a lot of this stuff is intentional, but a lot are just happy accidents. When he does it, it doesn't look as though he's doing it for the first time, or for effect.'

Nevertheless, the watching public noticed.

What he was really doing, was expressing camaraderie, not an affair. The most radical thing about the gesture, within the confines of male sexual politics, is the embracing of another man not on a sports field. It was non-competitive. It was also an exotic gesture, as there was nothing brotherly about it. This wasn't Jagger and Richards embracing each other at the end of some sweaty gig, sharing a bottle of Jack Daniel's together. This wasn't a bunch of denim-clad long-hairs holding hands and communing as they tried to find a perfect harmony, and this wasn't the rugby team throwing soap at each other in the baths after the game.

What it always wasn't was a coy piece of camp, a play-act for the camera. No, this was two good-looking, over-dressed young men embracing each other on national television, in an almost completely unselfconscious way, as if to say, 'Look at us, ha!' Or, more specifically (Mick Ronson not having a huge say in the matter), 'Look at me!'

'It's also a generational thing,' says Cooper. 'I think Jagger could have done what Bowie did, quite naturally, sidling up to Keith and throwing his arm around him onstage. But no one cared about Jagger as he was an old man. The notion of a singer interplaying with their guitarist was not necessarily a new thing. It was generationally new. Plus Bowie was one of the few artists [along with Roxy Music and Elton John] to play both *The Old Grey Whistle Test* and *Top Of The Pops* – he was both rock and pop, and so he straddled those two worlds, too.'

As the guitar refrain starts at the end of the chorus, Ronson drops down to his knees before bouncing back up again to play the lead. Frustratingly, the camera moves away, and we're left with a long shot of the stage, the BBC cameramen displaying their innate gift for focusing on the wrong player while someone else was performing a solo. Shots were worked out in blocks, with cameras being used for four bars, then six, then another four, etc.

Bowie then drops his arm, and the camera takes us across the stage, catching Trevor Bolder's dyed-silver sideburns (so voluminous were they that Bolder could easily have been related to Noddy Holder), as he concentrates on his burgundy bass guitar. His shirt glistens as well, open to the chest, and very, very blue.

'Even Noddy Holder's weren't as long as mine,' says Trevor Bolder, discussing his sideburns. 'Mine started out as [part of] a full beard. When I joined Bowie, I was in the Rats, with the rest of the Spiders, and because of the Beatles I'd grown a full beard. And I looked really odd compared to Mick and Woody, because they were clean-shaven. So when we started to put the Spiders show together I looked really strange. So I thought, "Well, I can't go on with a full beard, it looks really odd." So I shaved the middle out, so I had a 'tache and sideburns. And then I thought, "Well that looks really odd as well." So I shaved the 'tache off, and I was just about to shave the sideburns off when Angie Bowie said, "Don't you dare shave them off, that'll be part of your image." So it was her decision that I kept them, otherwise they would have gone as well. And then of course she decided that she wanted to spray them silver.' Which is exactly what she did.

Then we're treated to a back shot of the audience – dancing, if somewhat uneasily – until the camera shows us a seated pianist, his red shiny clothes looking far more important than whatever it is he appears to be playing (this would turn out to be Robin Lumley, who had just taken over from Matthew Fisher as the pianist on the *Ziggy* tour). Suddenly we're aware of a boy in a tank top who has appeared as if from nowhere, put directly behind Bowie, and who for some reason seems to be marching along to the song, all by himself (the Spiders' road manager was also in the audience, dancing in a canary yellow suit). This immediately adds a sense of the prosaic to the performance, as it brings the whole performance down to the level of the show. For the producers it was important to always have a smattering of badly dressed people in the audience; indeed when a couple of rather ordinary girls from our school scooted off to London one Wednesday, claiming they were going to be in the audience, we scoured the screen the following evening, and although we didn't see them (we were fairly sure they'd gone shopping in London instead), they wouldn't have been out of place.

Here was the Great British Public, on television! Baying for a good time!

Two-thirds of the way through the song, Bowie drapes his arm around Ronson's neck once more, this time with more conviction and feigning in ecstasy. And as the arm curls around Ronson again we notice the painted white fingernails on his left hand. Oh my word, what on earth was going on here? They're doing it again! Bowie then throws his head back, as though he and his friend are just about to set off on some great adventure, like schoolboys in a Victorian adventure yarn transported to the twentieth century for some gung ho glam. I can't say this gesture stirred any latent homoerotic feelings I may have had – far from it, as you were always on the lookout for the girls in the audience who *were* actually attractive – but the song was performed with such fervour, such enthusiasm, that it was difficult to concentrate on anything after it. When Bowie launches into, 'Let the children use it', he lurches backwards before stepping forward again, trying to inject a sense of energy into a song that was too much of a singalong to allow the band to move around as they were used to doing onstage. And when he sings, 'Don't tell your papa as he'll get us locked up in fright', there is an immediate sense that he's actually talking to the TV audience rather than anyone else. Too late, though, we'd already seen it!

The Ziggy Stardust character was meant to be detached and theatrical (the reference material that Bowie showed to the *Ziggy Stardust* album sleeve photographer, Brian Ward, included a perfect example of urban loneliness, an image of the Fifties cigarette advertisement, 'You're never alone with a Strand'), yet on *Top Of The Pops* Bowie looks almost aggressively tactile, so libidinous in fact that he couldn't have looked more human. Images of Bowie from this period make him look cold and austere, aloof and androgynous; as he performs 'Starman' he can't stop smiling, almost as if he can't quite believe he's back on television. This was artifice for artifice's sake, with a wink, a nod, and yes, a grin. He had had one of the longest apprenticeships in the business – nine years is a long time to wait for success – and you can almost see the relief in his eyes, as he knows he's finally done it. Here, there is no weary bitterness, just a genuine sense of enthusiasm for his work. Even though he looked like a genuine oddball, there was almost an innocence about his appearance. As Bowie's face first comes into focus, at the beginning of the song, he flinches, self-conscious for probably the last time in his entire career.

That night they were performing on a raised white platform, surrounded by a typically incongruous set design, which that week included large, polyurethane tablets suspended in mid-air, a string of molecular bubbles that weaved their way around the studio. As the song fades, Bowie approaches the audience behind him, encouraging them to clap, which they do, obediently.

Tony Blackburn then introduces Pan's People dancing to Frederick Knight, and the world moved on. However, even though the entire performance had taken only four minutes and five seconds, the world would never be the same again. Eleven minutes later the show was over. The credits started to roll – 'Top Thirty specially prepared for the BBC and *Record Mirror* by the British Market Research Bureau, *Top Of The Pops* Orchestra directed by Johnny Pearson, Vocal backing The Ladybirds, Musical Associate Derek Warne, Pan's People choreography by Flick Colby . . .' – and the world spun again.

This was glam rock in full bloom. When Marc Bolan wore glitter on his face during his performance of 'Hot Love' on *Top Of The Pops* in March 1971 (styled by *Nova* magazine's Chelita Secunda), he was partly responsible for the flowering of a new musical genre; Bowie's 'Starman' appearance was the full garden centre.

As *Top Of The Pops* at the time was an entrenched example of BBC early evening family viewing, so Bowie's appearance was deemed to be somewhat outside the show's prescribed comfort zone. Fathers shouted 'Poofter!' and 'Nancy boy!' at the screen, and wondered why Bowie and

Ronson were clinging so close to each other, why they had their arms draped around each other's shoulders so tightly. This was, 'A sweet moment of inclusion,' according to one critic, 'the alien embracing the rocker, and, by proxy, all of the nation's misfits.' Did they need to share the same microphone? Why were they both dressed so strangely? Did they really want to look like women? In 1972 there was still a generation gap. Our parents could remember the war (in January the Japanese soldier Shoichi Yokoi was discovered in Guam, having spent twenty-eight years in the jungle), and were still more than in thrall to *The Morecambe And Wise Show*.

Family viewing it may have been, yet down on Orchard Avenue, mine were nowhere in sight. Brother Dan was safely upstairs, and probably asleep, my mother was out in the garden, bent over her beds, down at the end of the long strip of sunlight that seemed to be squeezed between the semis, the chalets, and the bungalows that fanned out from the seafront, seemingly desperate to inch back to London (I know I was). Every house in our area appeared to have been built in spite of its proximity to the sea rather than because of it, which meant that no sun streamed into any of the rooms, upstairs or down, making you feel as though you were trapped and unable to get outside whenever you were indoors. Most were Victorian, or late Edwardian, but even those that weren't somehow adhered to a similar code of restraint. And Dad? He was away with the RAF, occasionally home at weekends, so I was glued to *Top Of The Pops* by myself, wondering what to make of it all, and growing up very quickly. Soon I would be bouncing around the living room, an HB pencil as my substitute microphone, wondering how I was going to convince my mother that I needed to dye my hair. Orange. Tomorrow.

Bowie's ambiguous sexuality was one of his shrewdest marketing ploys. A month earlier, on stage at the Oxford Town Hall, Bowie had sunk to his bodystockinged knees and fellated Ronson's sanded-down Les Paul Custom, a moment that had not gone unnoticed by the music press – namely the *NME*, *Sounds*, and the *Melody Maker*, all of which were selling upwards of 200,000 copies each week. Everything Bowie did was premeditated. When he stepped offstage that night in Oxford, he screamed at the photographer Mick Rock, who was covering the gig, 'Did you get it, did you get it?'

So what was all this? All the other pop stars around at the time were relatively benign. Marc Bolan was really only a spangly hippie, Sweet and Gary Glitter were just novelty acts, while Slade still looked like Black Country plumbers dressed up for a night at the local rugby club.

But Bowie? Well, Bowie looked transgressive, odd, dangerous. Bowie looked as though he might turn out to be trouble.

And he was. For all of us. Suddenly Bowie – a man called alias – had the world at his nail-varnished fingertips, and in no time at all he would be the biggest star in the world. All of a sudden we were collectively possessed.

'As soon as I heard "Starman" and saw him on *Top Of The Pops* I was hooked,' remembers Ian McCulloch from Echo and the Bunnymen. 'I seem to remember me being the first to say it, and then there was a host of other people saying how the *Top Of The Pops* performance changed their lives. In 1972, I'd get girls on the bus saying to me, "Eh, have you got lippy on?", or "Are you a boy or a girl?" Until he turned up it was a nightmare. All my other mates at school would say, "Did you see that bloke on *Top Of The Pops*? He's a right faggot, him!" And I remember thinking, "You pillocks", as they'd all be buying their Elton John albums, and Yes songs, and all that crap. It made me feel cooler. With people like me, it helped forge an identity and a perspective on things, helped us to walk in a different way, metaphorically . . .'

Bowie's appearance had a similar effect on Marc Almond: 'Next day, all hell broke loose in the playground. Bowie was a queer, and if you liked him you must be queer, too.'

For former Creation Records boss Alan McGee, the man who discovered Oasis, the performance was, 'The reason I got into rock 'n' roll.' Bowie's performance didn't just kick-start the Seventies, in a way it did the same for the Eighties, as many of those who saw him on television that day didn't get a chance to fulfil their own dreams until years later – John Lydon, Boy George, Sean Ryder, Dave Gahan of Depeche Mode, Dave Wakeling of the Beat. One was Gary Kemp:

'The first time I fell in love it was with a man,' he wrote

in his autobiography *I Know this Much: From Soho to Spandau*. 'Gender-bending was suddenly far more rebellious than drugs and violence. [The performance] became the benchmark by which we would forever judge pop and youth culture. It was a cocksure swagger of pouting androgyny that appealed to pubescent working-class youth across Britain – a Britain still dominated by post-war austerity and weed-filled bombsites. For us, the Swinging Sixties had never happened; we were too busy watching telly. The object of my passion had dyed orange hair and white nail varnish. Looking out from a tiny TV screen was a Mephistophelean messenger from the space age, a tinselled troubadour to give voice to my burgeoning sexuality. Pointing a manicured finger down the barrel of a BBC lens, he spoke to me: "I had to phone someone, so I picked on you." I had been chosen. Next to him, in superhero boots, his flaxen-haired buddy rode shotgun with a golden guitar. As my singing Starman draped his arm around him, I felt a frisson of desire and wanted to go to their planet. I had witnessed a visitation from a world of glitter. That night, I planned my future. After all, "If we can sparkle," he'd told me, "he may land tonight."'

The fifteen-year-old Susan Ballion – who, four years later, would re-emerge as Siouxsie Sioux – watched the show in hospital, recovering from ulcerative colitis, a life-threatening illness requiring her innards to be exposed through stitches in her stomach for several weeks until it was safe to reinsert them. 'It sounds horrific,' she says, 'and it was. Surreal. It completely de-romanticised the body for me.' She fell in love with Bowie, though. 'I just couldn't believe how striking he was,' she says. 'That ambiguous sexuality was so bold and futuristic that it made the traditional male/female role-play thing seem so outdated! Besides, I'd lost so much weight and had got so skinny that Bowie actually made me look cool . . .' She had just turned fifteen, and was starting to walk again after her operation. 'Gary Glitter's "Rock 'n' Roll" was also in the charts; so were Marc Bolan and Roxy Music who, like Bowie, didn't seem to be part of the mainstream. The music went directly to me. It was the first time I felt that it was music made for me. It was an amazing time. There were lots of things to get excited about during the next eighteen months, or so. I was still pretty much a loner, though. I never hung out with a gang of friends.'

Her friend was David Bowie. '[He] was incredible – the skinniness, the alienation, the otherworldliness. He was more than simply androgynous, though for the first time, I heard words such as "unisex" and "bisexual". I thought that was really interesting. He was aimed at both male and female audiences, and projected something very different to what most boys and girls were trying to conform to. It was definitely the man/woman of the future, and although nothing was ever said, you understood it instinctively, just by the imagery and the sounds that he used. It was about tearing down the old traditions and clichés. It was a brave new world, a springboard to accentuate your own individuality. But I was never a Bowie lookalike. I found it odd that so many people were content to merely copy.'

A few years later, when Bowie began to withdraw from it all, it really felt to Siouxsie that there was something missing. 'Until then, his albums had been eagerly anticipated. But by the mid-Seventies there was a vacuum. It was no coincidence that so many people involved in punk at the beginning had been inspired by him. Bowie was the catalyst who'd brought a lot of us, the so-called Bromley Contingent, together. And out of that really small group of people, a lot happened . . .' Including Siouxsie And The Banshees.

'I saw David Bowie on *Top Of The Pops* and immediately put on some of my older sister's make-up,' says the Cure's Robert Smith. 'I loved how odd it made me look, and the fact that it upset people. You put on eyeliner and people started screaming at you. How strange, and how marvellous!'

'I remember being frightened by "Starman" on *Top Of The Pops*, and my mum thought he was horrible,' says Bob Stanley of Saint Etienne. 'One of my favourite comments was someone's father asking, rhetorically, "Whatever will they think of next?" as though the whole thing were a conspiracy.'

'At school the next day nobody talked about anything else,' says Nick Rhodes. 'Not everyone had seen *Lift Off With Ayshea*, but everyone had seen this. It was so different. The approach, the look, the sound of him, the excitement that he was singing about aliens. At that point most people were still singing dull old love songs, and Bowie really came from such an obtuse angle, visually, conceptually, lyrically. He was unique. For me, at that time of my life, when I was just discovering music, it was so magnetic, and he was genuinely exciting.

'My parents would often watch *Top Of The Pops* with me, as they were quite turned on by knowing what was going on in the charts, and I remember they actually liked him.'

They liked Bowie so much they took Rhodes to see Bowie when he played the Empire Pool in Wembley, in London, in 1976, on the *Station To Station* tour, not once but twice. 'I'd become such a fan and he had become such a focus of what I thought I wanted to do with my life at the time. They were very indulgent of Bowie because this was the person who inspired me, and the rest of Duran Duran, and most of the rest of the British music industry that exists now, to do what we all chose to do. I told my parents when I was ten that I wanted to be a rock star when I grew up, which they laughed off and said, "Yes, well that's very nice darling, but let's not talk about it now." But when I was still saying it at fourteen it was a little more worrisome for them.' At fifteen he could play guitar, and a year later formed a band. Rhodes wore huge, wide trousers, bum-freezer jackets with wide lapels covered in Anabas badges, and shirts with unforgivably large collars. 'I accessorised and adapted everything. I remember during punk I would pin my tie back with paper clips to make it look thinner. You just adapted whatever you had. I remember in assembly at school, the headmaster announcing that, "Just because Nicholas Rhodes is doing this to his clothes doesn't mean all of you have to do it." '

He says that one of the most embarrassing moments of

his life was when he had just moved into a new house in London, and had a surprise visit from Bowie and his new wife Iman. 'They just happened to be in London, and popped round on the off-chance I was in. They both looked immaculate, but my house was full of boxes and piles of books and delivery cartons. There were no chairs, it was a complete mess, and there was junk everywhere. Anyway, my dad is there, painting one of the rooms, and when I introduced him to David and Iman, he put down his brush and said, "Hello David, could you give us a quick rendition of Major Tom, then?" At that moment I wanted the floor to open, but David took it in good grace, as he would, because he is so charming.'

Rhodes remains in awe of the man who became a friend, and who he spent much of the Eighties hanging out with. 'The thing about David Bowie is that he totally changed the whole game at that point. There were lots of other people who were equally as innovative at the time, some people maybe even further ahead – you look at Lou Reed, Iggy Pop, Bryan Ferry and Roxy Music, Eno, there were lots of people with progressive ideas – but it was David who managed to focus that Seventies energy into something that was irresistible. You bought into the whole thing. You didn't just buy into how great the songs were, or how strange the lyrics were, you bought into him being different, and it rubber-stamped you as being someone who thought about life in a different way. I was an incredibly young adopter, but having said that, most of my friends at the time were fifteen or sixteen. Bowie bonded a generation.'

As for myself, Bowie's invasion couldn't have come at a more opportune moment, although I appeared to be getting the better end of the deal. Quite literally. I wasn't wandering the boulevards of some oversaturated border town, swept away by all the innate romance and drama these places demand, but rather trapped on the perimeter of indifference, in the pebbledash and Anaglypta tedium of the Kent coast.

Deal wasn't a beginning, it was the end, almost as if the land mass had just suddenly stopped. It was as though our town had been cut in half by the seafront, and instead of being replaced by extravagant beaches, lush hotels, and the possibility of adventure, everything had been sealed up, cordoned off. True to our island mentality, if we could have erected – metaphorically or otherwise – some sort of edifice that cut us off from the rest of Europe, it would have been done. The English Channel wasn't the gateway to the rest of the world so much as a full stop. In Seventies Britain the world was flat, and you were doomed to fall off if you ventured into the water abutting anywhere on the coast.

Bowie and the Spiders watched *Top Of The Pops* the next night at Haddon Hall. And they loved it. They knew they were different, they knew they had made a step-change, knew that they'd made others on the show look immediately old-fashioned. 'Everybody thought it was great, and it was very, *very* different,' says Trevor Bolder. 'I mean we were different to what was going on at that particular point in time. And a lot of people who have talked to us, a lot of musicians who were young, they said it was such a big influence on them, to see this band all dressed up in colourful clothes, looking different to any other band and stuff, that everybody was like, "What's going on here?" They were used to seeing Fleetwood Mac and those sorts of bands on *Top of the Pops*, and Status Quo and all that, whereas we were totally different to anything going on. Plus, of course, we were on *Top Of The Pops*. That's why we felt so great, because we'd finally done it. We were all young kids. It was great.'

The word that crops up most whenever you mention the performance to those who saw it, is 'important'. Unlike, say, the Sex Pistols' appearance at the Screen On The Green in August 1976, which, due to collective selective memory, was apparently witnessed by enough people to fill the Albert Hall, there is no reason to doubt anyone who claims they saw it. The show was watched by upwards of fifteen million people, around a fifth of the population, and while you don't come across many people who enthuse about the performances that night of Dr Hook, Sweet, or Frederick Knight, those who remember Bowie's appearance remember it with reverence.

'It was the most extraordinary thing, something quite remarkable,' says one friend of mine, who watched the show in his parents' sitting room in Manchester. 'You always watched the show because that was what you did. It was just a completely passive experience, but when Bowie came on he made it impossible to treat pop music with anything less than respect. The right pop music, of course.'

That was it. Bowie's appearance was a proper bench-mark, as thereafter, every *Top Of The Pops* appearance, every single, every song, every album, every new release was judged against it.

What Bowie had was polish. Unlike his Bacofoil peers, Bowie's Ziggy Stardust looked as though he had catwalked off the pages of *Vogue*, *Honey*, or *Interview*; he looked like a fashion plate, using style not so much as a veneer but rather as currency.

After the *Top Of The Pops* performance was recorded on 5 July, the band waited for the stage manager to give them the signal to step down from the podium, and then they all smiled at each other, clapped the studio audience – who were mostly standing around watching Bowie and the Spi-ders rather than watching Tony Blackburn tee up his link – and started walking through the empty part of the studio back to their dressing room, Ronson and Bolder carrying their guitars, Woodmansey carrying his drum-sticks, and Bowie carrying a big fat smile, a smile almost too wide for his face. As soon as they closed the door of their dressing room, they all let out cowboy whoops of joy. The web had been spun, and in record time! Ziggy's little boat was still afloat.

They poured themselves some more wine – miraculously there was still some left, although it was warm – and opened the remaining cans of Red Barrel. They snapped at the remaining sandwiches, not caring that the crusts were curled, or that the cheese now tasted like ham, the ham like cheese. The limo was waiting outside, and it was time to disrobe and go. What a day!

Pierre Messmer became French Prime Minister, two young Protestant brothers were killed in Belfast, thirty patients were killed in a fire at Coldharbour Hospital in Sherborne, Air Canada cancelled options for four Concordes, the Queen and the Duke of Edinburgh visited the Royal Show at Stoneleigh, near Kenilworth, and in London W12 a star was born.

The music had sounded colder than most of the other stuff on the show that night – not exactly brittle as such, but less bumptious, less willing to placate. How wrong I was; Bowie had been desperate for success for nearly a decade, and would have probably given one of his Earth fingers for even a whiff of quantifiable success.

Some who watched it said it was as though a light had been turned on, although this wasn't like a sidelight or a torch, this wasn't a standard lamp, an overhead light, not even an outside light – the coal light, in our case – nor the porch light that announced to the neighbours how much electricity you were prepared to use. The Bowie light was bigger, spaceship big, canyon-sized mothership big, a light bright enough to fill the Wyoming flats, or at least the one in the National Park surrounding the Devils Tower. If Spielberg's Indiana electrical lineman could have his life skewed by encountering a UFO, then so could we (although I don't know anyone who had pre-empted *Top Of The Pops* by sculpting a Ziggy Stardust effigy out of mashed potatoes on their kitchen table).

'God, was I blown away?!' says Joe Elliott, the Def Leppard singer who would later go on to play with both Bolder and Woodmansey. 'The image, the song, the whole package ... when I got to school the next day I raved on and on, [and] I got beaten up by Slade fans.'

'I think it stands as one of the pivotal moments of modern music, or, if not music, certainly a pivotal moment in show business,' says Gary Numan, who would later appear to base his entire career on the first three years of Bowie's. He was fifteen at the time of the broadcast, watching from his parents' home in Middlesex. 'It must have taken extraordinary courage and/or a monumental amount of self-belief. To say it stood out is an epic understatement. Even as a hardcore T. Rex fan I knew it was special.'

Man And Boy author Tony Parsons watched it at home in Billericay. 'Missing *Top Of The Pops* would have been like missing church on Sundays – you just didn't do it. As soon as I saw him I knew it was my thing. Pop culture was still pushing at the frontiers, still pushing west, and Bowie was an extension of that. My dad would have been watching it with a tray on his lap, having just come back from work. He was the type of man who would leave the room when Danny La Rue came on the TV, so he can't have been impressed with Bowie. I was, though.

'The sexual ambiguity was there for all to see, but it

wasn't threatening, it was only like Jagger wearing his hair over his collar. It felt inclusive. It was like puppies. You've always had these guys like Marc Bolan or Mick Jagger or Russell Brand, who play with their sexuality, and they're always the ones getting all the girls. Plus you had Mick Ronson, who was clearly a brickie from Hull, so that was OK.

'Surrounding Bowie you had the likes of Sweet, Mud, and the Glitter Band, and they were oh so obviously geezers, even if they were wearing Christmas baubles on their ears. David Bowie wasn't a geezer. He wasn't overly concerned with socio-economic politics either, and was far more interested in the way that cultural touchstones influenced the zeitgeist. This was only a few years after the first moon landing, when space travel was suddenly no longer exotic, when the expectation amongst all of us was that trips to the moon would soon be as common as taking a number 19 up to the Arsenal. You couldn't watch the moon landing and not imagine that we would all soon be bouncing around between the planets.'

Bowie was one of those people, and the future became the way he defined his present. Look at the *Top Of The Pops* performances on YouTube today, and the tinfoil antics of Gary Glitter and Sweet are not exactly embarrassing, yet they feel distinctly parochial, displaying a professionalism and a dress sense you'd expect from a relatively proficient secondary school play.

However, we actually knew this at the time. Glam may have been quixotically subversive, yet even as twelve-year-olds we knew it was naff. Which is why Bowie's appearance on the show was so transformative, for us as well as him (which was ironic when you consider that, as a member of the Mannish Boys in 1964, he was banned from appearing on the BBC as his hair was thought to be too long).

When Ziggy was fully realised, you got a sense that if you touched him you might be rewarded with an electric shock. The visage was that powerful. However, while Bowie may have been responsible for the birth of glamour in pop – imbuing his creation with intimations of sex and sedition – the conception wasn't quite as immaculate as we were led to believe. In essence, he was the first proper post-modern pop star, for whom thievery was as important as melody. Almost every part of the Ziggy project was adapted from something else – the performance, the clothing, the hair, the bone china skin. To suffice, he was not the proverbial incandescent prodigy. He was a carpetbagging neophiliac, a sucker for the next big thing, always looking for something to use himself. He displayed a wonderful gift for melody, and his lyrics crackled with just the right amount of urgent melodrama. When Bowie looked in the mirror, even he was taken aback by what he had created. He was a dilettante, and proud of it. He was also a rather good-looking dilettante, not the kind that had ever been seen before.

Me? I didn't have anyone or anything to help context-ualise it. I was still buying *Popswap*, didn't know anything about the *NME* (that would come a few months later, when I read a Nick Kent review of an Alice Cooper record), didn't have any frame of reference. Bowie's decision to dump the

Oxford bag-sporting, singer-songwriter persona that had created *Hunky Dory* (the previous Bowie record, the one that owed rather too much to Elton John), and reinvent himself as a myth-making alien dovetailed perfectly with the ambitions of a generation of young men (mostly), who, while being completely unprepared for someone like Ziggy Stardust to land in their back garden, were more than happy to embrace the whole idea of him.

When David Bowie appeared on our television screens that Thursday evening, we were all there, captive, waiting for him.

In *To Major Tom: The Bowie Letters* (published in 2002), Dave Thompson imagines an obsessive Bowie fan's missives to his idol, all twenty-eight years' worth. The first letter, dated 10 July 1972, is the result of the 6 July *Top Of The Pops* performance:

Bournemouth, Hants

Monday 10 July 1972

Dear David Bowie

My name's Gary Weightman. I am twelve, and I'm at boarding school in Boscombe, near Bournemouth, although I live in Chatham, Kent.

I'm writing to tell you that 'STARMAN' is the <u>BEST RECORD OF THE YEAR!</u> I saw you on *Lift Off With*

Ayshea a couple of weeks ago. And then again on *Top Of The Pops* on Thursday, I couldn't believe what a fab song it was, and how brilliant you and your band, THE SPIDERS FROM MARS, looked. I loved the bass player's silver side-burns. Are they real? They must have taken him years to grow!

Is your hair really that red? Some of the boys in my school think it's dyed because it's so bright, but my aunt is Scottish and her hair is almost that colour. Are you Scottish? I'd love to have a hairstyle like yours, but I can't because my hair is a straggly blond mess that looks like a rat's nest. In fact, for a while, that's what some of the other kids called me, but then I had it cut really short, sort of skinhead but not quite, so they had to stop. Now they call me Fat Boy because of my surname, 'Weight-Man', and because I'm so skinny, but I don't mind that. At least it's better than what some of the other kids here are called. One boy with braces is named Tin Teeth and once, when a teacher told him to shut his mouth at breakfast, half the dining room shouted out, 'Clang!' Then there's Cripple Foot, who has a limp, and one boy with asthma, whose nickname is Iron Lung. So Fat Boy really isn't that bad.

Anyway, as soon as I was given my pocket money on Saturday I ran to WHSmith's on the High Street to buy 'Starman'. I was sure they'd be sold out, because EVERY-BODY agrees that it's a great record. I bought the last copy. You're going to go to No. 1 because the other side, 'Suffra-gette City', is just as good. I used to like T. Rex and Argent, and I bought 'Debora' (by Tyrannosaurus Rex) and 'Hold Your Head Up' during the last holidays. But 'Starman' is a million times better than both of them.

Is this your first record? My friend Jonathan James reckons you had another one out a few years ago, about an astronaut named Major Tom, but he says it sounded very different. He said you looked very different as well, with curly blond hair. Is that your real colour or was that dyed? Either way around, I don't blame you for changing.

How do you pronounce your surname? I've heard you called 'Bow-ee', like a dog (bow wow), 'Boo-ie', like a ghost, and 'Bo-Wee', but I wanted to make sure.

Nobody can stop talking about what you did on Bottom Of The Wellington Boot, when you put your arm around your guitarist's shoulders. Some of the older boys here say that means you're a queer, and that anybody who likes you has to be a queer as well, but that's a gormless thing to say. My school is all boys, and a lot of them like 'Starman', but I don't think they could all be queer, do you? Besides, the real queers here all like different sorts of music, and one of them doesn't like music at all, so he listens to jazz instead.

All pockets of the country were affected. Condé Nast's Nicholas Coleridge saw the programme in the back room of the Eton College tuck shop, Rowlands, aged fifteen. 'Doesn't everyone remember where they were when they first saw David Bowie? [With his] hips gyrating [he was] electrifyingly alien and disconcertingly sexy. Bowie's audience in the squalid, testosterone-rich Eton dive was largely unimpressed. Probably a hundred pupils were hanging out around the TV with plates of chips and saucers of ketchup, and there were catcalls of derision: "Poofter".

'It was summer term and the room was packed with boys in cricket and rowing kit, and these sporty pupils with their ketchup-dunked chips stared indignantly up at the screen. It was all so provocatively . . . queer. It was also the most exciting music I'd ever heard, and the most beguiling performance. I didn't realise, of course, that this was the beginning of a thirty-eight-year-long fandom, that I was to see him in concert a dozen times, that I would become virtually lyric-perfect on the complete discography. Or that I would come to regard David Bowie as the greatest enduring icon of all time.

'How rapidly obsessive fandom takes root. Within a day of hearing "Starman" on *Top Of The Pops*, I'd gathered the backlist, just four albums at that point: *David Bowie*, *Space Oddity*, *The Man Who Sold The World*, and *Hunky Dory*, and then the one that sealed the deal, *The Rise And Fall Of Ziggy Stardust*. I can't pretend my devotion differed in any important respect from that of any other fifteen-year-old Bowie fan. In those pre-Google days, I read whatever I could about the boy from Bromley. I confess that, in those barely liberated days, I preferred evidence that my bisexual hero was more straight than gay. So it was good news he was married to Angie, less good they'd reportedly first met when sleeping with the same guy. And the album cover of *The*

Man Who Sold The World, showing Bowie wearing a Michael Fish "man dress", was uncomfortable.

'What is the world record for listening to a Bowie song over and over? It is possible I hold it. His voice, with its range, passion, and yearning, had a spooky, Dalek quality, and the lyrics felt like poetry to my teenage ear.'

Yet for me it was all a fiction. Well, much of it anyway. Look at the YouTube clip and the vivid nature of Bowie's appearance makes it fascinating to watch even now. It is electrifying. Unlike most other *Top Of The Pops* performances featuring British rock bands that involved four or five smirking lads falling onto the stage and embarking on their foot-to-the-floor, heads-down-I'll-see-you-at-the-end narrative, Bowie's presentation that night was theatrical in the extreme, a performance played out in every colour imaginable. The thing is, like most people who saw the performance, I actually saw it in black and white. I had always assumed I'd watch the show in colour, until my father told me that as we didn't get a colour set until Christmas that year – another rented Rediffusion – Bowie's transgressive shaking and shimmering was a vision in grey. White greys, charcoal greys, warm greys, cool greys, and all the other greys in between. But still grey. Which meant that Bowie's performance of 'Starman' that night was even more impressive than I remember it, because it was not about colour and flash and the Spiders' meticulously assembled wardrobe. Instead it was all about style and sex and grace. And the way Bowie actually looked and sounded. I was a victim of False Memory

Syndrome, and this was my mutable past, a patchwork of dates, times, and pictures, images that rattle past like a scratched DVD, some lingering for seconds, some distressed and blurred, some skipped over completely, and others popping up earlier than they ought to. So much of my childhood is a blur, and often I recall emotion rather than events. This applies to the *Top Of The Pops* performance itself, as I remember how I felt about Bowie afterwards more than the show itself. The very idea of him, the thought of him, was more powerful than the reality. Which, if this was a sensation shared by others – and I can see no reason why it wouldn't be – might be why he became so successful so quickly.

It's easy to think that his appearance was so memorable because of the indefinite sexual role-play between Bowie and Ronson, but one of the most obviously conspicuous things about the performance is the extraordinary way Bowie looked. His face, his hair, the way he opened his mouth and bared his teeth in such an exaggerated fashion. Much the same can be said about Elvis's first appearance on *The Ed Sullivan Show*. When Elvis launches into Little Richard's 'Ready Teddy', it's not only his dancing and the way his elasticated legs weave around each other that is so mesmerising, it's the way he looks, the way he holds a camera, and the magnetic pull he has on those watching him. It really didn't matter if Elvis was usually filmed from the waist up on American television, because people could still see his hair. With every shoulder shrug, every probing of his tongue, and every coy little smirk, Elvis seduced the audience. Bowie did the same, using his sculpted orange feather cut instead of Elvis's greasy blue-black loaf.

And it worked: The following week, 'Starman' went up from No. 29 to No. 20, the following week to No. 18, and then its highest position, at the end of July, to No. 10. The performance was repeated on *Top Of The Pops* two weeks later, on 20 July, on a show that also featured Alice Cooper's 'School's Out', Bruce Ruffin's 'Mad About You', Gary Glitter's 'Rock And Roll Part 2', Labi Siffre's 'Watch Me', Mary Wells' 'My Guy', Middle Of The Road's 'Samson And Delilah', Terry Dactyl And The Dinosaurs' 'Seaside Shuffle', and the Supremes' 'Automatically Sunshine', as well as the Partridge Family and Donny Osmond.

David Bowie was suddenly, finally, a star.

FOUR

'When The Kids Had Killed The Man I Had To Break Up The Band'

HYSTERIA, GLOBAL SUCCESS, SUICIDE, 1972–1973

After their appearance on TV that night, Bowie and the Spiders became a sensation, fêted and idolised in almost equal measure. But when he retired Ziggy, he opened up Pandora's Box for all of us.

'And Robert was a big boy and he walked into the concert with Mummy and Vincent, and I was on Daddy's shoulders and we all had tickets to watch David Bowie be a person called Ziggy Stardust and that's why Mummy says Vincent hasn't been the same since'
Tiffany Murray, *Diamond Star Halo*

THE HULLABALOO OF ATTENTION started almost immediately, and if, on the Wednesday, David Bowie was just a signature, by the Friday he was an autograph. Almost immediately, Ziggy Stardust became a phenomenon, in the national press as well as in the music weeklies, as the country got all goosebumpy over Bowie. Could all this folderol survive the summer? Apparently it could. As Charles Shaar Murray said in the *NME*, he was hotter than a stolen atom bomb packed with pictures of Howard Hughes playing strip poker with Jacqueline Onassis. The concerts were now frenzied. Girls were hysterical, and boys too. The former wore leopard skin and expectant frowns; the latter mascara and Pierre Cardin Pour Monsieur. They were teenagers: the fourth sex.

The pandemonium and sexual energy appeared not to be so far removed from the frenzy that greeted Frank Sinatra at his early concerts in the Forties, and as Bowie stood, centre stage, at the end of each gig, as the crowd watched coils of steam stalk and twine above him, it was as if he were taking mass. As he ended his songs, he looked like Elvis, standing with his legs apart, crotch forward, before lifting his arms in an imploring way towards the audience, the hands slowly drifting ever higher until he looked like he'd been crucified. T. V. Smith, who would go on to form one of the most important, if short-lived, second wave punk bands, the Adverts, caught the *Ziggy* tour in the West Country. 'It was just astounding. I'd never seen anything like that. I'd seen a couple of gigs already. But that gig really . . . so, no way were the Sex Pistols ground [year] zero, and you're not gonna tell me that they weren't informed by the [New York] Dolls and Iggy and the Small Faces as well . . .'

'It all happened after that night,' says Trevor Bolder.

'We went out on the road and did a British tour, and where we'd been playing to maybe fifty, sixty people a night in small venues, we were selling places out. Friars in Aylesbury was the big one [15 July], as that's where we tested everything out. That was sold out, and then everything started to go . . . Everybody wanted to see the band. So that was when we realised it was taking off.'

Roger Taylor and Freddie Mercury from Queen saw the Aylesbury Friars show, and were blown away, too. 'I got Freddie out in my little Mini and I remember the lights didn't work very well and we were going around the roundabout and he was going, "Oh dear, I don't think you can see dear, can you?"' says Taylor. 'And I said, "Don't worry Freddie, it will be all right." Anyway, we got around the roundabout and we got out to Aylesbury, which seemed like the end of the Earth at the time. [The show] was so fantastic, like nothing else that was happening and so far ahead of its time. The guy, he had so much talent to burn, really, and charisma to burn as well. I hate to gush but he did have it like no one else did at the time.'

Bowie's coming-out gig was on 19 August, at the Rainbow in Finsbury Park, a 3,000-capacity former cinema that had been built in 1930. With its Moorish foyer – complete with a fountain – and its Spanish-style auditorium, the Rainbow felt almost exotic, which, seeing that it was situated on a busy junction in a rundown part of north London, was doubly ironic. In the audience that night were Elton John, Rod Stewart, Mick Jagger, Lou Reed, and Alice Cooper, all sitting towards the front of the stalls, and all having come to see if the Ziggy Stardust hype was justified. Supported by Lloyd Watson and Roxy Music – who, like T. Rex, were mixing the Fifties with space-age glam rock, but with far more subtlety and humour – when Bowie finally came on, he left no one in any doubt. All for the princely sum of 75p. It was also one of those nights when Bowie incorporated a line from 'Somewhere Over The Rainbow' into 'Starman'. In the magazine *Plays And Players*, Alexander Stuart wrote, 'Judy Garland hasn't left us! The entire evening seemed like a tribute to Judy. David Bowie, his delicate face made-up to look like hers, has the guts, the glitter, the charm [of] Garland, and yes, even the legs.'

Bowie played the Rainbow later in the year, too.

'One afternoon, my school friend, the satirist Craig Brown, announced he had two tickets to see Bowie at the Rainbow, Finsbury Park, during the Christmas holidays, and would I like to go?' wrote Nicholas Coleridge. 'We took the train up from Sussex and at some point must have changed into our Bowie gear. [Where? The train's loo, presumably.] Is it really conceivable I wore a striped matelot T-shirt under a denim shirt with silver nylon lamé sleeves? Half the audience had enviable Ziggy haircuts. Sunday 24 December 1972: my first Bowie concert, seats in the third row of the dress circle, and the man did not disappoint. All that remains is a memory of fuzzy orange light and loudness, a cover version of the Stones' "Let's Spend The Night Together", "Rock' n'Roll Suicide" as the finale . . . "Give me your hands . . . 'cause yer won-der-ful," please God, let this concert never end. And afterwards a kebab bought on Finsbury Park Road that stank out the country taxi that delivered us back to Sussex. During the long cab ride home, I sensed that Craig had not bought into the universal truth behind Bowie's towering genius and lyrics to the same degree that I had. He had reservations, even dared mock. Well, some people exist on a less sensitive plane and just can't get it.'

A few weeks after *Top Of The Pops* a bunch of American rock critics were flown over on a junket to see the Ziggy show, and the resulting reviews all had a similar feel: Alan Rich's piece in *New York* magazine was headlined, 'I Went To England And Saw The Queen', while Lisa Robinson in *After Dark* wrote, 'David's hand rests on his hip while he's belting out his tunes. The lights playing on his innocent, unlined face colour him an unearthly green . . . More unearthly than his face is his crotch, which seems unusually large, almost inhuman . . .'

It appeared that Bowie had enough cock for everyone.

Bowie's appearance that summer's evening said as much about his tenacity as it did about art. He had been trying to be successful as a singer for nearly a decade, and had reinvented himself so often, that what would become known as his great chameleon-like changes over the next decade or so were not remotely out of character, or, indeed, that prophetic. Bowie was simply doing what he had always done, the only difference being that almost everything he did after 1972 he would do with a modicum of success.

Those of us who were sufficiently pricked soon knew the cut of his cloth when we started exploring what he'd been up to before Ziggy Stardust; for me, the Bowie manifesto appeared to be contained in these words from 'Changes' on *Hunky Dory*, *Ziggy*'s predecessor: 'But I've never caught a glimpse, Of how the others must see the faker, I'm much too fast to take that test . . .' Oh yes, we thought, we wouldn't be taking that test either.

Here, finally, was a sound that was going to build a wall between me and whomever I chose to put on the other side (parents, teachers, the oik who kept ambushing me as I arrived at school each morning). This was slightly less successful than I hoped it would be, due to my mother's indifference and my father's inquisitiveness. Dad, when he visited, was always annoyingly tolerant of my teenage obsessions, and far from being outraged at Bowie's indulgences, actually found them intriguing. Any attempt I may have made to widen the generation gap was foiled later in the year when he returned from London with a 'recommendation'. Oh God, I thought to myself, and probably said aloud, 'What is it?'

What was it? 'Walk On The Wild Side' by Lou Reed.

Harrumph. I loved it.

Bowie's appearance was flattered by his success, and his success by his appearance. Nearly forty years later, Russell Brand said that his own persona didn't really work without fame. 'Without fame, this haircut could be mistaken for mental illness.' In Bowie's case there was actually nothing ironic about this.

Having seen Bowie on *Top Of The Pops*, I didn't write him a letter, didn't take a day trip up to London to try to stalk him, and didn't really go out of my way to go to a concert (I was twelve). Instead, I tried to emulate his haircut. It appeared to me that his hair was the element that personified Bowie, and in this respect I was uncharacteristically ahead of the curve. You weren't going to get hordes of teenage boys and girls wandering around my town centre dressed in the kind of get-up that Bowie wore on television (although for some reason it was extremely popular with travelling Manchester United supporters for a while), however, it was completely logical that they – we, us – could all copy his haircut (it was everywhere, and even the *Sun* gave Bowie's hair their centre-spread, with the caption, 'Now everyone wants the Bowie haircut'). Except that it wasn't 'me' at all, and it was always 'they'. I wasn't cool, wasn't in with the in crowd (not any of them), and the terms on which they acknowledged and accepted each other in the playground were not terms that had any bearing on me. Their parameters were, in fact, meaningless to me, as I wasn't affected by them.

So if I could get the haircut, then things might begin to change. A successful Bowie haircut could bestow countless wonders on me, or so I thought. In a matter of days the 'Bowie cut' had started to spread across the school, and those who could, went out and got their hair cut in a direct facsimile of DB's. As many girls as boys, and girls and boys of all ages, even down to nine- and ten-year-olds. I was still only twelve, and yet felt oh-so much older, as though I'd skipped the accelerated, colourful business-end parts of adolescence, and gone straight to the boring, thoughtful bits. I wanted to parade around town in bright clothes and high-heeled shoes, I wanted to smoke and pretend to drink and hang around street corners looking insanely modern. I wasn't interested in being reflective or introspective; the only problem was that being reflective and introspective was all I appeared to be good at.

Which meant I had to go out and get my hair cut.

The whole excursion was planned with an attention to detail that I certainly didn't employ at school. I was always very good at collective things, cutting things out of magazines and newspapers, filing and making lists, but none of this I put to any great use. But my Saturday morning trip to the unisex hairdressers was planned days in advance. I'd scouted the town for the various barbers and hairdressers who might offer this newfangled cut. I went through the local paper, looking for more, and methodically called them all up, asking if they indeed did offer a 'Bowie cut'. Most didn't know what I was talking about, but one said they could probably do what I wanted, so why didn't I come in and they would give me a free consultation. Gratis. And for nothing!

Having never made such an important trip to a hairdressers before – who am I kidding? I'd only ever been to a barber before, and then usually under duress – I can remember being unusually careful about what I wore. I can't remember exactly what I *was* wearing, but I've got a fair idea it involved either a pair of slightly flared plaid trousers or a cheap pair of Oxford bags, a round-collared shirt with a repeated print of a French café scene, and probably an extremely unfashionable canvas jacket, with aircraft carrier lapels and large silver buttons. I'm sure I looked as though I was going to the school disco, complete with my red glitter socks, my first real concession to glam (I had six pairs: red, yellow, black, pale blue, purple, and silver). I don't think I had a pair of spoon shoes yet – they were hideous but fashionable, and looked like a cross between a couple of ping-pong bats and a brace of duck-billed platypuses (which makes me think they were designed by someone with either a keen sense of humour or extraordinarily bad eyesight) – so more than likely I was wearing my school shoes, with embarrassingly low heels, the kind that by rights shouldn't have been pretending to be heels at all. In those days, it was better not to be in the high-heel game unless you were going to take it seriously, and seriously amp up the inches. My worst fashion faux pas of the time was a pair of four-inch, two-tone beige platforms, bought from my friend Bruce, that I painted two tones of green. I wore these with a pair of bottle green, high-waisted pinstripe trousers, a turquoise butterfly-collared shirt, and a chocolate brown tank top. I had lank, straight hair that almost brushed my shoulders. I'd like to say I looked like a member of the New York Dolls, but actually was a spit for Jimmy McCulloch, the guitarist in Wings.

Years later Jean Paul Gaultier would say that it's always the badly dressed people who are the most interesting, but in my case he would have been colossally wrong, as I was the prisoner of what I was wearing rather than the proprietor. Consequently it was the haircut which was going to save me, Bowie's haircut that was going to make me not just acceptable, but appealing.

Unsurprisingly, this was not to be. Having walked from Orchard Avenue to the hairdressers at the appointed hour – an arrangement completely constructed in my head, as I actually didn't have an appointment – I sat in the chair and blithely told the stylist what it was I wanted. And what I wanted was to have hair like David Bowie, to have a large quiff on top, with a feather cut beneath, and locks brushing passed the edge of my collar. Years later it would be called a formative mullet, but that's just about the most pejorative thing you could say about someone's hair, and Ziggy's hair most definitely wasn't a mullet. It was high, it was cut close to the side of the head, and it was full. Which was my problem, as I didn't have full hair. I had lank, floppy hair, the sort that wouldn't be interested in hovering above my head as though I were a day-glo Eddie Cochran.

'It won't work, 'cause your hair's all wrong,' the hairdresser took great delight in telling me. 'For this kind of haircut you need hair that goes up, and yours just goes down. No offence, but it just won't work.'

Which is how I ended up leaving the salon that day with a haircut that approximated the one sported by Dave Hill, the decidedly odd-looking, buck-toothed guitarist in Slade, the one who looked like Cleopatra in nine-eyelet

Dr Martens boots. When the hairdresser had finished I felt like saying that David Bowie wouldn't have his hair cut like that. To which the hairdresser would no doubt have said, 'Well he would do if he came in here.' It was this haircut – and my inability to have the one I actually wanted – more than anything else that would eventually force me down a path littered with patchwork denim, cowboy boots, and long hair, the inevitable alternative to the proscriptive nature of glam. My entire demeanour was the result of my failed attempt at transforming myself. The clothes would eventually come – fur-collared Budgie jackets, pinstriped high-waisted bags, platform shoes and high-collared shirts – but it was the haircut I wanted more than anything else, the haircut that could have helped me bridge the credibility gap.

Much later, reading his memoir *Take It Like A Man*, I saw that Boy George had exactly the same problem. The first time I set eyes upon George was on the dance floor at the Blitz in Covent Garden, in 1979 (I was terrified), when he was dressed as a deviant priest (and I was wearing a leather jacket, a pair of black leggings and skirt); how much more personal our relationship could have been if we had walked by each other in Lewisham or Hastings, both sporting our Slade-by-numbers haircuts.*

....

* Rock 'n' roll jeweller Stephen Webster was living in Gravesend at the time, and visited Deal in the summer holidays. 'I went to get the Bowie haircut, although I have to say it was an "approximation". It was short on top, and long at the back but to be honest, in the end, it looked more like a mullet.'

'The thing that really did it for us was the advert for "John, I'm Only Dancing" – the picture where he's got his arm outstretched,' says Neil Tennant from the Pet Shop Boys. 'It was a bit of a classic glam-era image, that. I had a Ziggy haircut – dyed red as well. I did get his autograph in 1972 . . . at the Newcastle City Hall in June, which I have to say was over half-empty! During "Suffragette City", when he sang "Wham bam, thank you mam", they showered the audience with pictures of David as Ziggy Stardust, which was just about to come out. And I got him to sign one of those on his way out, which I still have, funnily enough. My brother Simon and I used to tape [his BBC radio sessions] and by the time *Ziggy Stardust* came out we knew almost every song on it already. "Hang Onto Yourself", "Moonage Daydream", "Ziggy Stardust" I'd all taped off the radio. "Starman" had been on the single. "Five Years" he did on *The Old Grey Whistle Test*. I remember initially preferring those radio recordings. One actually forgets that "Starman" wasn't a particularly big hit. David didn't have a Top Three single until "The Jean Genie", and it seemed rather frustrating at the time. We did have *Ziggy Stardust* the week before it came out, though, because RCA's records were produced in County Durham and I had a friend whose father worked at the factory there.

'[As] I'd already seen Bowie play in Newcastle the previous month, it wasn't some sort of epiphany for me watching the *Top Of The Pops* performance, exciting though it was. I was already obsessed with Bowie and so were my friends.

It was *The Old Grey Whistle Test* performance in February of that year that made the big impact on me, the camera so close on Bowie's face at the beginning of "Five Years".

'The *Top Of The Pops* appearance just confirmed that the public was catching up and that Bowie finally had a hit. It was also rather thrilling that Bowie was so daringly "camp" on TV.'

One American fan called Madeline, who had seen Bowie on the US TV show *In Concert*, started water-colouring her hair red and green along with her friend Lisa, wearing glitter on their faces and fingernails, and wearing various homemade glam outfits and platform boots to school. These were what Bowie called 'the Wowies'. 'Nobody was doing this at the time. Now you can buy all kinds of crazy hair colours and mass-produced "rock 'n' roll" clothes, but this was the early Seventies – the drab age of denim. All the kids in school thought we were nuts. They had never seen the likes of glam rock, in fact they were the opposite – messy, sloppy, hairy, pimply Deadheads. Lisa and I would save our lunch money each day (we were both rail-thin to begin with, and we got thinner by skipping lunch) to buy records and magazines. We began to resemble our idol with our skinny bodies, anaemic complexions, and colour-streaked hair. Our teacher came back to class after a six-month illness. She was emaciated and pale, and we told her how fabulous she looked. We gave ourselves shag haircuts since there was nothing other than old ladies' hair salons at the time who refused to give us the Ziggy cut when we described it (layered on top and long on the bottom). They would say, "That's two different haircuts," and we'd reply, "So is there a law against that?" Why wouldn't they just do it for us? It was quite frustrating.' (Nick Rhodes tells a story about Mark Ronson going into a hairdressers and asking for a John Taylor haircut, but after an hour or so nearly bursting into tears as he realised he'd been given a Nick Rhodes haircut instead.)

'Mickie Bloomfield is a sixteen-year-old shipping clerk who lives in a tower block off the Old Kent Road and who, in order to "be great like David Bowie", has had his ear pierced, his hair restyled, and spends up to £17 for a pair of boots with four-inch platform soles,' wrote Steve Turner in an unpublished piece for *Nova*. 'Roger Swanborough is twenty-three, a postgraduate painting student at the Royal College of Art, and feels that by simulating Bowie he's found an outlet for a part of his personality which has been previously submerged.'

In 1976 and 1977, when the world spun again, and punks roamed the earth, the best examples, or at least the best ambassadors, were always girls. They did their hair properly, dressed in a way that was designed to arouse as much as confront, and they always looked unpredictable, always looked capable of punching you squarely in the thorax and thinking nothing of it. The memory I have of seeing my first proper punk is still incredibly strong – she had bright red hair, black bondage trousers, and gave the impression of walking on a strip of the pavement reserved for her and for her alone. I wasn't sure, but she may have been called

Sharon, may have been two years above me in school. She definitely looked as though she meant it; the only problem being, you couldn't tell exactly what she meant. And being sixteen, and wearing patchwork denim jeans and a velvet jacket, I wasn't about to ask.

My memory of seeing my first Bowie clone four years earlier is just as strong, and she looked as mean and as glossy and as confrontational as Sharon did in 1976. To a twelve-year-old boy who had only just got to grips with seeing a flame-haired pop star, I wasn't prepared for seeing a clone in the flesh, even if I had attempted to emulate his haircut only a few weeks before. I was going for the shape, and it hadn't occurred to me that I might dye my hair, too. But this girl had, and she looked like a princess – a princess from the planet Phantasmagoric.

She wasn't alone (wasn't that what Bowie promised?). Suddenly Bowie's influence was everywhere. Boys adopted the bogbrush hair, girls with feather cuts grew them out and dyed them orange. Clothes got a little glossier, a little bolder, a little more colourful. Not much, mind, but enough for it to be noticeable. It didn't galvanise us, we didn't become an army, but Bowie instantly opened up the decade for those of us who were touched by the performance. I was primed, impressionable, fresh meat. I was already into David Hockney, *Mad* magazine, art school, Americana, pop art, Radio Luxembourg, and brash white-trash iconography. My idea of a good view was the string of fast food outlets and gas station signs surrounding Las Vegas. Bowie chanelled a lot of this, but in a totally new and refreshing way. The only other person at the time who did it for me was Alice Cooper, who wielded his own – and in hindsight, not all that original – version of outrage; I remember once being asked by my form teacher why I liked Cooper so much, and, after telling her that it was obviously his music, instantly realising that what I really liked about him was the way he looked.

When you're a teenager you tend to think you're fully formed, both physically and mentally. Why wouldn't you? At the age of twelve or thirteen I didn't think I was going to be particularly bigger when I was older, or necessarily emotionally more mature. I suppose that's what being a teenager is all about. Photographs of my friends from the same period shock me, as they all look so small. A group of six boys on a lawn, all lying down and trying to look impassive for the camera, all wearing open-necked shirts (burgundy, pale yellow, and what one day would be called prune) with the sleeves rolled up to the elbows, all wearing slightly flared trousers in shades of brown or mauve, one wearing his watch with the face on the inside of his wrist. The hair (chocolate to tawny, lank, badly cut) is uniform: 1972 regulation near-shoulder-length, again just brushing the collar. Two are wearing striped tank tops, two more are sporting pale yellow socks, and two more are smoking (one cupping the cigarette between thumb and forefinger, pointing towards his palm). And – even though they're all wearing two-inch stacks – to a boy they look like hobbits in baggy trousers. They look *so* small. Too small to raise an army.

It's easy to forget that, as we live in such a heavily mediated environment, where glamour is a lifestyle choice with an exponential amount of entry points, and where the *idea* of luxury is available to all, that life in the early Seventies was incredibly dull, at least visually. Consumer magazines were thin on the ground – twelve-year-old boys didn't read *Vogue*, and didn't have a choice of comparable products – and the amount of glamour on television was finite. Glamour as a precept just wasn't available. Style as a prescription could only be bought through passive consumption. Participation wasn't an option.

In this environment it is easier to appreciate just how glamorous and otherworldly Bowie would have seemed. Just owning one of his records felt decadent. One day, about a year after seeing 'Starman', I arrived one morning at my new secondary school, just half a dozen stops from Paddington Station – I could hear London! – with the *Ziggy Stardust* and *Aladdin Sane* albums under my arm, with the back covers facing each other, all the better to advertise my allegiance. I can't remember why I brought them in – all the people I needed to impress would have already bought the albums and I don't think the school had a record player – but I remember doing it, which back then was often the point of seemingly random gestures. A trip to High Wycombe in a new pair of shoes was just that: a trip to High Wycombe in a new pair of shoes.

I was looking at my forty-year-old copy of *Ziggy Stardust* again the other day. I don't play vinyl any more, but

I keep the albums that are important to me. When I first owned it, the album was a vital cornerstone of my collection, even as that collection swelled from ten records to several hundred. When punk happened along, *Ziggy* was one of those records that was never going to be thrown away, and during the Eighties, when the new pop was everywhere (and with everyone from Simon Le Bon to Gary Numan professing their adolescent obsession with Bowie), *Ziggy Stardust* stood proud in my Battersea bedroom, a telephone call from 1972. And still it kept coming, in format after format after format. There were reissues (including ridiculously expensive Japanese ones), CDs, extended CDs, Mini Discs, and – much, much later – limited edition vinyl reissues for people like me who no longer played vinyl but who would never pass up an opportunity to buy something they already owned in a different format.

With such a huge back catalogue, with at least three great unheard albums, and a smattering of decent Sixties singles, overnight we became collectors. Bowie was the gift that kept on giving. We became his custodians, and we set about collecting everything he'd ever done, from *Hunky Dory* back through *The Man Who Sold The World* and 'Space Oddity', all the way to 'The London Boys', 'I Dig Everything', and the awful Anthony Newley-style jingles, 'The Laughing Gnome' included. God, we tried to like all that stuff, torturing ourselves by sitting around trying to work 'Love You Till Tuesday', 'Little Bombardier', 'In The Heat Of The Morning', and all of the other songs from *Images 1966–1967* into our freshly compiled Bowie canon. But it just didn't happen. At that age you could listen to almost anything and make it work; I reckon if I had been twelve or thirteen when Oasis released *Be Here Now*, in three days I would have thought it was the best record ever released. Objectively the Faces' *Ooh La La* is not one of the best albums of the Seventies, but it's definitely on my list, probably in the top ten – I must have played it fifty or sixty times when it was released, and I eventually came to love it in a way I'd never really loved another person, at least not one who wasn't a member of my immediate family.

There was a simplicity to these records that is usually only found in children's songs. In 1999, Bowie told Philip Norman about one of his earliest musical influences, the American singer and comedian, Danny Kaye. '"Inchworm" [from Kaye's 1952 film, *Hans Christian Andersen*] is a very important song to me . . . "Two and two are four . . . four and four are eight . . ." I love the effect of two melodies together. That nursery rhyme feeling shows itself in a lot of songs I've written, like "Ashes To Ashes". And maybe on my new album ['*hours . . .*'], "Thursday's Child".'*

I really loved *Ziggy Stardust*. 'There Is A Happy Land' and 'Sell Me A Coat' would have to wait (forever, actually),

....

* Philip interviewed Bowie in New York, and in the cab on the way back to the airport, he happened to mention to the driver who he'd been interviewing.

'No kidding. Say, what's he really like?'

'Search me.'

but 'Five Years', 'Lady Stardust,' and 'Starman' were able to satisfy me night after night after night. I'd finish my home-work, finish watching television, and then slope off into the dining room to do exactly as it told me to do on the back sleeve. TO BE PLAYED AT MAXIMUM VOLUME, it said, so whenever I could, that's exactly what I did. We'd moved by then, into a bigger house on an Airforce base closer to London, and the larger rooms gave the record an extra dimension. It would have filled the whole house if I had been able to turn the record up loud enough. My grandmother was in a new nursing home a few miles away, so for me – and I know in more fundamental ways, for my parents, too – there was a huge sense of freedom about the move.

The dining room – practically always empty, as it was in everyone's house when I was growing up – became my den, much more so than my bedroom. One night, lost in music, and bouncing around the room, a neighbour walked by the window, obviously perplexed as to why I needed to play 'Five Years' quite so loudly. As a family we seemed to have a thing for radiograms, and the one we had on the base was a fine example. It was made by Pye, was about four feet long, and made of teak, I think. The mid-Seventies ones had vertical faders, although I'm fairly sure ours still had dials – bass, treble, volume, and maybe tone (not sure what this was for, then, or indeed now). It had a com-partment for cassette tapes, even though it didn't include a cassette player or recorder; it can't have done, as one thing I do remember from my youth is the extraordinarily convoluted means you would use to try to make a tape recording from a record.

There was a long lid on the radiogram, operated from a single metal hinge, situated oddly about one-third of the way across the top. The speakers were on either side of the cabinet box itself, slatted, and much, much louder than they had any right to be. The deck had an autochanger spindle that was meant to allow singles to fall, in the way they used to in jukeboxes, but by the early Seventies they were already becoming superfluous. Tone arms would soon become ridiculously light, almost too light, which made playing a record incredibly precarious, as the arm could easily skip across the vinyl as though it had a mind of its own – seemingly wanting to edit the songs using a primitive form of scratching, dancing all the way to the label, never to come back. Ours had an arm like an anvil, and the reassuring thud it made as it fell onto the disc echoed the gong struck by the loinclothed bodybuilder at the beginning of old Rank films.

Stacked up against the cabinet was my rapidly expanding collection of LPs: *School's Out* by Alice Cooper, *Something/Anything* by Todd Rundgren, *Music In A Doll's House* by Family, *Glitter* by Gary Glitter, *Honky Chateau* by Elton John, both the red and blue Beatles compilations, some K-Tel albums, *Never A Dull Moment* by Rod Stewart, *Relics* by Pink Floyd, Genesis' *Nursery Cryme*, *Ride A White Swan* by T. Rex (the cheapy compilation), a few *Top Of The Pops* compilations (the February edition featured a smiling brunette wearing a red leotard, a floppy red hat, and a coquettish smile – was there any other kind? – while the songs included 'Telegram Sam', 'Where Did Our Love Go', 'I'd Like To Teach The World To Sing', 'Have You Seen Her', 'Poppa Joe', 'Baby I'm-A-Want You', 'American Pie', 'Son Of My Father', 'All I Ever Need Is You', 'Stay With Me', 'Let's Stay Together', and 'Horse With No Name'), a Middle Of The Road greatest hits ('Soley Soley', 'Sacramento', etc.), a whole bunch of my parents' soundtrack albums (*Oliver!*, *Zorba The Greek*, among others) and, of course, *The Rise And Fall Of Ziggy Stardust And The Spiders From Mars*.

Ever since the Forties, the designers of record players, like the designers of most household appliances, had tried to anticipate the future, always attempting to look at least five years more advanced than they actually were. In a way they were the perfect machines to play David Bowie records on, as they were already futuristic, with lots of black plastic and silver panelling. Did Gerry Anderson design this stuff when he wasn't puppet-deep in Supermarionation? Did he do this as a sideline when he wasn't designing *Joe 90* or *Space 1999*? Was my radiogram actually a scale model of a newfangled international space station? Even the Pye logo resembled a Spectrum crest, as worn by Rhapsody, Melody, Harmony, Symphony, and Destiny in *Captain Scarlet*. Actually, my Pye looked as though it should have had wheels. It looked like an Audi Quatro (years before there were Audi Quatros).

The window that Bowie opened was one I leaped through like an over-eager puppy. I remember buying every single after 'Starman', every album, and spent hours communing with the sleeves, searching for the clues that might add more data, more colour, to the memory bank I was rapidly developing that concerned itself with everything Bowie did. I've still got all the singles, all thirty-two of them – RCA, orange label, some with picture sleeves, most without – in several large black Dolce & Gabbana boxes that once housed leopard-skin cushions. I played them so often, knew them so well, that I could identify them from the scratches that preceded the intros. They're still in their makeshift sleeves, too, many of them – seven-inch canvasses covered in cut-out photographs, felt-tip, and dried Sellotape, the makeshift glamour of the ill-equipped.

My Bowie download was bulging right from the start. I can remember where I bought 'Life On Mars', 'Drive-In Saturday', and 'Rebel Rebel', remember how I was walking as I imagined listening to a particular song, remember what I was thinking about when I first heard a particular record, and how I carried the album home for the first time. The relationship didn't falter as I embraced other things, either, whether I was off listening to Genesis or going to see the Who in concert; I remember the train ride to Paddington immediately after hearing 'Sound And Vision' for the first time, and the Chelsea pub I was in the first time 'Heroes' came on the jukebox.

This was an especially epiphanic experience, and one that made my whole body feel as though it were expanding, as if I were being pumped up with air, and was now twice the size of everyone around me. Emboldened by strong drink, the glacial Germanic boogie swirling from the jukebox in the Bagleys Lane pub that day in 1977 (I was seventeen and dressed in my daytime punk garb of plastic leather jacket, matelot top, skinny jeans, and pointy shoes) made me feel as though at that very moment I was indestructible (like Captain Scarlet). More so than any punk record – save 'I Remember You' by the Ramones, 'Life' by ATV, and 'Complete Control' by the Clash, maybe – 'Heroes' was the song that encouraged a sense of immortality. I tried crack once, more as an experiment than anything else, and the sensation of expanding to fill the room – *rushing* to fill the room – was not dissimilar to how I felt when I first heard 'Heroes' stampeding out of that jukebox, trampling all before it. 'Heroes' had the added benefit of no side effects, unlike the crack, which left me feeling a lot smaller than when I started out that night. 1977 wasn't just the year of the Sex Pistols, the Damned, the Jam, and the Buzzcocks, it was also the year of the androgynous changeling. As I stood in my Chelsea pub – the one that was closest to the Foundation wing of Chelsea School of Art around the corner – I distinctly remember thinking I was exactly where I was meant to be. Heaving waited a year to get into art school (I had applied when I was sixteen and had been told I was too young), I was now here, walking to college every morning across Albert or Battersea Bridge from the Ralph West Halls of Residence on Albert Bridge Road, positively skipping down the King's Road, my head bursting with sensation. Most mornings I would walk by Bowie's old house in Oakley

Street, the house to where Angie claimed she came back one night to discover her husband in bed with Mick Jagger, although both men have denied there was anything going on and Jagger has said that Angie's claims were 'absolute rubbish'. (Bowie lived in Oakley Street in Chelsea from 17 October 1973 to April the following year.)

This was how it was meant to feel – being young, being seventeen, new in the city, new to the world, and escaping everything behind me. Each night before going out – to the Roxy, the Vortex, the 100 Club, the Marquee, the Red Cow, Battersea Arts Centre, the Hope & Anchor, the Rainbow, the Hammersmith Odeon – and after coming back home again, the 'difficult' sides of *Low* and *Heroes* would get heavy rotation on the turntable (competing with the first Talking Heads album and Steely Dan's *Aja* – there was no year zero in my room). Pye turned itself off when the needle reached the run-out groove – apparently suitable for any mood. Guiding me surely, surely on.*

'Heroes' made me dress differently, too, and towards the end of the year I invested in some army fatigues, a khaki

....

*To publicise 'Heroes', RCA came up with a career-defining slogan for their charge: 'There's old wave. There's new wave. And there's David Bowie.' The ad for *Ziggy* that I kept from *Zigzag* magazine has him sitting on a stool, wearing wrestling boots and the same haircut he wore on *The Old Grey Whistle Test*. The copy line reads: Can a young guy who went through truly incredible 'Changes' and made it all 'Hunky Dory' ever find true happiness as a 'Starman'?

top, and some baseball boots, as this was what I thought someone who listened to 'Heroes' on a daily basis should look like. It felt like a uniform, as I only had one set of clothes; a few extra shirts maybe, but that was about it. A certain amount of reinvention had been necessary, as I had spent much of the last two years wearing cheesecloth and patchwork denim, trying to disguise my adolescent funk with Fabergé's West, the thinking man's Brut. In my arrogance I hoped my garb might suggest that while I was embracing punk (spiky hair, et al), I was still going home to Bowie every night (hurrying with more purpose now, as I had *The Idiot* and *Lust For Life* to contend with too – two more abstract dystopian landscapes to feed into my hopelessly myopic and apolitical view of the world).*

In reality I was still completely aimless, as, like a lot of people I knew, I was concerned with sensation above almost anything else. At Chelsea, and then St Martins, I could design ad campaigns, photograph people on the King's Road, and produce posters for underground radio stations, but I was not exactly moving through life with any great sense of purpose. What was most important to me was how I

. . . .

*The *Heroes* album cover shot was actually taken during an Iggy Pop photo session on a promotional tour of Japan for *The Idiot*. Bowie had instructed the stylist to make the shoot very 'punky', asking her to bring as many leather jackets to the studio as she could find. In some shots he wore three jackets at once, reminding the photographer, Sukita, of a scene from Kenneth Anger's *Scorpio Rising*.

felt as I was doing all these things. I don't think I could have been more self-centered, and if I had any ambition at all, it was one borne of selfishness, self-absorption. We were Bowie's children, baby existentialists in pegged trousers. Self-possessed and cynical, Bowie had colonised our imagination.

Punk had barely started to flag before its early adopters began moving on, not by forming reductive power-pop bands, but by going back underground. Despite the world tagging them as the Blitz Kids, this generation of diehard clubbers were in reality Bowie's Kids. One day in the autumn of 1978, Rusty Egan, a member of the post-punk band the Rich Kids, was chatting with his friend Steve Harrington about how the London club scene had become stagnant. After a brief conflab they decided to open their own club, alighting on Gossips, a club just off Dean Street in Soho. Popular with local sex workers, it tended to be empty on a Tuesday, so the pair asked the owner if they could start a weekly club night. They called the club Billy's, printed flyers with the strap line 'Fame Jump Aboard The Night/Fame, Fame, Fame. What's Your Name?', and very soon they were full. It soon became known as Bowie Night, popular with a small group of clubbers who had briefly ended their affair with disco to embrace punk, but who had retreated when the scene became overrun by hordes of denim-clad rockers who nine months previously had been nodding their heads in unison to Thin Lizzy and Hawkwind. Harrington would change his name to Strange, and the club started to fill with other disenfranchised club kids intent on reinventing themselves. Fleet Street soon took an interest, called them the Blitz Kids, and a new movement was born, as Soho became overrun by eighteen-year-olds wearing tartan ball-gowns, pillbox hats, nun's habits, and deathly white make-up. The Blitz generation took punk and dressed it up, giving it a twelve-inch remix in the process. They anticipated the style-obsessed Eighties, when the world became a global catwalk. Narcissism plumbed new depths as haircuts reached new heights. Here, everyone had an alias, an ambition, and an aerodynamic haircut to match.

On the dance floor in Billy's you heard Bowie, Kraftwerk, the Human League, the Normal, Marlene Dietrich, and the theme from *Stingray*. Outside, Strange stood in his leather jodhpurs and German overcoat, deciding who could come in. 'I was strict on the door because once people were inside I didn't want them to feel they were in a goldfish bowl,' he said. 'I wanted them to feel they were in their own place, amongst friends.'

There were similar shifts in Birmingham, too, with Nick Rhodes being asked to DJ at the Rum Runner, a task which he undertook by playing his collection of David Bowie records (the other members of the soon-to-be-formed Duran Duran were all working at the club, although as they were cooking, cleaning, or washing up, Rhodes certainly had the best job). 'Duran Duran had a single vision of what we wanted to do,' said Rhodes. 'We wanted to mix glam rock and punk rock with a little bit of disco, although the prime motivation for forming in the first place was David Bowie. It always was.'

*   *   *

In late 2011, just a few days before Christmas, rare footage of Bowie performing 'The Jean Genie' on *Top Of The Pops* on 3 January 1973 was broadcast on BBC Two. The footage had been lost until just a few weeks before the broadcast, when retired TV cameraman John Henshall came forward with a copy of the performance. It was previously believed that every copy of the show had been destroyed. The unearthed footage showed a completely different Bowie from the one who performed 'Starman' the previous year, one who is totally confident of his powers, and of his ability to win over an audience. Wearing a loud Tommy Nutter-style brocade and folded silk jacket over a bare chest, along with a necklace, drop earrings, high-waisted speckled bags, and a greatly exaggerated Ziggy haircut (this one looking distinctly aggressive, as though Elvis may have worn it before going into the army), Bowie looked every inch the star. The song was performed live, with Bowie playing harmonica as though his parole depended on it. (In his harmonica solo he breaks into something that doesn't sound a million miles from 'Love Me Do'. Bowie put extra bars into the song, sending the *Top Of The Pops* producer, Johnnie Stewart, into a panic, instructing Henshall to 'Film it!') Whereas the 'Starman' performance looked tentative, this was almost sullen. What a difference six months had made.

Listen to those who were there, however, and they'll tell you that Bowie was, in fact, as nervous as he had been when he'd played 'Starman' the previous summer. For this *Top Of The Pops* performance, Bowie had actually invited along some of his 'piss-elegant, champagne-drinking entourage' (as he called them), not the New York bunch of hangers-on, but some of his old friends, those from the *Hunky Dory* days. There were three of them, Freddie Buretti, his flatmate Wendy Kirby, and Angie's friend, Daniella Parmar, and all had been invited along to BBC TV Centre as Bowie felt nervous. 'If you can believe that!,' says Kirby in an interview from one of the many Ziggy sites. 'He comes across as very confident, but he was always very shy and didn't really want to go on *Top Of The Pops* [again]. Angie was the one with all the energy.' Kirby had first met the Bowies at the Sombrero club in Kensington two years previously, 'We were the people always round David's house,' she says. Panda-eyed Daniella Parmar had constantly changing hair colour, and had helped convince Bowie of the importance of a synthetic hair colour for Ziggy, although it was Wendy and Freddie who Bowie had name-checked in 'All The Young Dudes': 'Wendy's stealing clothes from Marks and Sparks, And Freddie's got spots from ripping off the stars from his face . . .' When Bowie told Kirby, 'I said you could at least have made it Harrods!'

That evening Kirby was wearing a black fishtail dress,

'with an exceedingly low back', plus a long blond mermaid wig, 'The girl with a ton of make-up, huge eyelashes and the red flower in the hair – we piled on tons of everything then. We were the "young dudes" who shaved off our eyebrows just for camp, because you could paint them on higher up. That gave us a strange unearthly look which David adopted. He was always open to suggestions and went through our wardrobes like a magpie!'

She adds, 'Thing is, the fame happened seemingly overnight. People had thought of

'BOWIE DOESN'T SEEM QUITE REAL,' SAID THE NEW YORKER'S ELLEN WILLIS, WHO HAD BEEN FLOWN OVER TO SEE HIM PERFORM AT THE AYLESBURY FRIARS SOON AFTER THE *TOTP* APPEARANCE. 'REAL TO ME, THAT IS — WHICH IN ROCK AND ROLL IS THE ONLY FANTASY THAT COUNTS'

David as a one-hit wonder with "Space Oddity", then suddenly in 1972 "Starman" was a hit and everything went from ordinary to unreal. Nothing was the same again.'

Until the video was shown in 2011 Kirby had no idea she had been caught on camera. 'Pan's People had done their dance number and were heading out of the studio when

David went onstage. They all stopped to watch his act and were mightily impressed. I remember a couple of them were wearing red fox-fur coats . . .

'That's me between David and Mick, [and] that's Daniella dancing next to me. [It was] amazing to see myself on *Top Of The Pops* after all this time! I've never seen it before. And I haven't seen David perform live since . . . Those were great days and I was too young to appreciate them.'

I don't remember watching the 'Jean Genie' clip at the time, although it was obvious to anyone who was interested that by 1973 Bowie had become imperious, and rather grand. The critics certainly thought so. Many in the music industry hated the way that rock was being co-opted by people not prepared to just wear denim, hated the way in which Bowie had validated what they considered trivia. This was Roy Carr writing in the *NME* about the crowd at a Roxy Music concert at the Rainbow: 'There were droves of flat-chested femmes fatales and their frail skinny-hipped chaperones [Carr was rotund], heavy-boobed waterfront B girls with scarlet slashes for mouths and pug-nosed palookas for protectors, sixth-formers fresh from raiding their grandma's wardrobe, and fresh-faced fops in white tie and tails who looked like they'd be more at home throwing champers over each other at Lady Clarissa Minge-water's Coming Out Ball than washing down Jamaica Patties with Brown Ale [inverted snobbery here]. But then, Finsbury Park has never been the hub of café society.'

Ellen Willis, the *New Yorker* writer who was one of

those flown over to see Bowie play the Aylesbury Friars a short while after the *Top Of The Pops* appearance, felt there was something a little phony about him. She said he was all glitter and no grease, and that the Ziggy concept only really worked as a spoof. 'Bowie doesn't seem quite real,' she wrote on her return. 'Real to me, that is – which in rock and roll is the only fantasy that counts.' What Ellen didn't understand was that this was precisely why we liked him. Bowie may have been pretentious, but at least he wasn't earnest.

Throughout the Seventies, as Bowie's fame started to accelerate, it was obvious that he was obsessed with change, with moving on. Yet if this was the DNA of his identity, what wasn't apparent in 1972 was *why* he was doing this. What his public – us – didn't know was that Bowie had spent the previous eight or nine years running around in various different guises and costumes trying to find one that worked. Like Madonna and Lady Gaga after him, his reinventions weren't the motivating force behind his skittishness, it was the reinvention itself, the act of staying one step ahead of being found out. Bowie had hinted at this when he sang 'Changes', and had no qualms about breaking through the fourth wall and admitting as much. He wasn't driven by anything resembling ideology, but by instinct and impulse. (Conversely, back in the Sixties, when the creative wellspring was in full gush, the Beatles and their like – well, actually mainly the Beatles – pushed ahead driven by the changing nature of their passions, not because it might be a good idea to hire an orchestra or wear a pointy hat. Bowie was simply expedient.)*

Almost exactly a year after the *Top Of The Pops* performance, Bowie retired Ziggy, live from the stage of the Hammersmith Odeon. On 3 July 1973, in front of 3,500 of the faithful, he said, 'This show will stay the longest in our memories, not just because it is the end of the tour but because it is the last show we'll ever do.' This was the last date of the third Ziggy tour, by which time Bowie was physically and emotionally wrecked. He was exhausted, bored, wasted, and miserable. When he made the announcement, among Team Bowie there was a genuine sense of bereavement, even if we suspected he wouldn't be on rock-star gardening duty for long. Bowie had such specificity of intent, we suspected he'd already got whatever it was he was going to do next worked out in advance. It was all very well saying that Ziggy understood that he would have to die in order for his creator to live, but for Bowie, it was just another costume change.

As the Spiders From Mars left the stage that night, as Mick Ronson looked down at the red weals on his hands, his hair dripping wet against his forehead, Bowie's mind was

....

*'You're never who you think you are,' Bowie said once. 'Sometime in the Eighties, an old lady approached me and asked, "Mr Elton, may I have your autograph?" I told her that I wasn't Elton but David Bowie. She replied, "Oh, thank goodness. I couldn't stand his red hair and all that make-up."'

already elsewhere. Ziggy would soon become a discarded marionette, shoved in an ungainly manner into Bowie's already considerable closet. For the time being he'd finished with the palaver of dressing up.*

Almost immediately the concert became fetishised, and not just by those who weren't there. According to some who were there, the sexual abandon was rampant, with men and women throwing their clothes off, and then throwing themselves at each other. As soon as Bowie hit the stage that night there were rumours that this might be the Spiders' last gig, and the tension among the audience was high. Men were openly masturbating, and girls fell to their knees and fellated complete strangers as Bowie sprinted through his set. One girl, 'Julie', couldn't believe what she was seeing. 'I'd never seen so many cocks in my life ... A lot of fluid was flying about. One girl was actually sucking someone off at the same time as trying to listen to what was going on. I thought it was so extraordinary because nobody had any inhibitions.' Mike Garson, who would play piano with

----

*When Nile Rodgers worked on Let's Dance in the early Eighties, he was disconcerted by how ordinary Bowie could appear when he chose to. 'David arrived at the studio in a very upbeat mood. He looked so normal it made me more nervous.' Band member Sean Mayes has similar memories from the 1978 tour: 'David was a more elegant figure, a water-colour sketch of soft hues,' he says, describing Bowie's travelling wardrobe. 'Short hair with the translucence of the natural near-blond, his face a gentle tan, long trench-style raincoat in the palest olive, light JAL shoulder bag. This quite figure was the unconscious centre of the maelstrom.'

Bowie for years, says, 'I heard all those stories about what was going on in the audience and I tend to believe them. I remember seeing crazy stuff.'

D. A. Pennebaker filmed the final Ziggy show, and he talks about the gig with as much reverence as he talks about the Bob Dylan concert he shot for *Don't Look Back*, in the mid-Sixties. 'He [was] incredible to watch. I mean, I could see myself getting a hard-on just looking at him sometimes, which is ridiculous. But I think that the reason we made it was because RCA said, we have this guy and he's going to do a concert, maybe the last one he's going to do, and you've got to go make a film. I thought they said Bolan. I thought it was Marc Bolan I was going to do. And I was very excited because I really dug glitter rock. So I kind of set off with the wrong guy in mind. But I've spent time with Bowie, and I've seen him go into his head. He just disappears. He's like Dylan. He has some place where it's just all music, and he's all alone.'

The audience were all his people. Over-made-up girls with bloated faces and running eyes, under-made-up boys with skinny arms and billowing shirts. Bowie knew he'd attracted a somewhat eccentric audience, but he knew, too, that audience was also full of Little Noddy Holders and Little Iggy Pops. 'I feel like a Dr Frankenstein,' he told *Melody Maker*'s Roy Hollingworth in 1973. He was talking about Ziggy, though he may as well have been talking about the audience.

The gig smelled of pear drops and sweet white wine: a mixture of Ziggy's nail varnish and the mass of gigging teenagers (a fruity, chemical smell). And the sweet white wine? Well, Ziggy's rider backstage was a crate of Frascati.

When Bowie announced Ziggy's retirement, it was like Elvis joining the army, or like the Beatles announcing they would never tour again, an abnegation of only recently acknowledged responsibility.

'We didn't know anything about it beforehand,' says Bolder. 'I was a bit, like, "What the hell's he on about?" Woody thought about walking offstage before we did "Rock 'n' Roll Suicide". He told me later that if he'd known beforehand, he wouldn't have done the gig. 'That's why they didn't tell us. They couldn't take the risk we'd say "Up yours!" and walk. Everybody else knew. Mick Ronson knew. They just kept it from me and Woody.'

Like many celebrities, Bowie would go on to complain about his fame, and how it made him feel trapped, uncharacteristically oblivious to the Faustian pact that was made the night of 6 July; he was famous, having finally achieved what he'd been striving for for nearly a decade, and so to moan about the trials and tribs of recognition seemed silly and not a little ungrateful. However, when Mark Chapman shot John Lennon on 8 December 1980, the paranoid subtext of 'Fame' never seemed more prescient.*

. . . .

*'Fame' was the result of John Lennon mucking about with the guitar line from Shirley & Company's 'Shame Shame Shame'. 'Look, it's simple,' he told Bowie. 'Say what you mean, make it rhyme, and put a backbeat to it.'

Outside of Miles Davis and Bob Dylan, there are few other commercially successful artists who have gone to such lengths to distance themselves from their fan base. We don't really like our entertainers to break the social contract we think we have with them, but Bowie broke it time and time again.*

'It started out as a band, really,' says Trevor Bolder, describing the end of the Spiders. 'He asked us to join him and we said OK, 'cause we were on a record deal at the time and we gave that up to be with him. We were promised the same share of everything if we would do this, and it was, like, David Bowie And The Spiders From Mars, or Ziggy Stardust And The Spiders From Mars. We started out playing in clubs in London and, as a band, we went to all the gigs together in a car, but the bigger he got – and the band would go wherever he'd go – the less we actually saw him. We only saw him as we walked onstage. He separated himself from us towards the end, he was like a solo artist that didn't need us, while in the beginning he definitely needed us.

....

* Having finished his 1965 tour of Britain, Bob Dylan was physically and emotionally ruined. 'I realised I was very drained,' he said. 'I was playing a lot of songs I didn't want to play, I was singing words I didn't really want to sing . . . It's very tiring having other people tell you how much they dig you if you yourself don't dig you.' He got so angry with himself and with other people that he started treating interviews and press conferences as confrontational theatre, telling journalists he collected monkey wrenches, or that his songs were inspired by 'chaos, watermelons, and clocks'.

'We just sort of floated along with it. It didn't intimidate me, as I was married with two children and I had to get on with that side of life as well. So I really enjoyed what we did, I really enjoyed playing. We didn't have the sort of pressure that David had. He had all the interviews, and everything was on his shoulders and we were the band behind it all, and we just enjoyed it. We just got on and did what we always wanted to do since we first started playing as kids.'

Understandably, as Bowie got bigger, so the Spiders were pushed to the margins. Trevor Bolder has mixed memories, 'Really bad memories towards the end, when he changed as a person. He was really until then, just a regular sort of bloke, he was a nice, caring bloke, but the bigger he got, the bigger his head got, and the less important you were to him. From the stories I've heard, with all the musicians that were with him, he trod that line: when he didn't need you, he'd discard you, but while he needed you, he was very friendly towards you. I saw him do it to a few people as well – they used to do shows with him, and once he finished using them, he didn't want to see them, and if they came to gigs, he wouldn't let them in. They tried to see him play, and he'd be like, "I don't want them here tonight, I don't want them here!" That's just the way he worked.

'But the worst point was when it all finished – being out of work, being penniless; in the end, we had no money, and I had a family, and Bowie didn't really care about that. I'll never forget what he did then.' (It was always just about Bowie. Childhood friend Geoff MacCormack was recruited by Bowie as a backing singer and percussionist to play on the US tour of 1973, and he says that performing with Bowie was like having a backstage pass but not being allowed to join in.)

'He became quite grand towards the end,' says Bolder. 'He didn't really mix with others, you know. When we started out as a band we were playing pubs, dressed up as we were, and travelled up in the same car together. We set up the gear together, like a band does, but of course the bigger he got, towards the end sometimes we'd only see him when he walked onstage. And then we'd walk offstage and you were lucky to see him in the hotel afterwards. He sort of separated himself from the band. But by that time he had a lot of hangers-on with him, as well; there were all the Andy Warhol mob that were working for him and I think it went to his head a bit. Plus he had a lot of pressure on him; as I say, he was doing all the interviews and he was the one who was having to come up with all the songs, so the record company and the management were always pressurising him and stuff. So if he didn't see the band it didn't really matter, we still got on and enjoyed ourselves. But it was a shame really, that we sort of drifted apart.

'I think we could have gone another year. I think Bowie knew that as well; I think later on he thought it could have gone that bit further. And I always thought that the Spiders, with Mick, should have gone on as a band on its own, and done something as well. But it was all broken up and separated by the management, because they didn't want that.

They didn't want the Spiders to be out on the road as a band, because they thought it might have taken away from David, or whatever. They just wanted to give Mick his solo album, and me and Woody were left sort of in the lurch, and we didn't know where to go or what to do.'

'He became Ziggy and in the process became more distant,' says Ken Scott. 'Tony Defries had told David that he was going to make him a star, which is what he did. Defries was doing things in order to make David a star that no one had done before, and because it worked then I think David became more and more under his control. I think he believed other things that Defries said that weren't necessarily helpful, such as his insistence that Bowie separate himself from the rest of the band. I could never work out if the personality change was because he was adopting the Ziggy persona, or whether it was the result of becoming successful. Success changes everyone. The whole thing became intertwined. He basically became more distant, which was a huge issue with the band. In the early stage David wouldn't have allowed that to happen. It was bad for the band, but ultimately it made it easier for him to become successful in the States, as he changed his image so much.'

Over the next few years, Bowie would become a bit too pleased by his own transgression, usually keeping several steps ahead of his audience, in spite of that audience then wishing he had stayed exactly where he'd been. After Ziggy, and all the fractured versions thereof (Aladdin Sane, the Diamond Dog, etc.), Bowie went all Cubist, making the Berlin albums (enjoying the German clash between ego and melancholy), and dipped his head below the parapet. The new records were good, but they were dark. Gone was the shrill sound of *Ziggy*. When the *NME*'s Ian MacDonald first listened to *Low* he said that he got the impression he was listening to it sideways. Bowie invented a helix of characters – skinny men who, whenever the going got tough (mostly during the Eighties, when he turned away from the solipsistic content of his early records, and when in his world everyone else had caught up with him), tended to look back to the future for inspiration. Even when he was stealing. Not that anyone minded. 'It was true that Bowie swept into the Blitz scene and soaked up all the ideas,' says Boy George, 'but he was the reason that most of us were dressing up in the first place.'

So incendiary was Bowie that the critics were polarised. MacDonald said that, 'For good or ill, David Bowie's intellectualism (as manifested in his linked awareness of ideas and styles) is a revolution in rock. For the time being, David Bowie is incontrovertibly the most important figure in rock and I feel genuinely sorry for those people who can't or won't see why.' Richard Williams, writing in the *Melody Maker* – which for my money was always the most pompous music weekly – accused Bowie of shallowness, charlatanism, affectation, and using other people as vaulting-horses.

Bowie would become bloodless and emaciated, when the travel and the drugs and the constant costume changes eventually caused him to take a good long look at what he had become. However, he still knew what he was going to look like. Tom Kelley, the photographer who took the famous Marilyn Monroe 1949 nude calendar images, captured Bowie in the mid-Seventies (the picture was eventually used on the cover of *ChangesOneBowie*). 'Bowie took me back to the golden age of movie stars,' said Kelley. 'He's a visionary who looks into the camera as though he can see the finished pictures.' (At this point in the arc, Bowie was all angles; cheekbones, slash pockets, and high-waisted pegs.)

'I've shot David Bowie a lot over the years, and did some great pictures of him with Catherine Deneuve for their film, *The Hunger*, in 1982,' says David Bailey. 'He was always very reserved, though, and had a definite view of how he wanted to be portrayed. Which made it very difficult to take a picture of him if you're trying to be creative. In the early days it was easier to take a celebrity's photograph, because they didn't really know what to expect, but now they all know what they're going to get. The thing I hate is when someone phones and says, "I've got this great idea". I always say, "I've got a better idea. Why don't you come to the studio and I'll shoot you against a nice, white background." Bowie was one of the first to do that. And he was very definite.'

Bowie celebrated artifice, even elevated it, wearing not just his heart but also his influences on his capacious sleeves. He became more than the tasteful thief by using his influences to sculpt his own personae. The ideas he incorporated into Ziggy gave an indication of the way in which he would use the past to create the future for the rest of his career, paying homage to everyone from Fritz Lang and George

Steiner to William Burroughs, Yves Saint Laurent, and Derek Boshier. Being an autodidact, his sponge was bigger than most, sucking it all up – German Futurist, Expressionist, and Surrealist cinema, Japanese costume design, classic American pop art, and innumerable interpretations of British youth culture.

He even did normal. When he decided to reinvent himself at the tail end of the Eighties, after two decades of scene-stealing costume changes, he didn't try dressing up as a Bacofoil space elf, a Germanic troubadour, or a flame-haired kabuki sex slave. No, he'd already done all of these. For Bowie, the most unlikely, obtuse route to reinvention involved a black suit, donned apparently without irony, for the launch of his Tin Machine project in 1989. Tin Machine looked like they sounded: conventionally austere, clipped, careful, a tiny bit reductive . . . and very safe. Cool, studied, but safe. And they wore black.

Soon we would become accustomed to pop stars holding their hands up as if to ward off aggressive plant life or very large wasps, would get used to singers looking world-weary and all alone, trying to conjure up the requisite amount of existential angst. In the Eighties, record companies fell over themselves to sign neurotic boy outsiders who referenced Colin Wilson, J. P. Donleavy, and Jack Kerouac, pop stars who looked anxious and put-upon, wondering how they could possibly explain themselves to people so obviously less intense than themselves.

Well, DB did a lot of this first, and we didn't mind in

the slightest. If the skeletal vampire wanted to sit in his room in the dark, then so be it.

Ziggy has never really gone away, though. Bowie may have spent forty years thrashing around in an attempt to escape the confines of whatever alter-ego he was presently encased in, but he always came back to Ziggy. So many do (on the cover of Pulp's 2002 single, 'Bad Cover Version', is a hand-tinted photograph of Heddon Street. Instead of Ziggy standing in the doorway there is a child, the son of Pulp guitarist Mark Webber).

He swerved between veneration and sarcasm, though, and Bowie was ambivalent about his greatest creation, lauding the magnificence of what Ziggy achieved, and then denigrating the very idea of it, treating the whole process as an expedient exercise.

'For the likes of Roxy Music and myself, mascara was merely the conveyance by which great globs of non-rock flotsam and jetsam were to be delivered,' he said. 'Japanese kabuki, Dada, Dietrich and Leni Riefenstahl, Piaf and Futurism, and above all, "elegant gloom". We were wondering where to lay our hands on absinthe . . . puzzling . . . the big questions: greasepaint or pancake? Climbing the heights of what we felt was much-needed pretension, we were above common-or-garden chat-up lines to dodgy slappers. We craved the rarefied stratosphere from whence we dropped really heavy names: Burroughs, Brecht, and Baudelaire tumbled meaninglessly over Warhol and Wittgenstein in a blur of de- and re-constructed pop.'

Bowie had a habit of dismissing his past, as though he had a greater understanding of it than those who consumed it. But we are as important as custodians of Ziggy Stardust as David Bowie, because he is just as much a part of our lives as Bowie's. Five minutes after saying his creation was a badly amalgamated facsimile of second-hand ideas, he was espousing the intricacies of his alter ego, using as many artfully referenced themes and names as he had done back in 1972.

Ziggy had to go, though, as by 1973 he was already eating into Bowie's face, and he'd had enough. The conceit had become a burden. It wasn't as though he had to do six performances a week, plus a matinee on Wednesday and Saturday; Ziggy was a full-time job, twenty-four/seven.

'Ziggy, particularly, was created out of a certain arrogance,' said Bowie, after it was all over. 'But remember, at the time I was young and I was full of life, and that seemed like a very positive artistic statement. I thought that was a beautiful piece of art, I really did. I thought that was a grand kitsch painting. The whole guy. Then that fucker would not leave me alone for years. That was when it all started to sour. And it soured so quickly you wouldn't believe it. And it took me an awful long time to level out. My whole personality was affected. Again, I brought that upon myself. I can't say I'm sorry when I look back, because it provoked such an extraordinary set of circumstances in my life. I thought I might as well take Ziggy to interviews as well. Why leave him onstage? Looking back it was completely absurd. It became very dangerous. I really did have doubts about my sanity. I can't deny that the experience affected me in a very exaggerated and marked manner. I think I put myself very dangerously near the line. Not in a physical sense but definitely in a mental sense. I played mental games with myself to such an extent that I'm very relieved and happy to be back in Europe and feeling very well. But then, you see, I was always the lucky one.'

In the early Nineties I proposed a sequel to the wonderful Nik Cohn/Guy Peellaert book, *Rock Dreams*, in which the authors imagined rock stars in ironic and exaggerated situations and circumstances (albeit beautifully painted). Mine was going to be called *Pop Life*, and the first two pages were going to be devoted to DB. My notes included the following – '1. David Bowie: Onstage as Ziggy Stardust in a red/green catsuit covered in numbers, with his guitarist Mick Ronson pretending to give him head . . . Jealous, sexually excited, panting girls in the audience look on. 2. David Bowie: *Aladdin Sane*, sitting alone on his bed in an American hotel room, half a painted flash on his face. The floor is covered in notes for songs and bits of paper with phone numbers on them.'

As I wrote the proposal, I remember thinking the entire book could be about Ziggy Stardust.

FIVE

'Press Your Space Face Close To Mine, Love'

THE ZIGGY STARDUST LEGACY, 1972–2012

In the forty years since Bowie's most successful alter ego first crawled out of his spaceship, Ziggy's children have all had something of an enduring love. Sometimes it's been reciprocated, other times not.

'And I think my spaceship knows which way to go'
David Bowie, 'Space Oddity'

The first time I met David Bowie, he asked me for a light. We were standing in the downstairs pool room in a gay night-club called Heaven, down by the arches underneath Charing Cross Station in central London. This was back at the tail end of 1981. He was filming the designer vampire film *The Hunger*, and I was an extra, three months out of college, employed to wear a goatee beard, a zoot suit, and a key-chain, and to walk down a long flight of metal stairs as Bowie and his co-star Catherine Deneuve walked up them, knowingly nodding along to 'Bela Lugosi's Dead' by Bauhaus as I went. It was a fairly dismal film – in fact, it was something of a shocker – but I was only twenty-one, and couldn't quite believe that I was in the same room as someone who had meant so much to me in my youth. You can still see me, if you freeze the DVD at a certain point, although I realise that owning a DVD copy of *The Hunger* is about as likely as you owning *Rambo III* or *The Human Centipede II*. The *LA Times* called the film 'Stylish! Explicit! It'll take your breath away!', though I can only assume that the reviewer owed the director money because it really is a pile of dreadful old tosh, even if it was fantastically exciting to a twenty-one-year-old who had worshipped Bowie from afar for nearly a decade. (The movie also has one of the worst tag lines I've ever heard: 'Nothing human lasts forever', it proclaimed, as bold as brass, as if this was news to anyone.) There I am, a callow New Romantic barely out of my teens, dressed to the gills, with a drink in one hand and a cigarette in the other, standing around enigmatically as Dame David brushes by me. Oh, and they cropped my head out.

Brushing past my some-time hero would have been enough for me to brag about for months afterwards, although my anecdote moved up a gear around two o'clock that afternoon when everyone's favourite space-bloke marched up to me and promptly asked me for a light for his Marlboro Red. Now, this may not be up there with watching John Travolta rehearse the dance routine in *Pulp Fiction*, may not be up there with Robert De Niro asking you to help him with the mirror scene in *Taxi Driver*, but for someone from my generation, for whom David Bowie had been as revelatory as Elvis and the Beatles had been to the previous generation, it was a bit like sharing a beer with the Almighty, or at least his representative on Earth. Not only that, we smoked the same cigarettes! Spend half an hour on a film set and you'll hear that, 'Sean Connery told me this joke' (translation: I was standing behind him when he told the director the joke); or 'Al Pacino practically congratulated me on the way I walked into the room' (i.e. he didn't even blink). Celebrity encounters, however fleeting, or indeed, untrue, are the only currency extras have. Personally I was just thrilled to be in the same room as the man who'd sung 'Life On Mars'.

I would later get to know David Bowie, meeting dozens of times, and interviewed him in London, Switzerland, New York, LA, all over the place. We even watched the 1985 Notting Hill Carnival from the same first floor flat in Portobello Road (the home of my friend Cynthia Lole, who worked on *Absolute Beginners*). I've seen him backstage at concerts, in clubs, at gallery openings (including his own, in London). But none of this stuff means anything, because I am probably the only one who remembers the incidents. I wouldn't imagine Bowie had photographs of the two of us in silver frames on the piano in his downtown New York loft, if indeed he still had a piano.

If you spend a lot of time around celebrities, you can often begin to feel flattered, as though your proximity to true stardom is starting to rub off on you, as though you might yourself actually be beginning to be famous. But even when I started to move in those circles – I was a journalist, and bumping into celebrities was part of my job – I always treated the experience with a certain amount of circum-spection. If David Bowie wasn't rushing home and telling Coco (Bowie's assistant) or Iman that he had spent the day with me, then it didn't seem appropriate that I did it, either. Having a celebrity experience was no different from getting an autograph or a selfie, whether you asked for it or not. Nevertheless, I didn't feel any less excited about spending quality time with David Bowie.

Our lives were entwined, but then they weren't. He couldn't swim, and neither could I. We were both Capri-corns. We sometimes ended up in the same places – in the spring of 1978 I went to The Music Machine in Camden to see Iggy Pop play (I remember he wore fishnets and I arrived on the back of a large Norton), and Bowie was there, merrily chatting away to John Lydon, in what at the time seemed to be an implausibly volatile situation – yet he was David Bowie, and I wasn't.

I never failed to get goosebumps, never failed to get a little nervous, and never took him for granted. Yes, it was nice when he pretended to remember your name (he was one of the most professional pop stars you could ever meet, and got his management team to research people before he met them. Towards the end of the Sixties, Tony Palmer's reaction would start to be typical: 'He smiles; you melt. He winks; you disintegrate'), and yes, it's cool to have the occasional shared experience, but I never forget that he was a star, and I was the fan; I never forgot that he was the man I pretended to be as I danced around my bedroom at the age of twelve, singing along to 'Life On Mars', using an HB pencil as a substitute microphone, and wishing I had that shock of flame-red hair.*

'David Bowie is such a remarkably genial chap,' said

....

*For a while we sporadically corresponded, and sent each other Christmas cards, while my oddest Bowie encounter happened on the phone. It was one of those dark, miserable winter weekday afternoons at the *Sunday Times*, some time around 1994, one of those days when you spent most of the afternoon longing to escape Wapping and drive back to civilisation. That day was no different to any other: phones were ringing, faxes whirring, sub-editors screaming for copy, and couriers were coming and going and losing packages as though the whole idea of losing packages was coming back into fashion. It was raining heavily outside, as it always was in Wapping, even when it was sunny everywhere else in London, and the hail hit the windows like furious fingers on industrial PC keyboards.

My phone rang, I picked it up, and a more-than-familiar voice on the other end asked, 'Hello, is that Peggy?' although in the retelling (and in the weeks afterwards I told this story a lot) I always imagine it more as 'Helloooooo, is that Pigga-aay? This is your son David, the Cockernaaay in cyber-space,' in the sort of Mockney drawl that has been used by everyone from Anthony Newley to Damon Albarn via Mick Jagger, but which has been honed to perfection by my friend on the other end of the line.

'Er, no, this is Dylan Jones. Is that David Bowie?'

It seems Bowie's mother had just moved, and as I'd only recently interviewed Bowie for the *Sunday Times*, my number was on the same page as hers (her name was Jones, after all). Bizarrely, Bowie seemed as thrilled as I was flattered by this accident of serendipity, and stayed on the phone for twenty minutes, as I frantically made explanatory hand gestures, threw hastily scribbled notes at my

Nick Kent in 1973. 'You enter his suite at the Detroit Hilton armed with a horrendous opening line like "what's it like to be rock's prettiest neo-Nazi", but then you see this slight figure – red Oxford bags, checkered shirt [sic], red carrot-top coiffure, cheekbones like velvet dustbowls, with his

---

colleagues and mouthed, 'IT'S DAVID BOWIE!' to anyone passing through the office.

Peggy's boy was gearing up for another of his purple patches – and at the time he really needed one – and over the next few years would produce many records as good as those he made in the Seventies, when he was in his prime. The tin-pot Tin Machine had been thrown into the recycling bin (to be picked up by God knows whom), bouncing against the walls of a cast-iron box already full of the Glass Spider, the Laughing Gnome, the nightmare scarecrow of *Labyrinth*, and that weird guy from the 'Jazzin' For Blue Jean' video.

'I've got to stop mucking about and start making records for myself rather than for other people,' he told me on the phone that day. 'Anyway, I better call my mum before I get round to that . . .'

I like to think I would have been a little more dignified if he made the same mistake now, but I couldn't guarantee it.

(By the way. This is the same Peggy who called up the *NME* in October 1975, claiming that her son was 'a terrible hypocrite', and wanting to do an interview. Charles Shaar Murray, one of the paper's star writers, was duly dispatched, and returned with an extraordinary story about a woman slighted. She claimed she'd had only one telephone call from her son since the previous Christmas, and produced a sheaf of letters from Bowie's then manager, Tony Defries, 'All of which coldly interrogate her for production of receipts and a precise accounting of her expenditure as a prerequisite for the payment of any of her bills.'

Peggy said, 'Defries rang me up one day and said, "You must understand that David is under no legal obligation to finance you."')

decaying choppers pursed in a charming grin – and, well you just break down and act like a white man. Here is an English gentleman for sure, surrounded not by a host of mincing minions and lascivious youths as rumour would like to have it, but by a small entourage of close friends and carefully screened acquaintances.'

You never took anything for granted. Once, years ago, I was alone in a recording studio with Bowie in New York, listening to a playback of one of his albums. This is obviously an incredibly difficult situation, as you basically have to sit there for an hour telling someone how brilliant they are every four or five minutes. I started off saying that the album was amazing, and after every song had finished, would find some suitably fawning adjective. I wasn't being sycophantic, as the album was great. As I got to track five, the standard was slipping, as was my enthusiasm, and so I started tempering my comments with things like, 'I like it, but I don't like it as much as the other ones.' Wrong thing to say. Bowie didn't want my honesty, just my approval. (Apochrypha: a young composer had written two pieces of music, and asked the great Rossini if he would be kind enough to listen to them both before saying which one he preferred. The composer duly played one piece, whereupon Rossini intervened. 'You need not play any more,' he said. 'I prefer the other one.') The last time we spoke, Bowie told me, 'I've made over twenty-five studio albums, and I think probably I've made two real stinkers in my time, and some not-bad albums, and some really good albums. I'm proud of what I've done. In fact it's been a good ride.'

David Bowie was the first pop star to refuse to have anything to do with the past, even though the past informed so much of what he did. To him, the past wasn't necessary, wasn't particularly interesting, wasn't what he was about. In terms of presentation, there's never been anyone to touch him, even if Madonna has made a fairly good fist of it. Not only did Bowie invent glam rock, not only did he invent space-age rock, but in the last forty years or so he pretty much invented it all. He was a soul boy. He went ambient just as everyone else was going punk (after all, he'd already produced several seminal proto-punk albums for Lou Reed and Iggy Pop), and in the Eighties he went global – 'Let's Dance' – when everyone else was still copying all the old, esoteric stuff he did back in the Seventies.

He wasn't perfect. As we had done all that due diligence on his Anthony Newley songs of the Sixties, it was no surprise when, creatively, Bowie eventually turned out to be fallible. Nevertheless it was still shocking to see the Glass Spider tour in 1987, and while the album it was supporting was bad enough (*Never Let Me Down* was a record so bad you felt like saying, 'David, you haven't just let me down, you haven't just let yourself down, you've let the whole school down'; an album so dreadful that Bowie even tried to have one of its songs, 'Too Dizzy', deleted from its 1995 re-issue), the tour led me to think that Bowie had actually split – with his body going one way and his talent another. What surprised me was how much I still cared. Having invested so much of my youth in one man's vision I didn't want him to make it seem like a waste of time. In that respect I felt like those legions of Bob Dylan aficionados when they first heard his 1970 album, *Self Portrait* ('What is this shit?' asked Greil Marcus in his *Rolling Stone* review). Or indeed how fans of the Allman Brothers must have felt when they heard that Greg Allman was recording an album with (and marrying!) Cher.

At forty years of age – the point at which entertainers routinely announce that the best years of their life are about to commence – Bowie was rewarded with the worst reviews of his career, for a record he decided to publicise dressed like a junk shop Mick Hucknall. As maturity and sobriety set in, Bowie seemed ever more sane, reasonable, and at peace with himself. Yet the more personal stability he achieved, the more control he had over his life, the less interesting his music became.

He discovered perspective, though. I was editing *i-D* in 1987, when the Glass Spider tour crawled into view, and commissioned an interview with him in support of it. During the interview, many of his misdemeanors were discussed. 'I think we have to look back on [*Just A Gigolo*] with a certain amount of irony,' he said at one point. 'I had a wonderful time making that movie because by the second week we looked around at each other and said, "This is a pile of shit so let's have a good time!" So we had a good time . . . but it was an atrocious movie; but then again all it was was an atrocious movie, I mean, it's not the end of the world or anything like that. When one starts one's career with "The

Laughing Gnome" it's very easy just to put things down to experience.'

We got very blasé about Bowie in the Eighties. Opportunities to meet him were spurned, concerts missed, interest low. I was at *i-D* when Julien Temple was filming the 'Jazzin' For Blue Jean' video, and – what was I thinking? – refused to find time to take a cameo role. For five minutes it was my turn to be grand. Silly. But the Eighties belonged to us, and if anyone owned Swinging London it was the two hundred people tramping down to Leigh Bowery's Taboo in Leicester Square every Wednesday night, dressed up as day-glo post-apocalyptic stormtroopers, not an ageing rock god trading on former glories. At this point in his career, the self-certainty he had employed with such success during the Seventies was taking Bowie in all sorts of wrong directions, and to those of us who cared, he looked like a man decoupled from the Hadron Collider-sized radar that had made us admire him so much in the first place. (When voters start talking about a politician's appearance, it is less a cause of doubt than a symptom of doubt. With pop stars it's usually the other way round.)

I saw Bowie at Live Aid, and it was like watching a TV re-run. I'd started out that day up in the seats by the stage, not far from where Charles and Diana were sitting, and as the day progressed had moved towards the back of the stadium, trying to get a sense of scale, attempting to contextualise the enormity of it all. And it was immense. Queen were obviously the surprise success of the day – until that day I'd rarely had any time for them, but, like the other

71,999 people in the stadium on 13 July 1985, and the 1.9 billion TV audience, I was completely won over. U2 were impressive, too, although by the time they came on we were so far away from the stage that my girlfriend thought they were playing in Philadelphia. Oddly, Bowie was less impressive, somewhat anti-climactic, as he had to follow Queen. Seven-twenty should have been the perfect time for him to grab the audience, but Freddie Mercury's extraordinary performance – Queen's set that day is often referred to as the best stadium gig ever – made it impossible. Bowie stood no chance, appearing as though he had prerecorded the emotion as well as the music. In truth, he was shell-shocked.

The past isn't as easily dismissed as we sometimes might like to believe it is, and while Bowie built his reputation, his career, and even his prescience on relentlessly moving forward, occasionally he attempted to grab the second hand and swing, Harold Lloyd-like, back in time. I interviewed Trevor Bolder in early 2012, and I asked him – almost as an afterthought – if Bowie had ever tried to reform the Spiders. I already thought I knew the answer, and was about to stop recording when Bolder said, 'Actually yes. He rang me once, in 1978, at home, and he asked me would I go back and reform with the Spiders. And I said, "Well, if you can get Mick to do it, we'll consider it." Bowie was having problems with America, I think; he'd done *Diamond Dogs* and all that but I don't think his career had gone how he thought it was going to. I think he missed the band, in fact. He'd used other musicians but he missed the camaraderie of the band. But Mick wouldn't do it, as they weren't really speaking at the time, so it never happened.'

In truth, Bowie and Ronson had barely spoken since the break-up of the band in 1973.

'Everybody wants to talk to me about the Spiders,' says Bolder. 'When I'm out on the road with [Uriah] Heep I meet loads of people who are Spiders fans. My daughter went to see Moby and she went backstage a couple of years ago, and he wrote a song called "Bring Back The Spiders From Mars", and he was doing the "I am not worthy" routine to her.'

Towards the end, Bowie was a lifetime away from the androgynous android of the Seventies, when he could be found lolling about in the back of large American limousines, a crumpled heap of black kamikaze silk drinking Tequila Gold from a brown paper bag. This was when his ambition and ego were most blind. 'I get so much fan mail it has to be handled by a computer,' he said in 1975. Computers? What were they? Any one of Bowie's Seventies personae might have been apocryphal, yet they were all excessive.

Being acutely aware of the history of schizophrenia in his family, Bowie would occasionally freeze whenever he found himself straying into areas he couldn't control, whether that meant undue popularity and the strain of success, overindulgent drug ingestion, or elements of his creative work that disturbed him. Would his own psyche eventually shatter? 'One puts oneself through such psychological damage in trying to avoid the threat of insanity,' he said. 'You start to approach the very thing you're scared of . . . There were too many suicides [in my family] for my liking . . . As long as I could put those psychological excesses into my music and into my work, I could always be throwing it off.'

Of course, the worst thing a paranoid potential schizophrenic could do is create an alter ego that won't let him alone, but then Bowie knew that when he retired Ziggy on 3 July 1973.

In the forty-odd years that Bowie was a star, he recorded some of the most important music of the post-Beatles era, and although he is still largely known for the raft of ground-breaking albums he released in the Seventies, his work since then was equally fascinating, if not always as ground-breaking. If you were to compile Bowie's alternative greatest hits, many of them would be from the last twenty-five years, little known songs that are equally as good as anything he recorded before: 'Loving The Alien' (one of the few good tracks from 1985's *Tonight*, and – crappy production aside – as haunting as much of the space-age stuff from the early Seventies, and with a lyric that explored Bowie's intense dislike of organised religion), 'Dancing In The Street' (the much-maligned cover version recorded with Mick Jagger for Live Aid, again in 1985), 'Absolute Beginners' (the intricate long version, from another mediocre film, Julien Temple's 1986 take on Colin MacInnes' book of the same name), 'Shades' (the hilarious song he wrote for Iggy Pop's 1986 album *Blah Blah Blah*), 'Amazing' (yes, a Tin Machine song, from the first album in 1989, and a great one), 'Pretty

Pink Rose' (a song he gave to guitarist Adrian Belew in 1990), 'Real Cool World' (from the 1992 movie *Cool World*, and a song that's almost been forgotten), 'Sound And Vision–David Bowie Vs. 808 State' (a souped-up remix from 1991), 'Looking For Lester' (from 1993's generally over-praised *Black Tie White Noise*), 'Buddha Of Suburbia' (a 1993 song that is one of the best things he's ever made), 'Strangers When We Meet' (1995's rather more orthodox single version), 'Hallo Spaceboy' (the Pet Shop Boys remix, from 1995, which pays homage yet again to Major Tom), 'I'm Afraid Of Americans' (from 1997's *Earthling*, and a tes-tament to the fact that he's not forgotten not to deliberately kick up dust), 'Seven' (from 1999's '*hours*'), 'Thursday's Child' (ditto), 'This Is Not America' (from 2000's *Bowie At The Beeb*, and proof that his Sinatra phase was one he could have seriously and successfully exploited had he chosen to), 'I Would Be Your Slave', '5.15 The Angels Have Gone', 'Slow Burn', 'Everyone Says "Hi"'' (all four from 2002's magnificent *Heathen*), 'New Killer Star' and 'Fall Dog Bombs The Moon' (both from 2003's *Reality*), 'Changes' (with Butterfly, from the soundtrack of 2004's *Shrek 2*), and 'Rebel Never Gets Old' (yet another 'Rebel Rebel' remix, a mash-up from 2004, and a great record from gun to tape). Strangely, 'Rebel Rebel' is the Bowie song with perhaps the most endurance, the song that has entered the vernacular perhaps more than any other, even though it was thought to be little more than a half-hearted 'Satisfaction' knock-off when it was first released back in 1974; it is even the basis for one of Manchester

United's most popular terrace chants, about one of their most beloved ex-players, the incredibly partisan Gary Neville: 'Neville Neville you play in defence, Neville Neville your play is immense, Neville Neville like Jacko you're bad, Neville Neville is the name of your dad!' (Leyton Orient also had a Bowie-related chant, this one based around 'Starman' itself, and concerning an in-form player called Matty Joseph: 'There's a starman waiting in the sky, His name is Matty Joseph but he's only four feet five, There's a starman waiting in the sky, He'd like to come and meet us cause he knows it's all worthwhile . . .')

Then of course there are the late blossoms, *The Next Day*, *Blackstar*, and *Lazarus*.

And my favourite album of his? Well, if *Desert Island Discs*' Kirsty Young ever held a gun to my head I'd have to admit that *Young Americans*, his infamous 'plastic soul' record from 1975 (originally called *The Gouster* – black slang for 'cool dude' – and eventually released in this form in 2016), is my favourite-ever Bowie album, a slab of heartbreaking sophisti-soul that might just be the best seduction record ever made. Although he was criticised at the time for turning his back on Britain and for embracing the insincere world of Seventies soul (so much less authentic than the Sixties version, carped critics), this record proved that he could be as romantic as Marvin Gaye (with strings based on those used on Barry White records), or as funky as Sly Stone. The album remains underrated, a right turn for critics who always wanted Bowie to go left. It is full of heart-rending strings, searing and soaring sax, and enough minor chords to melt the coldest of cold hearts (even though he made the album on cocaine – one of the coldest of all drugs – it has an enduring warmth to it). Bowie called it his 'plastic soul' record, and 'the squashed remains of ethnic music as it survives in the age of muzak rock, written and sung by a white limey.' When critic Lester Bangs heard Bowie's falsetto on the record, he was incensed, and suggested that some of Bowie's fans thought he had turned them into 'veritable women'.

After his heart attacks in 2004, Bowie greeted every day with a resigned smile. The first attack happened on 25 June, backstage at a concert at the Hurricane Festival in Scheeßel in Germany. He had emergency angioplasty surgery for a blocked artery, and there were rumours that he had a second attack the following day.

During the Noughties Bowie lived in New York, on the top floor of a former chocolate factory in Lafayette Street, in an apartment designed by Jonathan Reed. Here he tended to his daughter Lexi, his website, his wife Iman, and – sporadically – his back catalogue. If you wandered around NoHo you'd probably see him, in his quilted black Belstaff, his skinny jeans, workman's boots, and peaked cap, looking like a cross between a gamekeeper and Lou Reed circa 1966. Blending in with almost everyone around him, he was invisible. Unless you were looking for him, of course.

On any day when the air was crisp and there was a chill between the buildings, you could see Manhattan's downtown quilted army out in force, drinking peppermint mochas, shopping for clothes, or simply convening with their smartphones. They all dressed in black quilted jackets, pea coats, or puffas, with their collars pulled up, scarves tied in fat knots, and buttons tightly fastened. Oh, and as it was winter, they would be wearing sunglasses, too, just in case. You couldn't miss them: they'd be wearing black caps, and matching jeans, maybe with a pair of designer biker boots (diker-boots?), or some hybrid trainers. Oh, and they'd be carrying a man bag of some description, and maybe walking a dog (a little black one, sporting its own quilted jacket). These men were anything between sixteen and sixty, and not only did they all look the same, they all looked like David Bowie.

Until he rush-released *The Next Day* in January 2016, he hadn't released a new album since 2003's *Reality* and not played live since 2006, when he sang onstage with Alicia Keys in New York City. He gave no indication he was likely to tour again. He was asked to participate in most global pop events – Live 8, the Princess Diana tribute, Glastonbury, on an annual basis – but preferred to spend his time analysing his future rather than exploiting the past. David Cameron asked him to participate in events, as did the Royal Family, but he wasn't interested. He was also rather dismissive of his fan base's obsession with his otherworldliness. A few years ago I asked him what people most misunderstood about him.

'What's to misunderstand?' he said. 'I mean, honestly,

I'm just a bloke doing his job, and it's not terribly complicated. What I do is I write mainly about very personal and
rather lonely feelings, and I explore them in a different way
each time. You know, what I do is not terribly intellectual.
I'm a pop star for Christ's sake. As a person, I'm fairly
uncomplicated. I don't need very much – I'm not needy in
that way. I'm not as driven as I once was.'

The thing is, for two years between 2009 and 2011,
Bowie actually did go out on the road, as part of U2's mammoth 360 tour. Their 110-date 360 tour was not only the
grandest tour ever staged by a rock band, not only the most
technologically innovative, and not only the most expensive, but by the end of their two years on the road, the band
would have performed in front of a staggering seven million
people. Initially scheduled to support their 2009 album, *No
Line On The Horizon*, the tour had taken on something of a
life of its own, dwarfing the achievements of anyone else
who had previously embarked on a stadium tour (including
the band themselves). Each night, as the vast video screens
showed Bono, the Edge, Adam Clayton, and Larry Mullen
Jr walking up from behind the stage, almost as though they
were astronauts walking onto their rocket, the PA started
blasting out 'Space Oddity', resulting in huge cheers from
the 100,000 people who were usually in the stadium. One
night towards the end of the tour, as I spoke to Bono in Guy
Laliberté's house, twenty-three kilometres east of Montreal,
in Mont Saint-Bruno, in the beautiful Monteregian Hills, he
explained that 'Space Oddity' had always been the song

they'd wanted to introduce the show. Having always seen the stage as a space station, he liked the idea of immediately setting the scene with the song. It reminded him a bit of the Only Ones song, 'Another Girl Another Planet', a song that evoked travel, escape, and moving on.

Ziggy is Zelig in his own life story. Bowie was always a keen advocate of printing the legend, and if he read something about himself that wasn't true, but that he liked, it became a fact. He read all the books about himself, occasionally contacting the authors to congratulate them, or – more often – correct them for some minor inaccuracy. He monitored the work of all those he worked with over the years, and, it has to be said, took umbrage when umbrage was not necessarily warranted. Eno went in and out of favour (how could he not when he worked with so many people Bowie thought had ripped him off?), as did Tony Visconti, Morrissey, Nile Rodgers, and Reeves Gabrels. His days were spent monitoring the successes and failures of his peers, not that Bowie considered many people to actually be his peers.

In the Nineties he became a *Commandeur de l'Ordre des Arts et des Lettres* in France, although in 2003, he declined a knighthood.

When you consider that Bowie was one of the most inventive, most influential, most commercially daring entertainers of the last forty years, it would have been churlish to deny him some reflection, or even a semi-retirement. Still, ever since he stopped taking drugs at the end of the Seventies, he became good at downtime. In the mid-Nineties, he told me he was almost proud of wandering around Manhattan, pootling about at home, visiting the occasional gallery: 'I do virtually nothing. I walk about a bit, that's about it. I'll drag my wife from museum to museum, that's about the only exercise I get. I mooch around.'

In the last twenty years or so, Bowie embraced most forms of multimedia, and was one of the first pop stars to seriously understand the possibilities of the Internet. But although being a renaissance man can be a full-time occupation, it was always the music that fired Bowie's soul, music that brought out the best in him. Like his former hero Scott Walker, Bowie had a way of walking around a song instead of addressing it head-on. 'I know my strengths and one of them is creating atmosphere,' he told me once, in a Midtown recording studio in New York, in the mid-Nineties. 'John Lennon was good at telling people off, but not me. Whenever I do didactic stuff it always seems ham-fisted. I often pull myself back if I feel something is becoming too melodic.' I had interviewed Scott Walker about his most recent activity about eighteen months earlier and he'd given me an almost verbatim quote.

'But then melody comes in many forms,' said Bowie. 'He'll hate me for saying it but the person who is better at hooks than almost anyone is Eno, and the solo on "Virginia Plain" is probably one of the greatest three-note hooks in the history of pop. Some people call me pretentious for working like this, but I don't think there's anything wrong with thinking of pop as an art form, you've just got to think of it without a capital A. Lower case art is always best. And anyway, a lot of what was considered art in 1978 is now just part of our vocabulary.'

Actually, when I read the interview again, for the purposes of this book, I was struck by how much I still expected from him. The final two paragraphs from that article (*Arena*, March 1997), are simple, but oh so telling, indicating that I still expected him to do what he had done twenty-five years ago, which was shock the living daylights out of me: 'There may be those who can't forgive David Bowie,' I wrote. 'Won't forgive him for growing up, older, wiser. And although he can still conjure up the dark and the unseemly when he wants to, he no longer has to carry them around with him.

'Just because we have bad dreams doesn't mean he has to have them, too.'

The fourth time I met David Bowie was just before his Serious Moonlight gig at the Milton Keynes Bowl on 1 July, 1983. I was backstage, wolfing down the free drinks and exotic canapés, standing with Cynthia Lole on the elevated walkway that stretched from Bowie's dressing room all the way to the stage. He had perfect 'Let's Dance' hair, a beautifully-tailored, baggy, pale blue suit, a white shirt, braces, and a Paul Smith old-school tie (I know about stuff like this), and he looked as though he'd just stepped out of his own ad campaign – fully formed, and aesthetically indestructible. And as he walked up to the stage, he stopped, turned to Cynthia and me, and said, apropos of nothing,

'You know, at times like this, it's great to be surrounded by your friends.' I wasn't his friend. I was an acquaintance, hardly knew the man (although Cynthia had worked fairly closely with him on a variety of projects), and if I'd known him better it would have been unbearably presumptuous for me to call him a friend. But in those few seconds – seconds before he was due to give one of the defining concerts of his career – he made both of us feel like the most important people on Earth. Which I suppose is why he was David Bowie, and we weren't. It wasn't us who were special, it was him. When Bowie was recording *Young Americans*, a pre-fame Vandross was employed as one of his backing singers. Bowie wanted to work on one of Vandross's songs, which would eventually become 'Fascination'. In the studio one day, Bowie asked him if he minded if he rewrote some of the lyrics. Vandross's response was perhaps the only one suitable: 'You're David Bowie, I live at home with my mother. Yes, you can do what you like.'

He did, and he continued doing so.

During the Noughties I often wondered what Bowie might do next, if he decided to step out of his torpor. His sense of self-preservation was keen, and having purposefully stayed ahead of what he witheringly still called the crowd (only faltering when he decided to second-guess his audience in the Eighties), he knew the value of 're-entry'. Back in the Sixties, when he was just starting out, he was a convincing London dandy before morphing into an effete singer-songwriter with stars in his eyes. Five minutes later he invented glam rock with *Ziggy Stardust*, and then kept reinventing himself throughout the Seventies with each subsequent record. With Tin Machine he even reinvented the yuppie, dressing like a banker who had decided to form a rock band. He was the quintessential rock chameleon, the archetypal pop changeling, everyone's favourite space face. But – and, like Luther Vandross in his pomp, this could be a very big but – he'd never been fat. Bowie had been thin, and he'd been skeletal. He'd been blond, and he'd been flame-haired. He'd wrapped himself in Bacofoil, worn the sort of thigh-high boots that would have shamed Madonna, and, in *Labyrinth*, he even looked like something out of *Fraggle Rock*. He'd done it all.

But he'd never been fat. Which is something he obviously could have done very well. I used to imagine that when Ziggy eventually crawled out from his lair, he would return as the Fat White Duke. How refreshing it would have been to see Bowie waddle up onto the stage looking like Alfred Hitchcock or Peter Ustinov. Imagine him Falstaff fat. John Candy fat. So fat he has his own postcode fat. I'm not for one minute suggesting that he may have reappeared as a tragic and bloated version of his former self, not suggesting he may have paraded around as a twenty-first-century Vegas-period Elvis, popping out of his rhinestone jumpsuit as he hurried his way through 'Life On Mars', 'Absolute Beginners', or 'Let's Dance'. I'm merely suggesting that, as the master of reinvention, he could have pulled it off with gusto. He could have descended on us looking grand, groomed, and incredibly well manicured, like Orson Welles promenading in Paris – an unlit cigar in his mouth, his hands pushed deep into his suit pockets, and his belly stretching all the way from here to over there. He would have been wearing a bespoke suit (obviously – how else was it going to fit?), bench-made shoes, and possibly a purple suede fedora. He would have super-sized himself.

The only problem, as far as I could see, was that Bowie was banned from enjoying all the good stuff that would have made him look this way. Orson used to consume four or five large portions of caviar every day, along with at least twenty cups of coffee, and many more tumblers of one hundred per cent proof vodka. And those were just the snacks between meals. A typical lunch might start with a bottle of champagne (for himself, mind), followed by *Boudin Noir aux Pommes* (blood sausages with apples), then a bottle of hearty red to ease down a *Terrine de Canard*, followed by something sickly and sweet along with a treble calvados. Bowie rarely ate anything that wasn't organic and hadn't drunk (or smoked) in years. If he had attempted to 'do an Orson' he'd have probably exploded before the fortieth anniversary of his *Top Of The Pops* appearance.

When I put this to Bowie, he laughed, but not with his eyes. 'The fat Bowie. Well, maybe when I move into the Las Vegas circuit . . . I have various photographs of me looking skeletal, which remind me how badly behaved I was back in the Seventies. They're Polaroids as well, which makes it even worse because they're badly lit. I occasionally look at them and think, "How did I ever get to that state? How did I survive?" Yeah, you can be too thin!' When prodded previously about this period of his life, he said that his insides must have been like perished rubber.

Occasionally over the last few years, when Bowie was photographed out in New York, he had looked a little heavy, which had caused some speculation that this might be the result of medication. Towards the end of the Noughties, his refusal to re-enter the world he created for himself, or to re-engage with his public – or indeed anyone's public – meant that speculation about his health was rife. He was still in almost daily contact with his management team, however, and appeared not to care what the press said about him.

I figured that Bowie's most obvious route of re-entry would be electronically, via our computers, tablets, or handhelds, as a hologram maybe, or a 3-D viral, bouncing around our laptops and our iPads as though he were Max Headroom reinvented as a cyber cipher. Doubtless, he would be digital. In the end I was right. He was certainly less precious about his image. Bowie famously appeared in an episode of Ricky Gervais's *Extras* in 2006 ('Little fat man who sold his soul, little fat man who sold his dream . . .'), and when he appeared on the BBC's *Comic Relief* in 1999, he made a film which involved him performing a parody called 'Requiem For A Laughing Gnome': 'Hello boys and girls, I'm David Bowie, and I'm talking to you for Comic Relief. Tonight I thought I'd do something a little different, so I thought I'd play a new composition for you, that I think you may enjoy. It's for recorder ... and it has some choreography, that I picked up from a Navajo Indian that I met last week [from] the Croydon chapter. It's in four movements, and I should probably begin with the first movement. Thank you ...' He then proceeds to play an awful recorder solo, followed by some shoe tapping. A sign flashes up: 'THIS LASTS FOUR HOURS'. Bowie continues playing, and then, in the voice of puppeteer Harry Corbett, says, 'Oh, put your clothes on, Sooty.' Then, as Bowie starts playing again, another sign crosses the screen: 'WE'LL GO ON SHOWING IT IF YOU DON'T CALL ... PLEASE ... PLEASE. PLEASE.'

Bowie loved this spoof, and included a link to the You-Tube clip in his Christmas Day message in 2011. The message also contained an 'unseen' photograph of 'Cool Hand Duke', a digitally altered picture of Bowie wearing a speckled suit and a green fedora, and playing a 'medieval magic pipe hewn from the helical tusk of a male narwhal, though it was originally presented as having been taken from a live unicorn, thus giving it its "magical" qualities'. The photograph is obviously a composite, yet Bowie had been doing this for years. The last time he was photographed for British *GQ*, in October 2002, he was shot by Markus Klinko with a variety of real wolves in an homage to the original Terry O'Neill cover-try for *Diamond Dogs* in 1974 (which featured Bowie sitting down against some Colourama in a photographic studio, dressed as an uptown gaucho guarded by a snarling mastiff). At Bowie's suggestion, Klinko – who was responsible for the image of Bowie on the cover of *Heathen* – was commissioned to create something for the cover of the issue celebrating Bowie's *GQ* Lifetime Achievement Award. 'Markus already had loads of heads in his fridge, as he put it, since he'd shot portraits of Bowie for his new press campaign,' said one of *GQ*'s art directors. Together, Markus and Bowie decided to construct an intricate montage using those head shots superimposed on a model who was holding the wolves. Bowie himself was intrigued by the notion of photographs of himself that were not, strictly, of him at all. 'It's an interesting dilemma,' he said. 'Does this carry the same weight as a genuine photograph, and is that important to you?'

In 2006 he even sanctioned a collection of David Bowie clothes, designed by the British designer Keanan Duffty for the chainstore Target. 'The third meeting was at the Isolar offices on Lafayette Street in SoHo,' said Duffty. 'This time it was just David, Coco, and myself. I had come to present the marketing ideas. Target were very keen to have David perform a song at an opening party. Not going to happen. "I'm not Posh Spice," he said.'

Irony actually became one of Bowie's closest collaborators. In 1995 he launched his own small range of wallpaper with Laura Ashley. Apart from some interior decoration in *The Man Who Fell To Earth*, where he is seen hanging a Japanese kite from the ceiling of his gargantuan lakeside villa, up until this launch Bowie wasn't known for his home improvement skills. 'I chose wallpaper because of its status as something extremely incongruous, particularly in the world of art,' he told me. 'I haven't completely lost my sense of irony, you know! I suppose I'm midway between high art and low art – I'm a mid-art populist and postmodernist Buddhist who is casually surfing his way through the chaos of the late twentieth century.' Fittingly, one of his designs featured a minotaur, whose genitals were erased by Laura Ashley, for fear of causing offence. 'I wasn't allowed to show my genitals on the inner sleeve of *Aladdin Sane*, nor on the cover of *Diamond Dogs*, nor on the cover of one of the Tin Machine LPs. I've been deballed four times! It says a lot about Western attitudes towards male genitalia. I mean, breasts don't seem to be hacked off in the same cavalier fashion.'

THE ARCHIVE WAS EVENTUALLY MOVED, AND ALL THE COSTUMES (GROUPED BY TOUR), ALONG WITH BOWIE'S VAST COLLECTION OF MASTER TAPES, ARTWORKS, HANDWRITTEN LYRICS, ETC. WERE KEPT IN VARIOUS BUILDINGS NEAR HIS HOME IN MANHATTAN.

There was a time around the end of the century when I thought Bowie was going to flout his own conventions by turning into a bona fide Sinatra-style crooner, a role in which his voice (deeper and more honeyed than in his heyday, and the result of his 'Ciggie Stardust' nicotine addiction) was the centre of attention rather than his clothes or his production partners. In many ways he had hidden behind his singing technique for years, and for a while that technique – the sombre way he used his rich baritone on the likes of 'Wild Is The Wind', 'Heroes', and 'Absolute Beginners', compounded by the mockney lilt that insisted on swapping vowels ('day' for 'die', etc.) – had become his calling card.

This was also the period during which he intended to bring back Ziggy Stardust, for a Ziggy Redux film. When he refused to allow the producers of the 1998 film *Velvet Goldmine* – which featured a Ziggy-type character – to use any of his Ziggy-period songs, he announced he was preparing his own glam-rock extravaganza, and this was meant to be it. He was adamant that he wouldn't be donning the catsuits and platform boots himself, even though, as he sat in the lounge of the Halkin Hotel behind Buckingham Palace, he looked as though they would still fit.

'I won't be in it, let's make that clear. Not me, mate! I won't even be Ziggy's dad!'

'So, this won't be *Ziggy Stardust And The Last Crusade*?' I asked him.

'Yes! Indiana Stardust! Yes, but unfortunately, no.'

Nor was Bowie writing new songs for the Ziggy project.

'I've pulled out a good deal of scraps that were never

used at the time. Some of them are only thirty seconds long, but I'm extending those. I thought, "OK, is this crap and is that the reason why it never appeared on the first one or is it OK and should I try and do things with it?" So I've taken those six tracks and thrashed them out and made them into songs that will support the original. One's called "Black Hole Kids", which is fascinating.'

Bowie found all this stuff languishing in one of the many boxes of archive material he kept at his home in Switzerland before he moved to New York. He had over 800 cassettes of recordings, including dozens of conversations with Incredibly Famous People, hundreds of concert recordings ('I found virtually the whole of the soundboard tapes for the '74, '76, '78 tours. Every one!'), superstar jams with the Stooges and the Stones, and a pristine recording of a long conversation he had with Iggy Pop when he went to visit him in hospital in LA in the early Seventies. Most of this material was recorded during Bowie's infamous post-Ziggy 'Warholian' period, when he would record and Polaroid everything that happened to him. Including, it's alleged, the odd sex sessions (he raised one of the famous Bowie samphire-thin eyebrows when I mentioned this). One of the funniest recordings involved Rolling Stone Ronnie Wood visiting Bowie in LA. The duo are sitting in the den, idly playing 'Golden Years' while, every so often, Ronnie stops to hoover up huge lines of acceleration powder. 'It's hysterical,' said Bowie. '*Very* rock 'n' roll.'

The archive was eventually moved, and all the costumes

(grouped by tour), along with Bowie's vast collection of master tapes, artworks, handwritten lyrics, digitally copied TV shows and concert films, tour paraphernalia, bootlegs, and everything else he has collected about himself over the years, were kept in various buildings near his home in Manhattan. This was a museum in its own right, one of the greatest pop cultural collections of the late twentieth century, and the collection was the basis for the extraordinary David Bowie exhibition at the Victoria & Albert museum in 2013 (which toured around the world until it ended up in Brooklyn in 2018).

Bowie often considered resurrecting Ziggy (occasionally he revisited him in his paintings), tentative where others were obsessive. One of the last projects I initiated at *Arena* before I left for the *Observer* in 1992 was a Bowie special, and I arranged for the magazine to get permission to photograph all Bowie's old Ziggy costumes. Robin Derrick, the magazine's art director, then flew to Lausanne, Bowie's home in Switzerland. Almost all of the clothes from his tours from the last twenty years were stored and archived there, and the day after arriving, having hired a watch photographer's studio half-an-hour away, Coco Schwab, Bowie's long-term assistant, turned up in a van with dozens of outfits, all hung perfectly, and draped in cellophane. Bowie had put the outfits together himself. There was the kabuki kimono, the pale blue suit from the 'Life On Mars' video, the circuit-board jumpsuit Bowie wore on *The Old Grey Whistle Test*, and the quilted one he wore on *Top Of The Pops*.

Two things were remarkable about the outfits, the first being that this was exactly what they were, outfits, not street clothes. The red boots, copied from Kansai Yamamoto, were literally held together with tape. 'I always imagined that the outfits would look more like the things you'd find in stores, but all of them looked like stage costumes,' says Robin. 'Reinforcing the idea that Ziggy wasn't Bowie, he was an act.' When Robin looked through the costumes, some hadn't been touched since they were last worn, and there was even a beer stain on one of the kimonos.

Robin was another Bowie devotee, and distinctly remembers his older brother bringing the album home for the first time. 'I remember staring for hours at that image of him on the back cover, and reading the TO BE PLAYED AT MAX-IMUM VOLUME line and thinking it was so otherworldly. To be sitting on a sofa in my parents' house in Keynsham and being transported like that ... it was quite extraordinary. Also the way in which the lyrics applied to both Bowie and Ziggy, the whole thing was fascinating. Up until then you had a singer and you had songs, simple as that.'

The second thing that shocked Robin was how small the clothes were: 'I was able to wrap my hands around most of the waists. They were absolutely tiny.'

In 2003, Robin called in the costumes again, this time for a *Vogue* cover shoot with Kate Moss. In half-a-dozen pictures by the photographer Nick Knight she wore: 1. Ziggy's embroidered satin kimono top and shorts, designed by Kansai Yamamoto, along with patent leather kabuki boots; 2.

His blue, three-piece satin suit made by his long-term confident Freddie Buretti, the one he wore in the 'Life On Mars' promo; 3. The Yamamoto asymmetric knitted jumpsuit and armbands that he wore repeatedly onstage during the 1972 tour. The circuit-board jumpsuit had disappeared, been stolen or lost. The pictures themselves were typically extraordinary (such is the world we live in now), yet more interestingly, Kate Moss didn't fit the clothes. A swing-tag chameleon she may have been, but it was all too small. She was Queen Waif at the time, and still she was too big to wear the outfits. Thinking that the powder blue 'Life On Mars' suit was made by Antony Price, Kate called the designer and asked him if he'd mind if it were let out. Price was forced to admit that the suit had actually been made by Freddie Burretti.

Over the years there were many undeveloped projects, especially in the ten years since 2002 and 2012 when EMI owned his back catalogue. Most of these projects were initiated by Bowie, and then dumped: a *Hunky Dory* box set, a *Ziggy* box set, *Toy*, *Pin-Ups II*, the follow-up to *Reality*, at least six mixing-desk quality live sets, an album of dance remixes, a Neil Young-style archive box, blah blah blah. He was proud of his career, yet seemed strangely reluctant to add to it. He saw everyone around him releasing bits and pieces from the past, yet in relation to his own work thought that if something wasn't good enough to release at the time, then it probably wasn't worth releasing at all.

So the Ziggy project was shelved, sitting, like many of his projects, in the bottomless drawer of unresolved and unmanageable Bowie projects. 'I did sit down with a couple of guys about two or three years ago,' he told me. 'We endeavoured to put a shape to it as a theatrical piece and it was a non-starter. The more I wrote into it, the smaller and smaller it just seemed to be. And one of the guys actually posed the question, "Why are you doing this?" He said it means a lot to people – didn't I feel that by developing him, I would be closing up all the possibilities to the character? He said if I devised a formidable storyline, I'd probably be doing the whole idea of Ziggy a disservice by nailing it. I think its major strength is that there was such an ephemeral quality to the whole business, and it left so many options open for people to read into themselves. That was his valuable service to humanity: I'm Ziggy, use me.'

Having painstakingly worked my way through all of the Bowie press cuttings I kept from the early Seventies, I found a scrap of an interview in a long-forgotten music magazine, and saw that he'd actually said something similar back in 1973. Asked whether there could ever be a Ziggy movie, he said, 'A lot of people I've talked to that have been to the shows have got a very, very definite idea of what Ziggy is and what he represents. They know how he works for them. I would not want to shatter anybody's private movie. I would not care to do that, because, not having heard their versions, I agree with them as well as I agree with my own version. I see what they mean, and I would hate to destroy all of that because it's all real. It's all valid.'

Ziggy Stardust remains David Bowie's most significant

achievement, his most perfect creation. As a character, Ziggy never really died; to echo the words of Ralph Ellison, like a fire in a peatbog, he would smoulder intensely and deeply, long after the flame had burned off the surface of public consciousness. Ziggy Stardust: the hungry ghost.

Bowie didn't see it that way, and you wouldn't have expected him to. The prism through which he looked at his career was his and his alone, and there was no way his sensitivities regarding his work were going to dovetail with ours.

'My career has benefited so much more from the mistakes than from the things I've got right,' he said. 'I can always learn something from the cock-ups! I see myself as something of a blunderer. I get carried along on tides of enthusiasm. My whole life has been like that. If I'm introduced to something that fascinates me, within three hours I'm the world expert.'

How did he feel about the 'new Sinatra' tag that I'd suggested. Could he easily hang it on himself?

'Oh, he would not [have been] happy with that. Sinatra's daughter, Nancy, once stupidly suggested I play him in a movie. God, he hated that. "I don't want a fag playing me!" He was absolutely terrified that I might be taken seriously. He hated long hair, hated anything limey! I do relate to Sinatra in that my tours are getting fewer and fewer. I don't tour just for the sake of touring any more.

'There's an awful lot of luggage that comes with [my songs] for both the audience and myself. [Once] I said I didn't want to sing my big hits again. I walked away from my older songs for years because I'd been doing them for so long, there was no resonance in them for me any more. But I've changed. I started feeding old songs back into the show around '97 when we were doing the festival circuit. With festivals you have to presume not everyone's there for you. You have to think, "Fuck me, I'd better give them something they know!" Then I'd play a few songs from *Scary Monsters*, *Low*, and *Heroes*, and throw in things like 'Fame' and 'Under Pressure', which is an irresistible festival song because of the association with Freddie [Mercury].'

And what of *The Rise And Fall Of Ziggy Stardust And The Spiders From Mars*? What of the record that accompanied all this fuss? 'Well, we made a record; that's it,' says Ken Scott. 'If people chose to use it to change their lifestyles then that's their business. I love the *Ziggy* album, but I don't think it's this classic album that people have taken it to be. We had no idea that people would be talking about it forty years hence. It's ridiculous. We made it to last six months. Which is what you did in those days. It worked because David caught people's attention. He was different because he was different from everyone else at that particular moment in time, and it gave something for people to grab hold of and find something more exciting in their lives. We'd gone through the big changes of the Sixties, the Beatles had broken up, and it was time for something new. And David was the person who came up with it.

'Is it the best album of 1972? Well, I didn't hear every album that came out in 1972, so I don't know. A lot of it is down to personal taste. I love the record, and the effect it's had on my life has been unbelievable. But I don't know how good it is. That's for other people to decide. It started some people along a particular course, that's all . . . Paul McCartney says the Beatles were a good rock and roll band, and that's what they were. People take these things for what they mean to them, and I can take no responsibility for that, it's their own personal issue. *Ziggy Stardust* is just a good rock and roll record. Technically Supertramp's *Crime Of The Century* is a better record, but there are some great things on it. A few years ago I went back to Abbey Road to produce a 5.1 version of the record and I was blown away by how much was on the record that I'd forgotten about.

'It's just a bunch of songs, really. Some of them fit the Ziggy story, but not all of them. It's not really a concept album at all.'

Ziggy Stardust was David Bowie's great escape, the character that finally freed him from a decade of failure, and if, in the years since, he found it difficult to shake him, that's hardly surprising. As a conduit, Ziggy delivered more than Bowie could have ever wished for, and, perhaps predictably, more than he ever bargained for.[*]

....

[*] On 27 March 2012, to celebrate the fortieth anniversary of *Ziggy Stardust*, the Crown Estate placed a commemorative plaque in Heddon Street, although it was almost unrecognisable as the scene of David Bowie's greatest triumph; pedestrianised in 2009, it had been gentrified with palms and olive trees, and turned into one of Regent Street's two 'food quarters', and home to nine restaurants and bars.

He still had strong views about what constituted a David Bowie song, a David Bowie performance, and, indeed, a David Bowie quote. There were things like 'Young Americans' and 'Space Oddity' which he recoiled from performing, and 'Starman' had never been one of his touring favourites, 'but when I feel I've left those songs alone for enough, maybe I'll sing them again,' he said.

Of course he never did, and was probably never going to. Ziggy was his, he said, and his alone. His to reintroduce to the world when he saw fit, his to remodel and re-make at will.

Yet Ziggy Stardust belongs as much to us as it does to his creator, and our collective memory of him is equally as important as Bowie's original ambitions for his alter ego. We own Ziggy Stardust, whether David Bowie likes it or not.

Ziggy is owned by all of us who were touched that day in 1972. Indeed, he's owned by anyone who fell hard for him at the time. Bowie's boy cut across all class delineations, and across all sexes. He may have inspired a generation of pop stars and smarty pants, but he inspired everyone else too: doctors, engineers, shop keepers, shop assistants, bus drivers, journalists, florists, nurses, photographers, carpenters, footballers, pilots and plumbers, and anyone else who still to this day puts on *Ziggy Stardust* and smiles. That moment in the summer of 1972 is one owned by us all.

Bowie was responsible for our emancipation in the first place, using rock 'n' roll – or at least his version of it – for what it does best: to liberate those who had previously been without liberation, in the words of Mikal Gilmore, to give voice to those who had been without it. Saliently, he did what all the best rock 'n' roll does, namely shine a light on those grey souls hiding in the corner, those of us who need a little more coaxing to stumble out into the sunshine. By reaching out his hands, and by giving us the kind of permission we weren't even allowing ourselves, he empowered all of us.

That's the sort of thing we don't forget in a hurry. Which is why we're still reluctant to hand Ziggy back. It was hardly a selfless act, as in 1972 Bowie probably wanted fame more than he'd ever wanted anything in his life. He could also have had no idea what an effect his funny little composite would have on those of us who bought into the idea. Yet the by-product of Ziggy's success was the validation of identity, our identity. What Ziggy did was create an army of misfits under the aegis of community. Of course, we weren't a community at all, just a collection of lost souls who wanted our sermons accompanied by some toe-tapping hymns. It's often said that David Bowie encouraged people to be different; he didn't, he simply allowed them to think they were.

Bowie spent much of the time surrounding the fortieth anniversary of Ziggy in his Downtown loft, tinkering with the minutiae of his legacy, moving cellophane packets of space dust from the drawers of one plans chest to another. Out there, right now, on the streets, in the bars, embedded on Spotify, flying around the net, in the luxury department stores of Omotesando, in cars, in the slums of Buenos Aires, on our iPods, and in our heads, leaning back on our radios, Ziggy Stardust lives on, a space face in aspic, really quite outta sight.

ACKNOWLEDGEMENTS

With many thanks to David Bowie, Trevor Bolder,
Woody Woodmansey, Ken Scott, Trevor Dolby,
Ed Victor, Laurie Ip Fung Chun, Becky McCarthy,
Jonny Geller, Bono, Nick Rhodes, Alan Edwards,
Charles Shaar Murray, Nick Kent, Robin Derrick,
Peter Florence, Terry Jones, Neil Tennant, Mark Cooper,
Nicholas Coleridge, Tony Parsons, Luciana Bellini,
Stephanie Sleap, Tony Blackburn, Nicola Taplin,
Melanie Haselden, Ray Langstone, Murray Chalmers,
Allan Jones, Michael Jones, Daniel Jones,
Julian Stockton, Siouxsie Sioux, Tiffany Murray,
Michael Watts, James Hale, Devon Blaine, Sarah Walter,
Edie Jones, Georgia Jones, and to Jonathan Newhouse.

BIBLIOGRAPHY

All of the following have proved useful in some way:

Bowie, Angie, *Free Spirit*, Mushroom Publishing, 1981.

Bowie, Angie, *Backstage Passes*, G. P. Putnam's Sons, 1993.

Bracewell, Michael, *When Surface Was Depth: Death By Cappuccino And Other Reflections On Music And Culture In The 1990s*, Da Capo, 2002.

Bracewell, Michael, *Re-make/Re-model*, Faber & Faber, 2007.

Buckley, David, *Strange Fascination*, Virgin, 2005.

Cann, Kevin, *Any Day Now: The London Years 1947–1974*, Adelita, 2010.

Carr, Roy and Charles Shaar Murray, *David Bowie: An Illustrated Record*, Eel Pie, 1981.

Charlesworth, Chris and Miles, *David Bowie Black Book*, Omnibus, 1988.

Collins, Jim and Morten T Hansen, *Great By Choice*, Harper Business, 2011.

Collis, John, *Chuck Berry: The Biography*, Aurum Press, 2002.

Cryer, Max, *Love Me Tender: The Stories Behind The World's Best-Loved Songs*, Francis Lincoln, 2008.

Currie, David (ed.), *The Starzone Interviews*, Omnibus, 1985.

Decharne, Max, *Kings Road: The Rise And Fall Of The Hippest Street In The World*, Weidenfeld & Nicolson, 2005.

Doggett, Peter, *The Man Who Sold The World: David Bowie And The 1970s*, Bodley Head, 2011.

Echols, Alice, *Hot Stuff: Disco And The Remaking Of American Culture*, W W Horton & Co, 2010.

Gillman, Peter & Leni, *Alias David Bowie*, Hodder & Stoughton, 1986.

Gittins, Ian, *Top Of The Pops: Mishaps, Miming And Music*, BBC Books, 2007.

Guralnick, Peter, *Last Train To Memphis: The Rise Of Elvis Presley*, Little, Brown, 1994.

Haslam, Dave, *Not Abba: The Real Story Of The 1970s*, Fourth Estate, 2005.

Hopkins, Jerry, *Bowie*, Hamish Hamilton, 1985.

Jones, Dylan, *Haircults*, Thames & Hudson, 1990.

Juby, Kerry, *In Other Words… David Bowie*, Omnibus, 1986.

MacCormack, Geoff, *From Station To Station: Travels With Bowie 1973 – 1976*, Genesis, 2007.

Miles (ed.), *Bowie In His Own Words*, Omnibus, 1980.

Mulholland, Garry, *Popcorn: Fifty Years Of Rock 'n' Roll Movies*, Orion, 2010.

Napier-Bell, Simon, *Black Vinyl White Powder*, Ebury Press, 2001.

Park, James (ed.), *Icons: An A-Z Of The People Who Have Shaped Our Time*, Collier, 1992.

Paytress, Mark, *Ziggy Stardust*, Schirmer, 1988.

Paytress, Mark, *Bowie Style*, Omnibus, 2000.

Pegg, Nicholas, *The Complete David Bowie*, Titan, 2011.

Pepper, Terence (with Jon Savage), *Beatles To Bowie: The Sixties Exposed*, National Portrait Gallery, 2009.

Pitt, Kenneth, *David Bowie: The Pitt Report*, Design, 1983.

Rock, Mick, *A Photographic Record: 1969–1980*, Century 22, 1995.

Rock, Mick, *Blood and Glitter*, Vision On, 2001.

Rock, Mick, *Moonage Daydream*, Octopus, 2005.

Rock, Mick, *Raw Power*, Palazzo, 2010.

Seabrook, Thomas Jerome, *Bowie In Berlin: A New Career In A New Town*, Jawbone, 2008.

Scott, Ken and Bobby Owsinski, *Abbey Road To Ziggy Stardust*, Alfred, 2012.

Shepard, Sam, *Rolling Thunder Logbook*, Viking, 1977.

Sheppard, David, *On Some Faraway Beach: The Life And Times Of Brian Eno*, Orion, 2008.

Sounes, Howard, *Seventies*, Simon & Schuster, 2006.

Spitz, Marc, *David Bowie: A Biography*, Aurum, 2009.

Stevenson, Nick, *David Bowie: Fame, Sound And Vision*, Polity, 2006.

Stern, Jane and Michael, *Encyclopedia Of Pop Culture*, HarperCollins, 1992.

Sukita, Masayoshi, *David Bowie*, Tokyo FM Books, 1992.

Thomas, Gareth, *David Bowie: The Illustrated Biography*, Transatlantic Press, 2011.

Thompson, Dave, *Moonage Daydream*, Plexus, 1987.

Thompson, Dave, *To Major Tom: The Bowie Letters*, Sanctuary, 2002.

Thompson, Dave, *Hallo Spaceboy: The Rebirth Of David Bowie*, ECW Press, 2006.

Thompson, Dave, *Your Pretty Face Is Going To Hell: The Dangerous Glitter Of David Bowie, Iggy Pop And Lou Reed*, Backbeat Books, 2009.

Thomson, Elizabeth and David Gutman, *The Bowie Companion*, De Capo, 1996.

Tremlett, George, *The David Bowie Story*, Futura, 1974.

Tremlett, George, *David Bowie: Living On The Brink*, Arrow, 1997.

Trynka, Paul, *Starman*, Little, Brown, 2011.

Visconti, Tony, *Bowie, Bolan And The Brooklyn Boy*, HarperCollins, 2007.

Welch, Chris, *We Could Be Heroes*, Thunder's Mouth Press, 1999.

Welch, Chris, *David Bowie: The Stories Behind the Classic Songs*, Carlton, 2010.

Zanetta, Tony and Henry Edwards, *Stardust: The Life And Times Of David Bowie*, Michael Joseph, 1986.

INDEX

(the initials DB in subentries refer to David Bowie)